RURAL COMMUNITY ECONOMIC DEVELOPMENT

RURAL COMMUNITY ECONOMIC DEVELOPMENT

Edited by Norman Walzer

PRAEGER

New York
Westport, Connecticut
London

Library of Congress Cataloging-in-Publication Data

Rural community economic development / edited by Norman Walzer.
p. cm.
Includes bibliographical references and index.
ISBN 0-275-93942-1 (alk. paper)
1. Rural development—Middle West. 2. Middle West—Economic conditions. 3. Middle West—Social conditions. I. Walzer, Norman.
HN90.C6R765 1991
307.1'412'0977—dc20 91-23637

British Library Cataloguing in Publication Data is available.

Library of Congress Catalog Card Number: 91-23637
ISBN: 0-275-93942-1

First published in 1991

Praeger Publishers, One Madison Avenue, New York, NY 10010
An imprint of Greenwood Publishing Group, Inc.

Printed in the United States of America

The paper used in this book complies with the Permanent Paper Standard issued by the National Information Standards Organization (Z39.48–1984).

10 9 8 7 6 5 4 3 2 1

Contents

Tables, Figures and Maps

TABLES

FIGURES

MAPS

Preface

Slow growing rural economies have been a concern of state and local public policy makers as high unemployment, relatively low incomes, and population outmigration threaten the quality of life in many rural counties. Policies by federal and state governments to improve economic conditions have had limited success and the disparity between urban and rural areas continues to persist.

This book examines rural conditions in the Midwest, a region which was hit particularly hard by the recession in the early 1980s. A combination of a depressed agricultural economy, employment declines in mining and resource-based industry, and loss of manufacturing employment to foreign competition brought hard times to many rural midwestern counties. The authors of this book review these trends and describe the policy responses of state and local public officials as they attempted to improve the local economies.

Many persons assisted in the preparation of this book. Don Norton and Louis DiFonso of the State of Illinois Governor's Rural Affairs Council helped identify authors and assisted in raising revenues to finance the conference at which these papers were presented. Lt. Governor George H. Ryan provided financial support for this project. Nancy Baird and Poh P'ng, Illinois Institute for Rural Affairs, worked many hours to prepare the manuscript for publication. Without the help of these individuals, this project could not have been completed.

Introduction

Historically, major regions of the United States have lagged behind other areas in economic and population growth. For example, the Southeast, especially the Appalachian region, has long been a concern of federal policy makers. Northeastern states underwent a major transformation in the 1970s and in the early 1980s, losing population and industry to other areas. In the 1980s, the Midwest faced similar economic and population declines. Heavy dependence on agriculture and the presence of old manufacturing firms set the stage for significant setbacks during the national 1980–2 recession.

Many factors work against the possibility that small rural communities will ever return to their former heydays as retail trade and employment centers in sparsely populated regions. Transportation improvements, shifts in agricultural mechanization, and innovations in technology that changed manufacturing techniques adversely affected small towns in remote rural areas. Historically, these areas lagged in consumer comforts, such as electricity, paved roads, and numerous other services that urban residents have long accepted as basic necessities. For these and other reasons, it is not uncommon to find steady population declines in rural counties for a century or more.

In discussing rural conditions, it is important to distinguish between a long-term economic transformation of the American economy and relatively short-term economic problems triggered by a national or state downturn. Rural areas, especially those not close enough to an employment center to support residents, have experienced a significant decline since the 1950s. Although the 1970s brought the possibility of a rural economic revitalization, this reversal was short-lived.

The 1981–2 recession was particularly hard on areas relying on manufacturing, bringing high unemployment and causing manufacturing plants to close. Furthermore, the long-term decline in agriculture during most of the 1980s, partly due to changing overseas markets and increased foreign competition, caused the dislocation of many farm families. Residents in these communities, faced with loss of employment or a bleak future, migrated to urban areas, searching for better opportunities.

During the 1980s, with the Reagan Administration, the philosophy of the federal government was to reduce federal involvement. State and local governments assumed control of their own destinies, instead of relying on the federal government for support. This attitude sparked state and local governments to be creative in seeking out industry and developing programs that might set the stage for economic prosperity.

State and local governments created many programs to promote local economic development. Tax incentives or reductions, educational assistance and retraining efforts, capital subsidies, and low-cost loans became popular. Interest in creating businesses increased and states worked with universities, small business incubators, and other agencies to identify entrepreneurs and finance their projects. Some of these innovative programs were created by midwestern states, in response to persistent economic stagnation (Osborne, 1988).

PURPOSE OF BOOK

Problems facing rural areas are complex and often difficult to analyze. Some regions of the United States, such as the Southwest, have done well. Other regions, such as the Northeast, seemed to recover from a long-term decline in the latter 1980s (the Massachusetts Miracle) only to encounter major economic downturns in the early 1990s. There are many explanations for these differences, including energy costs, foreign competition in agriculture and manufacturing, movements of jobs to off-shore locations, changes in the age distribution of the population, interest rate differentials, and other characteristics.

This book examines rural conditions and practices in the Midwest, a twelve-state region of the United States, with 17.3 million residents (Map 1). The states include Illinois, Indiana, Iowa, Kansas, Michigan, Minnesota, Missouri, Nebraska, North Dakota, Ohio, South Dakota, and Wisconsin. The area is an amalgamation of manufacturing, agriculture, and service industries. It contains the third largest city in the United States, but also 4,974 communities of fewer than 1,000 residents. This region supports more than 38,000 units of local government, spending $90 billion annually on public services.

This region is of interest because it was particularly hard-hit by the recession and has been relatively slow to recover. It is undergoing a long-term economic adjustment and some of its industries will never return to their former status. The region has had to replace aging industries in a time when manufacturing jobs are going to off-shore locations. Startups in the region have been slow, partly because of the relatively high energy costs and population shifts to the South, West, and Southwest. Population increases in the Midwest also have been slow, and during the 1980s, at least three midwestern states were among the largest national losers in population.

Not all of the economic changes, of course, have been negative. There are

Map 1
Census Geographic Regions and Divisions of the United States

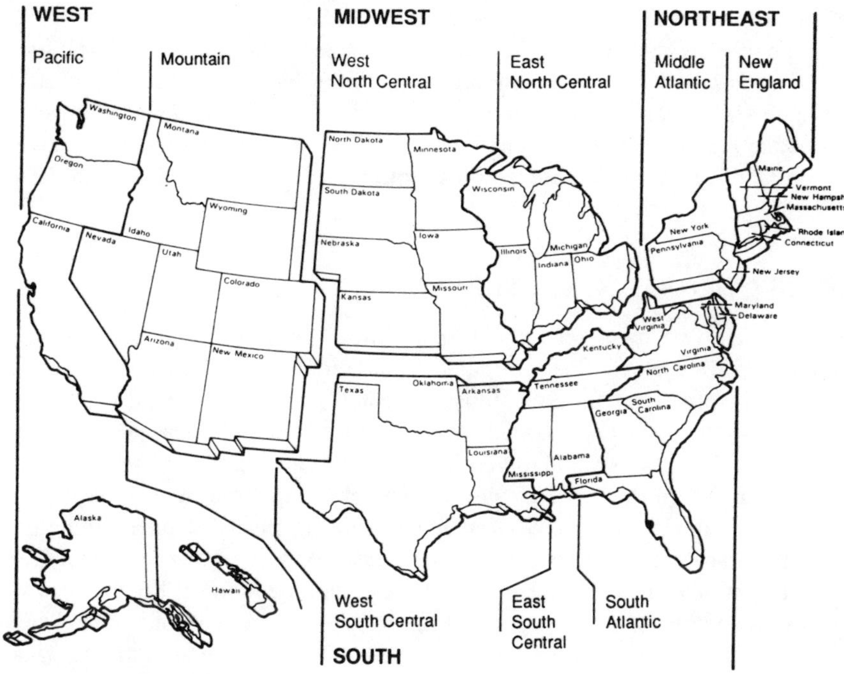

Metro counties:

1. *Greater metro core* counties include the central city or cities of large Metropolitan Statistical Areas of at least 1 million population.
2. *Metro fringe* counties are the other or suburban counties of large MSAs.
3. *Medium metro* counties are counties in MSAs with a population of 250,000–999,999.
4. *Small metro* counties are in MSAs of less than 250,000 population.

Nonmetro counties:

5. *Urbanized adjacent* counties have urban populations of at least 20,000 and are adjacent to an MSA. An urban place is defined as any place (such as town, city, or township) with a population of 2,500 or more. An adjacent county is defined as both touching an MSA at more than one point and having at least 2 percent of its labor force commuting into the central county of the MSA for work.

signs that the Midwest is rebounding; it is attracting business investment, and may emerge in the 1990s a stronger place to do business and earn a living. This trend, if it continues, however, is not likely to be true throughout the Midwest. In particular, rural counties continue to lag behind urban counties by virtually every economic index. These counties are adversely affected by both the relatively short-term recession and by much longer-term economic change.

This book elaborates on trends that have affected rural midwestern counties and examines how institutions within these counties have adjusted. This clearly is an aggressive agenda. It is impossible to gain a detailed understanding of a twelve-state area in a relatively small project. However, an analysis of available data can identify trends that are useful in finding solutions to problems in these states.

ORGANIZATIONAL STRUCTURE

This book has two main sections. First, demographic and economic changes during the 1980s are examined. Population and employment changes, industrial shifts, and income trends are examined. Second, policy responses by local officials to population and economic shifts demonstrate how local governments have become more actively involved in economic development efforts.

Rural midwestern states participated in several changes during the 1980s. The national recession closed many rural manufacturing plants in cities and rural areas alike. At the same time, the agricultural economy did not perform well and midwestern farmers faced greater foreign competition. With the loss of agricultural employment and depressed farm incomes, local businesses in small rural communities suffered economic declines. These changes, although relatively short-term, brought unemployment, population decline, and loss of local services. These changes elicited responses from local public officials.

While the 1970s brought renewed hope for rural areas, it did not reverse the long-term economic transformation that had been underway for decades. Rural areas were no longer able to compete with urban counterparts in salaries and employment opportunities. Populations and economic activity in rural areas had declined relative to urban areas for many years. Thus, rural midwestern economies, troubled by the long-term relative declines faced another major setback with the national recession in the 1980s.

Demographic and Economic Changes in the 1980s

Discussions in the first part of the book focus on three main issues—agriculture employment, population, and business establishments. Changes in these groups are especially important in rural areas. Detailed information on rural counties often is difficult to obtain because of disclosure, and therefore, some of the analyses are limited in this regard. The main focus is on trends that have created difficulties for rural counties.

Rural areas experienced major declines in their main employment sectors—resource-based industries—agriculture, mining, and forestry. The recession brought significant declines, and these industries did not respond well in the postrecessionary period.

Mazie and Killian examine national trends and show that rural areas were adversely affected by manufacturing trends. The relatively high dollar during the 1980s meant that, even though wages in rural areas could compete effectively with urban areas in the United States, they were high compared with those in other countries. The result was a shift in manufacturing jobs to overseas locations. The type of manufacturing found in rural areas was fairly routine and low-skilled, precisely where foreign competition is greatest. New industries relying on the latest skills and technology are more attracted to urban areas that contain a broader range of services and larger labor markets.

The growth in jobs in the 1980s clearly was in services, but this industry contains two segments. Producer services—those provided primarily to businesses—tend to be relatively better-paying than consumer services—provided mainly to consumers. Unfortunately, much of the growth in rural areas has been in the latter. These jobs pay substantially less, even than the producer services that pay less than manufacturing jobs lost. Thus, even though some of the employment lost during the early 1980s was regained, the income generated is less.

The Midwest suffered many of the same economic problems experienced nationally, but because of the heavy dependence on agriculture and resource-based industries, the effect was much greater. Population declines during the 1980s were especially severe, as documented by Sofranko, and these losses are not likely to be regained in the future. The population declines, of course, are a result of concentration in agriculture and the exodus of manufacturing and retail businesses from rural communities. Even during the 1970s when rural areas, nationally, were doing well, midwestern states grew at approximately one-half the national rate. During the 1980s, based on preliminary census data, rural counties in the Midwest had zero population growth, compared with approximately 0.5 percent growth nationally. The Midwest is the only region expected to report no growth. Preliminary evidence also suggests that midwestern states will report substantial outmigration during the 1980s.

Shifts in population are also linked to economic issues. Continued outmigration of the younger populations, in search of better employment, means that the remaining labor force is less attractive to incoming industries or businesses. Population declines shrink markets for retail stores. It may be difficult for the remaining population to afford the resulting higher costs of services, especially if the wage rates or incomes generated are reduced.

Commercial agriculture, in the past, was a dominant industry in both employment and income in many rural areas in the Midwest. Times have changed, however, as agricultural mechanization and a poor farm economy displaced many farm operators and families. These changes, of course, involve a long-term trend toward larger farms and more mechanized operations. Low farm prices in the early 1980s, coupled with high debt levels incurred during the late 1970s, forced many to leave farming.

The agricultural industry, as pointed out by Lins, underwent several more subtle changes. Small farm operators had relied on local sources to market produce and purchase feed, fertilizers, and supplies. Large farms, however, more likely purchase supplies and inputs from large suppliers and often are able to purchase in bulk quantities. Thus, even though the same number of acres is under cultivation, the purchasing patterns have shifted from small retail trade areas to large regional centers.

A clear example of the effect of changing farm operations is the loss of farm equipment dealerships, so common in small farming communities. The closing of these dealerships in small towns shifts retail trade activity to large regional centers as well. Retail and wholesale businesses cannot compete with large discount stores, which offer a wider selection of merchandise at lower cost. Small town residents, as well as farm families, are attracted to these centers.

Farm families also have come to rely more heavily on off-farm income. This shift was necessitated during the early 1980s when off-farm employment often meant the ability to continue farming. Off-farm employment, however, also strengthened economic ties to larger urban employment centers and directed economic activity away from small rural communities.

The importance of the link between small communities and commercial agriculture, however, can be overplayed. The growth in economic activity in large centers is part of a long-term economic transformation and is not likely to reverse, without unforeseen major changes. Shrinking agricultural employment indicates that, even if purchasing patterns had not shifted, business losses in small rural communities could not have been averted.

In addition to commercial agriculture, trends in other industries have affected the Midwest. The fact that the Midwest lost employment, relative to the United States, is well-known. In addition, however, small and medium-size businesses contributed relatively more to the employment growth in the Midwest than in the nation during the 1980s. Phillips and Miller show that more than 60 percent of the net employment growth is represented by small and medium-size firms, but the growth rate of these businesses is well below that for metropolitan areas. They also show that large-size operations actually increased more rapidly in nonmetropolitan areas than in either metro areas or in counties adjacent to metro areas.

Employment trends show some bright spots for rural areas also. Phillips and Miller demonstrate that manufacturing jobs shifted from metro areas to nonmetro areas in the 1980s. The growth in manufacturing, however, tends to be offset by declines in agriculture and related industries. In fact, manufacturing has replaced agriculture as a major income source in some rural counties. The East

North Central region, in particular, has benefitted more from this employment growth than have the more agricultural West North Central states.

The difficulty, though, is that the manufacturing jobs tend to be low-technology and low-paying. Many are branch plants of larger firms, which have taken advantage of lower labor and land costs in rural areas. The ties with parent corporations do not cause the stimulative effect that might occur if more inputs were purchased locally.

The service sector represented almost three-fourths of the employment increases in the rural Midwest, but this increase has been generated by large companies or chains, rather than by locally owned businesses. Much of this employment is part-time and pays relatively low wages. Such employment tends to dampen local investment and may limit traditional employment-generating effects.

There is some evidence to suggest that nonmetropolitan areas may benefit from a shift to smaller plant sizes. The areas most likely to benefit, however, are those within commuting distance to larger urban centers. Rural and remote counties are less likely to attract producer services, because of limited markets, and there is increasing concern about shrinking labor markets in these areas also.

Demographic and economic shifts in the rural Midwest have raised havoc with tax bases and other resources used to finance local public services. In turn, good quality public services are necessary to attract residents and industry into rural areas. The decline in farm income and property values in the early 1980s strained local government resources. At the same time, federal assistance to local governments declined during the Reagan Administration, at least in constant dollars, adding to fiscal problems faced by rural governments. The early 1980s also brought inflation, which increased the cost of providing public services.

What was the upshot of declining real fiscal resources and increasing costs of public services? Walzer and Deller identify several trends in methods of financing services in rural areas. Overall, governments in nonmetropolitan counties experienced real increases in revenues and expenditures, but metro areas, except for townships, increased at a much higher percentage. The expected shift from federal revenues toward own source revenues is clearly evident. The national trend for a shift to user fees is less clear, however, and, in some instances, just the reverse was found. Counties, when classified by economic base, differ in revenue and expenditure changes. Agricultural counties depend more on property taxes and state aid than manufacturing counties.

The differences in finance patterns also suggest changes for the future. Those counties with past growth are likely to participate even more in the economic recovery. Thus, one might expect rural areas to continue to lag behind their urban counterparts. The differences in revenue and expenditure growth, most likely, will be attributable to differences in economic base.

Public Policy Responses

The second section of the book examines public policies used in response to demographic and economic changes. Of special importance to rebuilding local economies is the quality of the labor force. The labor force partly determines attractiveness of rural areas for business investment. The issue of education, therefore, is of major concern to rural communities from several perspectives. First, it often is one of the largest employers in the city or county. Second, local policy makers are concerned that without a high-quality educational system, entrepreneurs will not be attracted to the region. From this claim follows the argument that investment in education is an investment in the future of the community.

Crihfield examines the issue of education as an option for improving the labor force and, therefore, the economic potential of rural communities. Specifically, he tests whether additional spending on education results in better student performance on standardized test scores and local economic growth. He also questions whether education is an appropriate public policy tool for promoting economic development within an area. Many studies of the relationship between spending on education and economic development, measured by employment growth, have found virtually no correlation. Crihfield's analysis of Illinois supports this view. Student performance and employment growth are not correlated with spending on education.

Evaluating the importance of spending on education is difficult at best. Student test scores do not always correspond to job performance and payoffs to students from an expanded curriculum may come many years later. Population losses in rural areas are threatening many rural school systems and are alarming for community residents.

While many rural residents and policy makers are genuinely concerned about the future of their communities, relatively few rural communities have a strong economic development program underway for several reasons. The staff available for economic development in small communities is not sufficient to embark on an active program. Financial resources typically won't allow spending large sums to attract outside investment. Economic development leadership is not sufficiently experienced to maintain a prolonged thrust in industrial or business recruitment.

Walzer and Gruidl examine small rural Illinois communities to identify community characteristics associated with economic development activity. They find that city size is crucial to continued support for economic development. Dissatisfaction by the mayor with performance of the city economy often provides an immediate spur to involvement in economic development. Presumably, mayors communicate this dissatisfaction to other members of the city government. Also important is the relative pressure on property taxes to finance services. Communities in which residents are asked to pay higher property taxes are more likely to be active in local economic development.

Although studies in Illinois and Nebraska have found that few small communities typically pursue economic development, there are examples of innovative programs in small towns. In Illinois, for instance, successful community projects have included forming a corporation and selling stock to purchase a company and relocate it within the community, and providing property tax reimbursements to incoming residents who purchase a house in the community. Other groups have built on natural or locational attractions to increase traffic through the community or have conducted special events to attract tourists.

Not all economic development efforts are mounted at the community level. It is equally important to understand the success of specific projects attempted by cities. These projects range from annual events to boost community pride and attract visitors to major undertakings, such as attracting industrial plants. In any case, some communities are more successful than others in these efforts.

Flora and Flora examine economic development approaches used by local governments and factors that differentiate units having successful economic development projects from those that do not actively engage in these endeavors. Special attention is paid to creation of a social infrastructure that will support projects versus other factors that foster economic development. They provide case studies of Kansas governments that have undertaken economic development projects and examine these efforts in light of the professional literature on economic development.

Successful community projects are built on strong, local leadership. This leadership can come from many sources and may or may not involve established organizations, such as the city government. Nevertheless, some person or group of individuals has the interest and foresight to organize the community and pursue economic development goals. The leader also must be able to garner community support toward a common aim, and, in some instances, even cause community residents to invest large amounts of time and money in projects.

Hustedde describes several leadership models and summarizes state programs initiated in the Midwest that implement each of these approaches. He separates leadership programs into three types and explores which might be most suitable for rural areas, given their needs and capacities. Community-based leadership programs appear to have the best chances for success in rural areas and examples of success are provided.

In small communities, local leadership usually is not sufficient to bring about economic development. During the 1980s, state governments tried to entice industry to locate within their boundaries and to work with communities to prepare for industrial development. These programs range from infrastructure improvements and expansion of public facilities to leadership development programs. The 1980s also saw the introduction of aggressive economic incentive and benefit programs for private industry. Businesses became adept at working the system and eliciting competition among states.

Much of the economic development competition missed rural communities. Many, if not most, of the communities are too small to compete effectively for a large industrial plant. An alternative, and more successful approach, is to create and nurture small businesses, using entrepreneurial talent within the community. Business incubators, flexible manufacturing programs, and other approaches were initiated to stimulate the business creation process.

Unruh examines approaches and strategies adopted by midwestern states in promoting rural economic development. He focuses on the processes that assist state governments to formulate goals and enact successful economic development programs in the Midwest. The state programs are compared on the basis of their overall approaches and direction. Some of these programs involve funding creative local economic development projects and others work on local capacity building.

Communities, in many instances, do not have sufficient resources to carry out economic development programs alone, and are more successful when they cooperate in a regional effort. Unruh examines these programs in several midwestern states to illustrate their effectiveness in bringing rural communities together.

Although there are encouraging signs, there is little doubt that rural areas in the Midwest, generally, are facing difficult times. Many long-term economic trends documented in earlier chapters will continue and will be very difficult, if not impossible, to reverse. Rural areas must adjust and policy makers must manage the economic transformation so as to optimize quality of life for residents. They must recognize that effective solutions will come from within the communities and cannot be created by the federal or state governments.

Drabenstott contends that effective rural policy should contain several main elements. It must be targeted to meet the needs of diverse rural areas. Small communities do not have the staff and finances to participate in extensive development activities. The programs must be broad enough to allow communities to build on special talents and resources.

Because attracting large manufacturing plants is not feasible in many rural communities, appropriate federal and state policies should encourage entrepreneurship in rural areas. Starting small businesses with local talent and finances, however, often is possible and can form the basis for an effective local economic development policy.

To participate in economic development and be prepared for the future, the rural work force must be prepared for future employment opportunities. This will be even more difficult for rural areas with a declining tax base. Nevertheless, rural populations, in the future, must compete in an increasingly complex labor market.

Clearly, if rural midwestern communities are to survive, efforts must build on the main resource available in rural areas—farm products. Future research should be directed toward increasing the value added of these products and toward the promotion of industries that can bring this increased productivity to rural areas. Universities and other research agencies are an important component of this process.

Community economic development in the Midwest and other regions will be one of the most important rural issues during the 1990s. Long-term trends, many of which adversely affect rural areas, will continue, as residents migrate in search of better job prospects. Only through an understanding of rural trends and the direction in which rural areas are heading will effective policy initiatives be forthcoming.

RURAL COMMUNITY ECONOMIC DEVELOPMENT

1. Growth and Change in Rural America: The Experience of the 1980s and Prospects for the 1990s

Sara Mills Mazie and Molly Sizer Killian

Social scientists don't have an impressive record in reading crystal balls. Just as they think they understand what is going on and have some confidence in talking intelligently about the future, everything seems to change and they are reminded again that "while forecasts usually run in straight lines, history often generates bends and curves" (Perspectives, 1989, p. 2).

This reality holds true when considering the future of the rural economy. In the latter 1960s and early 1970s, social scientists were surprised that rural areas were attracting more people than they were losing and were growing faster than urban areas. Just as this trend became recognized and understood, the tides reversed and trends of rural net outmigration and slower growth returned.

Recognizing the limitations of the field, however, has not and should not keep social scientists from trying to understand what has happened in rural areas and what these past patterns might mean for the future of rural America. In this chapter, then, we examine the performance of the rural economy during the past decade and the changes in the structure of that economy that, to a large extent, characterize the rural experience of the 1980s. This analysis provides a basis for considering the rural economy and its performance in the 1990s.

THE RURAL ECONOMY IN THE 1980s: GROWTH VERSUS DEVELOPMENT

Rural areas suffered badly, and to a greater extent than urban areas, during the back-to-back recessions at the beginning of the 1980s. They also took longer to recover, essentially stagnating in the middle of the decade as the urban economy expanded. Only in the past few years have there been signs that employment growth has returned to prerecession levels and parity with metro areas. This improvement is misleading, however, for the parity is in terms of the numbers of jobs created only, not in the quality of those jobs.[1]

Major economic and demographic indicators clearly reflect the trends of the decade. Employment growth in nonmetro areas lagged behind metro areas through most of the decade, and, in several years, was slow in both areas (Figure 1.1). Between 1980 and 1983, nonmetro employment levels remained below those of 1979. Between 1979 and 1987, nonmetro employment increased only about 8 percent. In contrast, metro employment grew almost 20 percent, or more than double the nonmetro rate between 1979 and 1987.

Changes in earnings per job (an indicator of growth in the quality of jobs) did not follow the pattern set by employment in returning to prerecession levels. Little gain in this measure of economic well-being has occurred nationally, but rural areas have done particularly poorly. Historically, earnings per job have been significantly higher in urban areas; the margin increased in the 1980s. By 1987, nonmetro real earnings per job ($16,737) were about 7 percent less than before the recessions in 1979 ($17,845), whereas metro earnings per job had returned to prerecession levels in urban areas ($22,285 in 1979 and $22,404 in 1987) (Figure 1.2).[2] The rural decline in earnings per job coupled with an increasing rural–urban gap provide evidence that many of the new rural jobs created during the decade were of poor quality. In 1987 (the last year for which data are available), as rural employment grew substantially, there was actually a slight decline in earnings per job.

The overall poor performance of the rural economy during the 1980s, especially relative to the urban economy, is the product of developments in many sectors of the rural economy. Some of these developments were cyclical, such as the recessions in the early 1980s. Others were part of long-term shifts in the structure of the rural economy, such as the decline in the importance of agriculture and other resource-based rural industries. Equally important, but perhaps less understood, were structural changes that involved the increasing concentration of lower-paying, low-skill jobs in rural areas and better-paying, high-skill jobs in urban areas, a trend evident in both manufacturing and service industries.

These diverse developments help explain not only the poor performance of the rural economy during the early and mid–1980s, but also they suggest reasons for the slow recovery of the rural economy. Further, they provide insight as to why that recovery was primarily in terms of growth in the number of jobs and less in terms of improvement in economic well-being.

DECLINE OF RURAL RESOURCE-BASED INDUSTRIES

The resource-based industries of agriculture, mining, and forestry traditionally have been the heart of the export base of rural economies, bringing capital resources into local rural economies by selling natural resources (e.g., food, heating oil, lumber) to urban areas. The importance of these industries to both the national and rural economy, however, is continuing to decline. This can be seen most clearly through decreases in employment during the 1980s (Figure 1.3). In addition, each of these industries came upon hard times during the

Figure 1.1
Total Employment Change, 1979–87

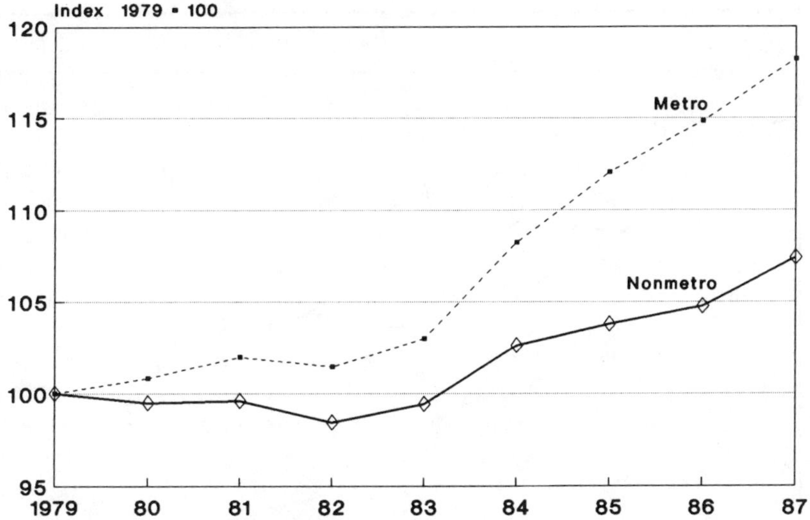

Source: U.S. Department of Commerce, 1989.

Figure 1.2
Total Earnings Per Job Change, 1979–87

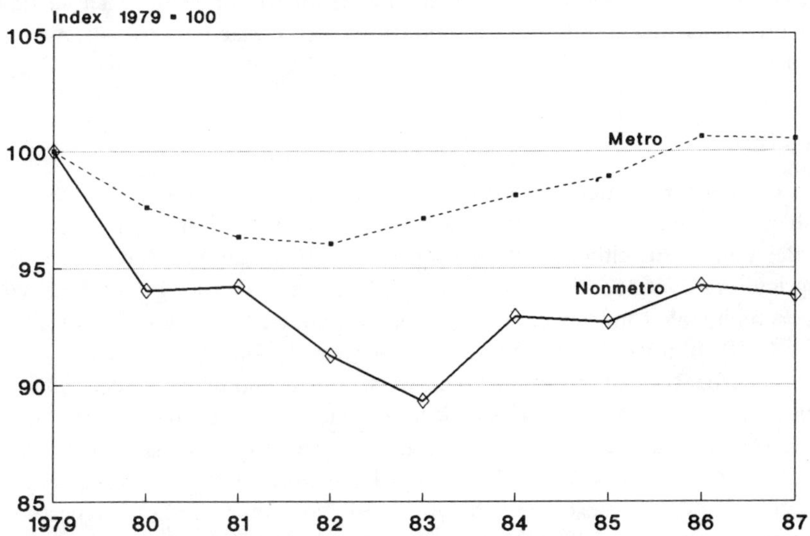

Source: U.S. Department of Commerce, 1989.

Figure 1.3
Nonmetro Workers in Resource Industries, 1969–87

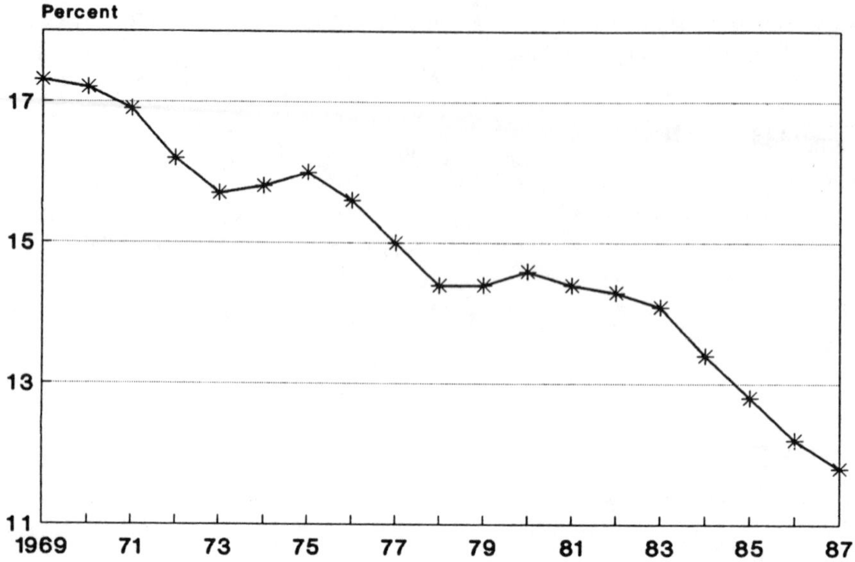

Source: U.S. Department of Commerce, 1989.

1980s, for reasons not obviously related to the long-term decline. These short-term problems in natural resource industries exacerbated the trends over the decades.

Agriculture

The experience of agriculture during the 1980s epitomizes this phenomenon as much as any industry. Consolidation and mechanization of farms over many decades continued, although at a slower pace. The result was that employment in agriculture continued to decline. The industry also did not grow at the same pace as many other industries and therefore accounted for a declining percentage of the GNP. In a word, agriculture is not a growth industry, whether measured by employment or total net income, so as the economy expanded after the recessions, rural areas could not look to agriculture as a source of growth.

The severe financial stress in agriculture in the early and mid–1980s, while primarily creating changes in the financial structure of the industry, certainly brought about a decrease in employment in the sector. USDA suggests that between 200,000 and 300,000 people left the sector during the worst period, a sizeable number, but not nearly as high, either in absolute or relative terms, as in earlier decades.[3] By 1988, agriculture had basically recovered from the financial travail earlier in the decade, but it was left once again with fewer people. In areas of the country where agriculture is dominant and there is little other industry, such as the western Cornbelt and the Plains, the effect has been crushing for individual families and for communities struggling to provide community services to a declining population.

Mining

The early years of the decade were golden times for mining and energy. Prices and demand were up, as were profits and employment. However, the collapsing energy prices and reduced production that hit soon thereafter devastated areas dependent on these industries. Employment and income dropped dramatically, creating major dislocations. Both mining and energy have rebounded somewhat, but have still not recovered to early 1980s' levels. Employment in mining continues to decline, although at a slower rate than middecade.

Forestry[4]

Forestry jobs are among the highest paying jobs in the natural resource industries. However, given the industry's strong relationship to construction, and construction's sensitivity to the national business cycle, forestry wages and employment levels are markedly cyclical. Not surprisingly, the industry was hard hit by the national recessions in the early 1980s. In addition, for the first time in more than 30 years, the early 1980s saw real interest rates exceed the rate of inflation by more than 5 percent, resulting in significant decreases in the demand for new housing, and, thus, for the forest products used in construction.

Renewed conflicts between ecological and economic interests in the 1980s also had a significant impact on the forestry industry, especially in the Northwest, where new requirements for selective harvesting of trees (as opposed to clear-cutting) led to higher production costs. Last, as in many industries, a considerable number of forestry jobs have been lost to automation.

The net effect of these changes in agriculture, mining, and forestry is that the traditional economic base of many rural areas no longer stimulate the growth or provide the employment base that they once did. When the national economy began to expand in 1984, these natural resource industries did not expand, and therefore, they did not help to pull rural areas out of the recessions. For this reason, these industries indirectly contributed to the stagnation of the rural economy, just as the urban economy began to pick up steam.

MANUFACTURING STRUGGLES

In the 1970s, much of the growth in rural areas was fueled by manufacturing, another important export base in many rural areas. Particularly in the rural South,

Figure 1.4
Manufacturing Employment Change, 1979–88

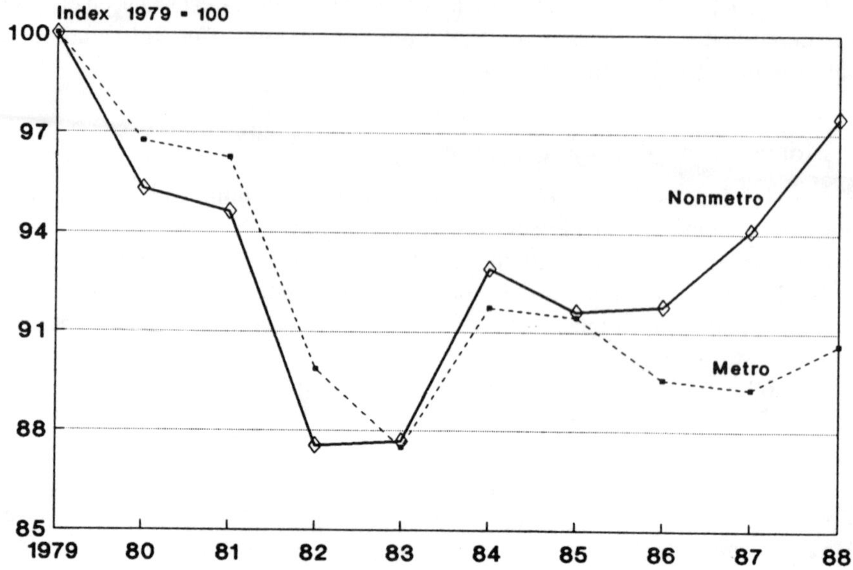

Source: U.S. Department of Commerce, 1989.

where labor costs were low, growth in manufacturing not only filled the employment vacuum left by declining agriculture employment, but generated overall employment growth as well.

During the 1980s, however, manufacturing in both rural and urban areas floundered. The national recessions seriously undercut domestic demand for manufactured goods, including those made in rural areas. Added to the problems of manufacturing during the early and mid–1980s were a dramatic growth in the value of the dollar relative to other currencies and a restructuring taking place within the sector.

The advantage of a rural location for manufacturing diminished significantly as the value of the U.S. dollar rose to an all time high, reaching its peak in mid–1985. This meant that the cost of rural labor, as low as it was compared with urban labor, was too high when compared with labor costs in other countries, especially the developing nations. In order to remain competitive in world markets, some of these rural manufacturers moved their production overseas, whereas others simply shut down altogether. Either way, rural areas lost jobs. Thus, just as the national economy began to grow again, the high value of the dollar didn't allow rural products to be competitive with the same products produced in Taiwan or Colombia or Haiti.

Figure 1.5
Change in Complex and Routine Manufacturing Employment, Total United States, 1979–89

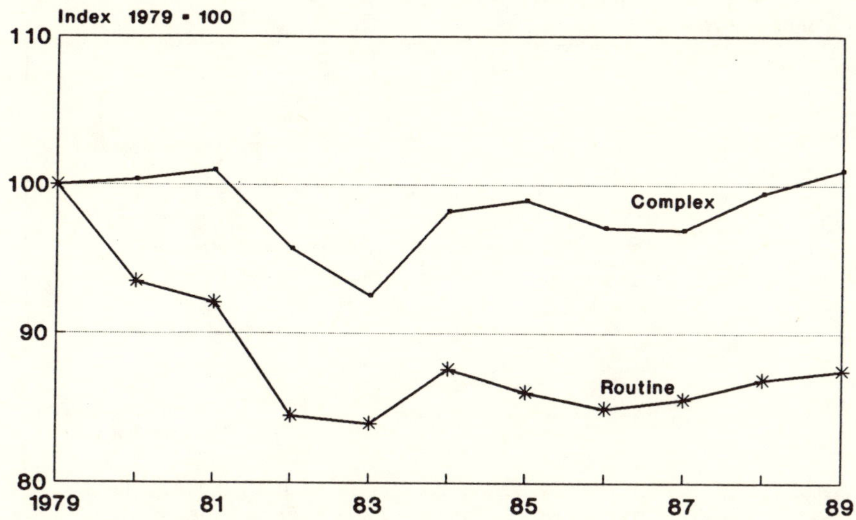

Source: U.S. Department of Labor, Bureau of Labor Statistics, 1990.

The net result is that rural manufacturing employment grew moderately between 1982 and 1984, only to drop again with the rise in the value of the dollar. It wasn't until 1987, roughly 18 months after the dollar had hit its peak, that employment showed signs of growth again. Nevertheless, as late as 1988, manufacturing employment still had not returned to 1979 levels, in either metro or nonmetro areas (Figure 1.4).

Equally important for rural economies, however, has been a restructuring within manufacturing.[5] To a large extent, rural manufacturing is concentrated in older, low-skilled, low-wage industries. The actual production process in these industries tends to be machine-paced and fragmented into many relatively simple, repetitive, and routine tasks, allowing firms to take advantage of the relatively low-skilled and low-wage labor forces in rural areas.

In contrast, complex manufacturing industries, those that depend heavily on advanced technology, more likely will locate in metro areas. Such firms need access to skilled workers and engineers, because of the complexity of the manufacturing process. A major component of the competitiveness of these manufacturers is their ability to respond quickly to changing needs of the companies and individuals to whom they sell. The success of these manufacturing industries

Figure 1.6
Change in Complex and Routine Manufacturing Employment, Metro–Nonmetro, 1979–88

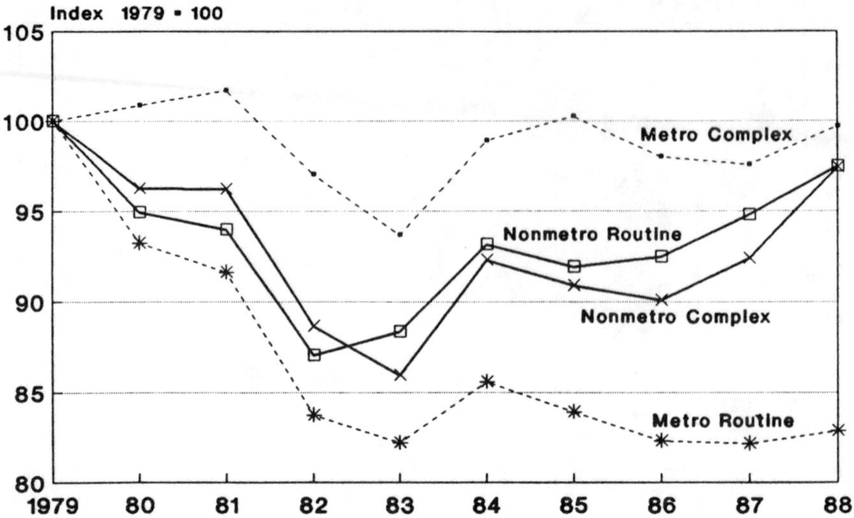

Source: U.S. Department of Commerce, 1989.

is less likely to be based on competitive prices and low wages, and is, therefore, less vulnerable to fluctuations in the value of the dollar.

Nationally, complex manufacturing did not suffer nearly as much from the recessions as did routine manufacturing, which actually was slumping even before the recessionary periods (Figure 1.5). By 1989, employment in complex manufacturing was back to prerecession levels. In contrast, although experiencing a sustained 3-year growth period, 1989 employment levels in routine manufacturing were still less than 90 percent of their 1979 levels.

Comparing complex manufacturing employment growth in metro and nonmetro areas shows that this bright spot of the 1980s failed to boost the rural economy (Figure 1.6). Complex manufacturing employment in metro areas weathered the recessions better than routine manufacturing, and had recovered by 1985. In contrast, complex manufacturing employment in nonmetro areas performed only marginally better than nonmetro routine manufacturing. Consequently, urban areas captured more than their share of growth within the complex manufacturing sector.

The net effect of these differential growth rates during the decade was a sorting-out process within manufacturing. By the end of the 1980s, an even greater and disproportionate share of the less attractive, lower-paying routine

Figure 1.7
Spatial Distribution of Complex and Routine Manufacturing Employment, 1979 and 1986

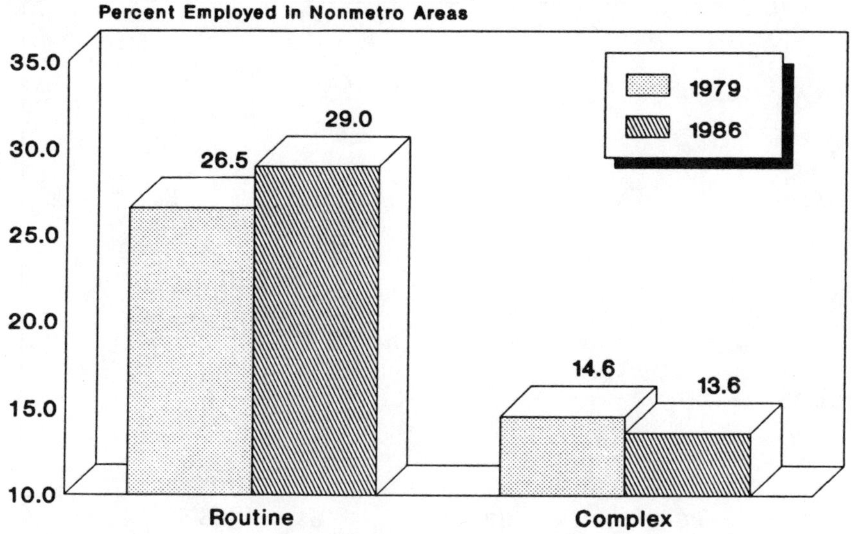

Source: U.S. Department of Commerce, 1989.

manufacturing jobs was found in rural areas and a higher share of the more desirable, better-paying complex manufacturing jobs was found in urban areas (Figure 1.7).

These cyclic patterns and structural trends in manufacturing employment had significant impacts on the changing quality of rural jobs, as measured by earnings per job. Earnings per manufacturing job grew fairly steadily in urban areas throughout the decade, reaching a peak in 1986 that was almost 8 percent higher than that in 1979 (Figure 1.8). Even after a decline between 1986 and 1987, earnings per manufacturing job in urban areas were 5 percent higher than in 1979. In contrast, earnings per job in rural manufacturing remained at or below 1979 levels until 1986. A decline in 1987 returned rural manufacturing earnings to 1979 levels.

STEADY GROWTH IN SERVICES FAVORS URBAN AREAS

While manufacturing faltered in both urban and rural areas during the recessions, the service industry, the fastest growing sector of the economy and the one contributing the most new jobs, barely missed a step (Figure 1.9). Service

Figure 1.8
Manufacturing Earnings Per Job Change, 1979–87

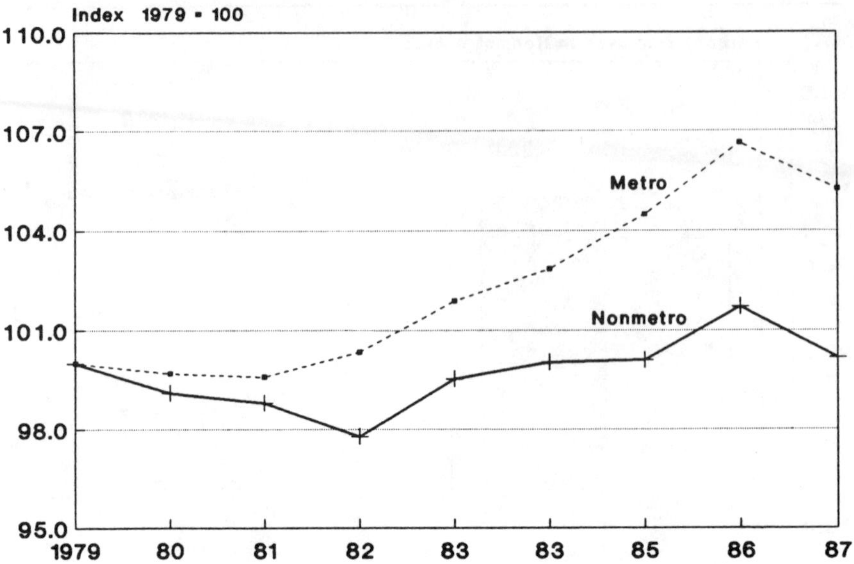

Source: U.S. Department of Commerce, 1989.

employment in metro areas grew more than 30 percent between 1979 and 1988, and almost 20 percent in nonmetro areas.

A closer look at service industries suggests that a significant sorting-out process occurred within services during the decade. The service sector can be divided roughly into two types, those that generally provide services to individuals as private citizens, or consumer services, and those that provide services to businesses, or producer services.[6]

Consumer services, such as dry cleaners, grocers, and car dealers, are marketed to local residents, and, therefore, are generally distributed according to population and are strongly influenced by changes in the size of the local population. These services recirculate money within the local economy rather than bring in money from outside the area. Thus, they do little to stimulate growth in the local economy. Also consumer service jobs generally are low-wage and often part-time.

Producer services, including wholesale trade, transportation, communications, banking, and other business and professional activities, support firms of all types, including manufacturers, and, therefore, locate where there is a sufficient number of potential clients. This location pattern means that a disproportionate share of producer services are in urban areas, where there is

Figure 1.9
Service Employment Change, 1979–88

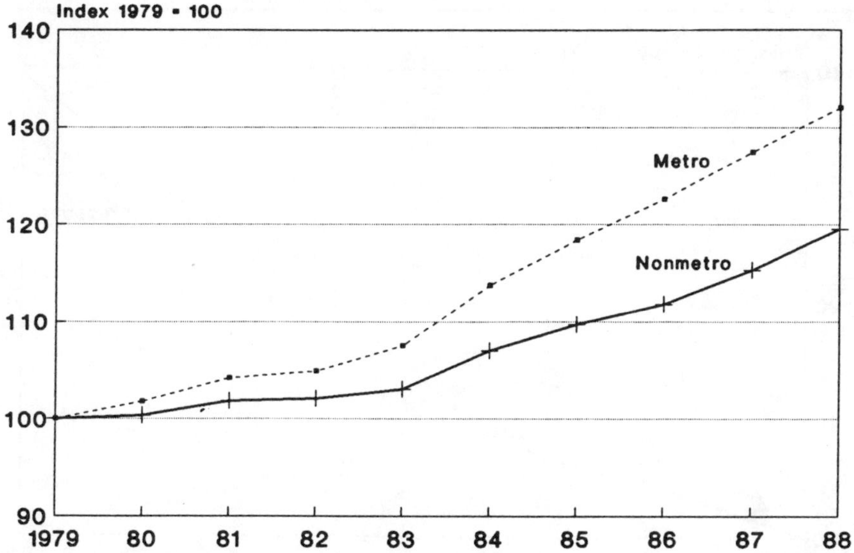

Source: U.S. Department of Commerce, 1989.

a larger market for their services. Because producer services often market to export-base firms that typically sell a product outside the local economy, they are also considered export-base industries. They attract funds into an area indirectly through the firms they serve, stimulating growth in the local economy. Producer service jobs, on average, also pay higher wages and are more desirable than consumer service jobs.

Both consumer and producer services grew quite rapidly during the 1980s (Figure 1.10). However, there was a distinct spatial pattern to that growth. The growth in consumer service jobs was distributed between rural and urban areas roughly in proportion to the areas' share of the national population. Consumer services in rural areas, while growing less rapidly than in urban areas, did grow throughout the decade. At the end of the 1980s, there was a slight shift in jobs toward urban areas. This approximates a small shift in the distribution of the population (Figure 1.11).

The experience with producer services differed markedly. The growth was much faster in urban areas than in rural areas. During the depth of the recession in 1982, employment in producer services declined slightly, but rapidly recovered after 1983. This growth, along with that in consumer services, boosted urban areas and, to some extent, mitigated the negative effects of declines in manu-

Figure 1.10
Change in Producer and Consumer Service Employment, Total United States, 1979–89

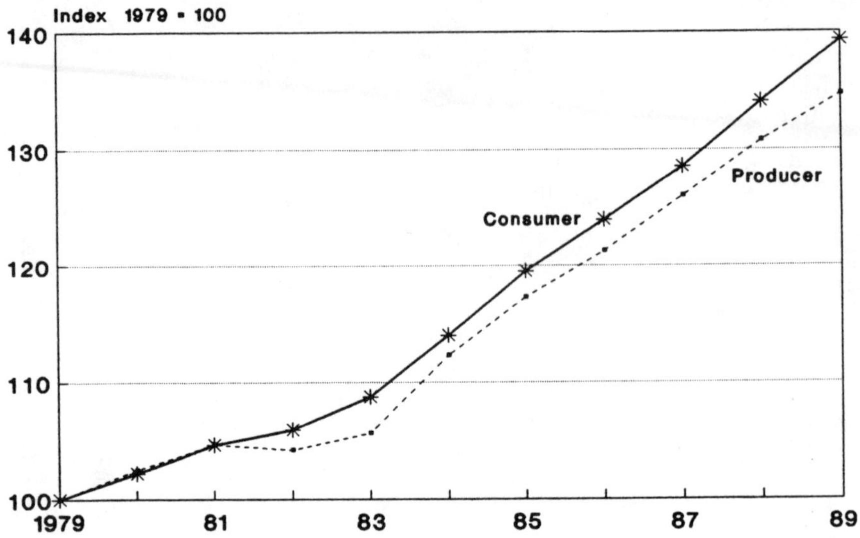

Source: U.S. Department of Labor, Bureau of Labor Statistics, 1990.

facturing during the recessions. The same phenomenon did not occur in rural areas, which explains some of the gap between the urban and rural economy, particularly during the mid–1980s. Producer services in rural areas grew at about one-fifth the rate of urban areas.[7]

The net effect of the difference between the metro and nonmetro growth rates was that producer services became even more urban-oriented. Whereas roughly 24 percent of the U.S. population is in nonmetro areas, only 12 percent of producer services were located in nonmetro areas in 1986 (the latest year for which data are available). Again, the scales were tipped toward urban areas and urban growth during the 1980s (Figure 1.12).

As with manufacturing, these differential patterns of service employment growth in metro and nonmetro areas had significant impacts on changes in the quality of jobs in rural areas. In urban areas, earnings per service job declined during the recessions, but grew steadily after 1982 (Figure 1.13). By 1986, due primarily to thriving producer services, metro earnings per service job exceeded 1979 levels. In contrast, earnings per job in rural services declined or stagnated throughout the decade. In 1987, nonmetro earnings per service job were no better than they had been during the worst of the recessions—only slightly more than 90 percent of 1979 levels.

Figure 1.11
Change in Producer and Consumer Service Employment, Metro–Nonmetro, 1979–88

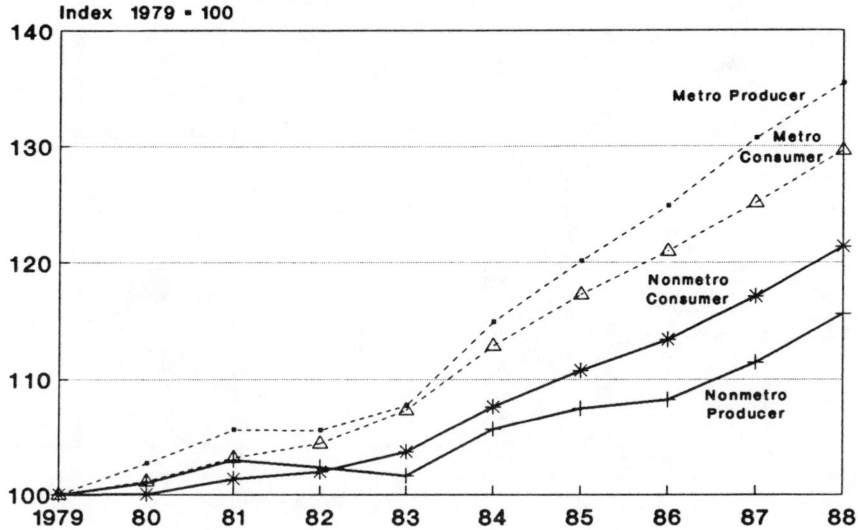

Source: U.S. Department of Commerce, 1989.

The diminishing importance of traditional resource-based rural industries combined with the poor performance of rural producer services and weak performance of rural-oriented routine manufacturing explain much of the overall poor performance of the rural economy during the 1980s. The next section briefly examines some of the social and demographic effects of these changes in the rural economy.

POPULATION RESPONSES TO CHANGING ECONOMIC CONDITIONS[8]

As the rural economy suffered through the difficult times of the early and mid–1980s, many rural residents decided to search for ways to improve their well-being. They responded to the changing distribution of employment opportunities. Data on population growth and migration during the decade support the notion that people adjusted to the recessions, the slow rural recovery, and the structural shifts transforming the rural economy by moving where they could maximize their personal skills and earning capacity (Mazie, 1990a).

A time lag occurred between when rural conditions deteriorated and when people made personal adjustments to worsening conditions. The two recessions

Figure 1.12
Spatial Distribution of Producer and Consumer Service Employment, 1979 and 1986

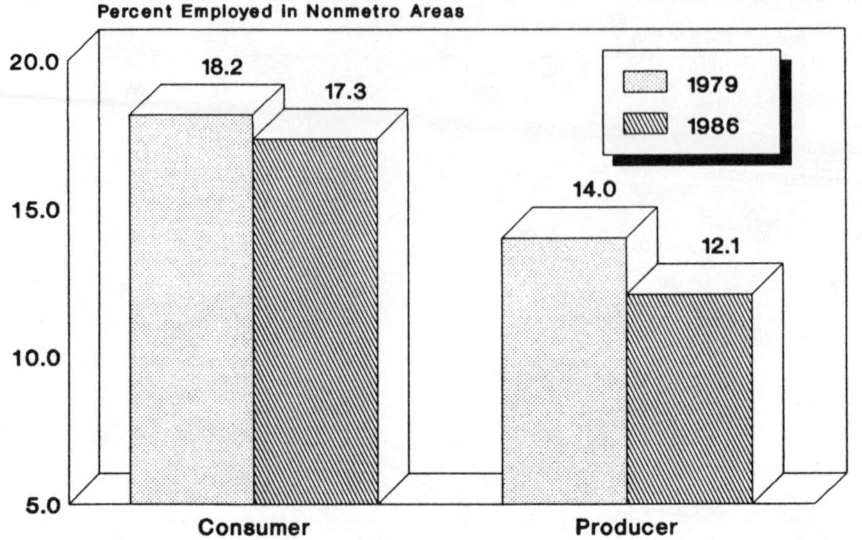

Source: U.S. Department of Commerce, 1989.

in 1980–2 followed a decade of relative prosperity, one in which both rural employment and population growth were higher and the gap between rural and urban per-capita income had narrowed. This, coupled with the fact that people don't move at the first signal of deteriorating conditions, explains why the significant movements out of rural areas did not become apparent until about 1983.

Rural residents may have hoped to wait out the national recessions. However, when their effect continued in rural areas much longer than in urban areas, rural residents began to respond to a lagging rural economy. Many responded by moving to cities or suburbs with an expanding economy and more and better jobs. In contrast, few metro people could move to rural areas, no matter what the attractions. The result was that, after more than a decade of net movement or migration into rural areas, there was net outmigration. During the mid–1980s, when the rural economy performed especially poorly, relative to the urban economy, the outmigration was particularly high, and, as a result, rural population growth was very low, far below the urban rate (Figure 1.14). Since 1986, the growth rate has improved somewhat, but through 1988, the most recent year for which data are available, the rate has continued to be lower than during the first half of the decade. Between 1986 and 1988, over half of the roughly 2,400 nonmetro counties nationwide lost population.[9]

Figure 1.13
Service Earnings Per Job Change, 1979–87

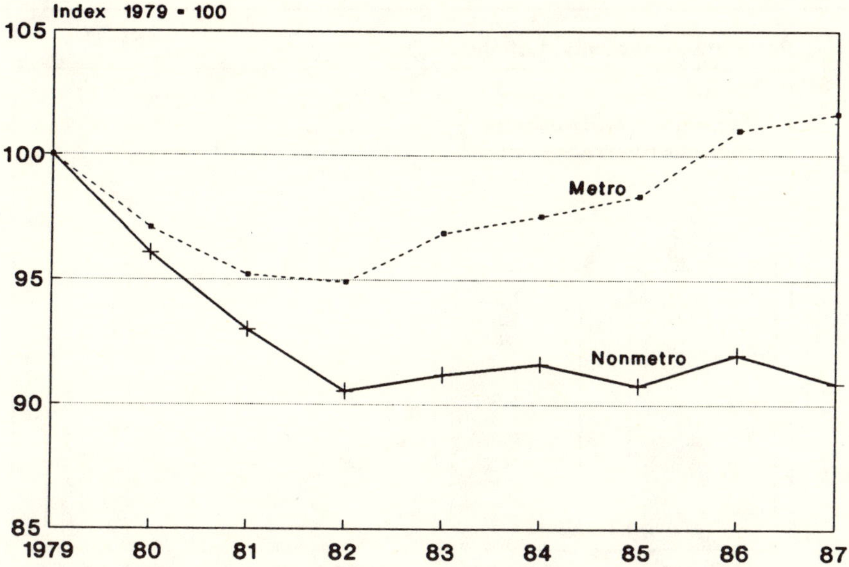

Source: U.S. Department of Commerce, 1989.

As the rural economy picked up toward the end of the decade, consistent with improved rural population growth, net outmigration slowed considerably, particularly between 1988 and 1989. The outmigration and population growth rates, however, have been very uneven across the country, reflecting the considerable diversity in local or regional economies and geography. Each of the three groups of counties, in which farming, mining, and manufacturing are dominant, experienced net outmigration between 1984 and 1988, a trend consistent with the decline in employment in each of those industries. A disproportionate number of farming-dependent counties lost population.

Those nonmetro counties adjacent to metro counties attracted more people than they lost throughout the decade, almost certainly because of proximity to urban areas, and to an expanding urban economy. They also had growth rates that, although only roughly two-thirds the metro rates, were much higher than in the more remote nonmetro counties. Moreover, the advantage of being close to a metro area seems to be growing. Net outmigration in the more remote counties increased from 1983–6 and 1986–8 and net inmigration to adjacent nonmetro counties increased during the same periods. The penalty for remoteness seems to have increased (Figure 1.15).

Migration trends in rural areas during the 1980s exhibit diversity, not only in

Figure 1.14
Nonmetro Population Growth Rates, 1980–8

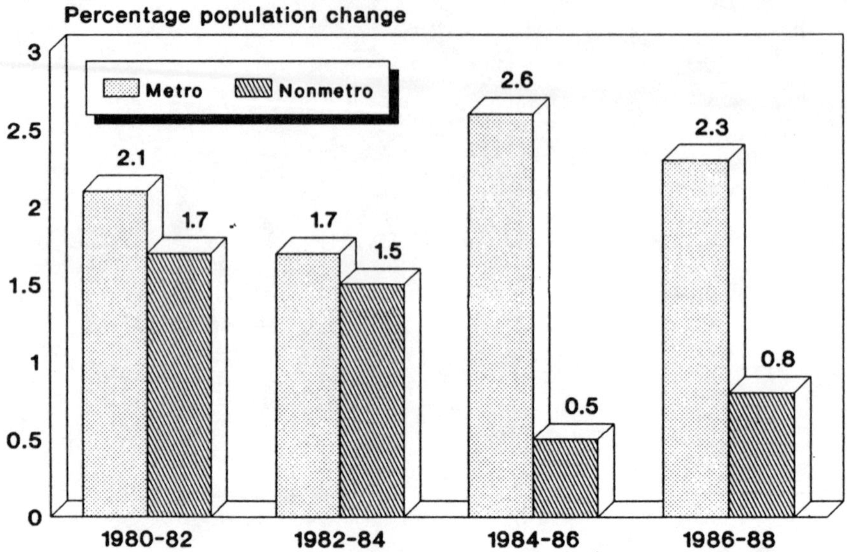

Source: U.S. Bureau of the Census, 1990a.

the type of areas left by rural people, but also in terms of who was moving, and, specifically, their educational level. A disproportionate number of people with some higher education left rural areas. In the middle of the decade, net outmigration was evident for all rural residents, regardless of education level, but was highest for those with the most education. By 1988, this situation had changed somewhat, with rural areas experiencing low levels of net inmigration for those with lower levels of education, whereas outmigration continued for those with more education (Figure 1.16).

The shift in the rural–urban distribution of jobs by skill level almost certainly contributed to this selective outmigration. If one can assume that people move to where employment opportunities are best, then the fact that the rural share of lower-skilled and poorer-paying jobs increased and higher-skilled and better-paying jobs decreased during the decade attracted better educated rural residents to urban areas and less educated urban residents to rural areas.

This tendency is enhanced because the rural–urban wage differential increases with level of education.[10] Not only are more highly skilled jobs disproportionately concentrated in urban areas, but they tend to pay better than do similar jobs in rural areas, requiring the same level of education. The economic penalty for

Figure 1.15
Net Outmigration from Nonmetro Counties, 1980–8

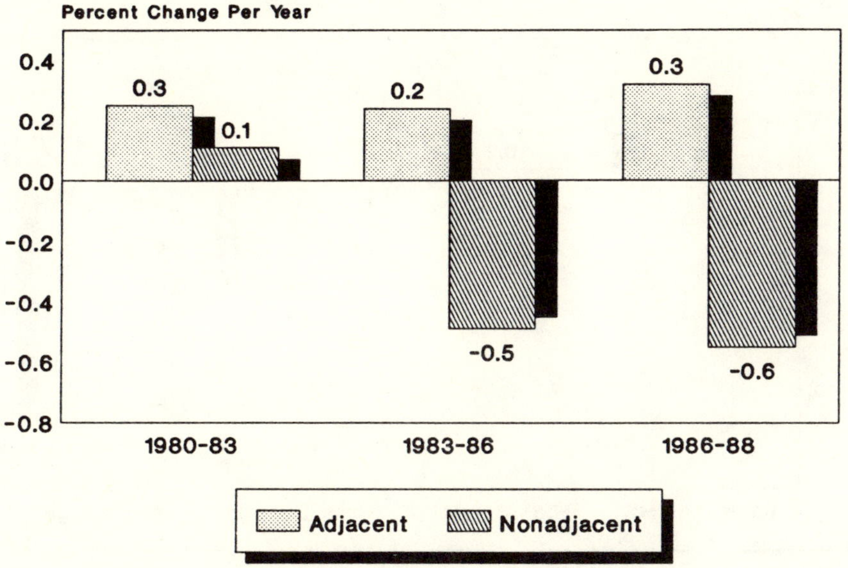

Source: U.S. Bureau of the Census, 1990a.

living in a rural area is higher for a highly educated person. In contrast, the penalty for living in rural areas is relatively low for those with little education. When the somewhat lower cost of living in rural areas is considered, the economic penalty may well become insignificant for the less educated. The facts that the differential migration by education level is not found in the 1970s and that the differential wage levels by educational level were much less significant support the argument that the shift in the distribution of jobs by skill levels has at least encouraged these migration and wage trends.

SUMMARY OF 1980s AND IMPLICATIONS FOR 1990s

In laying the groundwork for looking into the 1990s, several long-term structural shifts in the U.S. economy have been described: (1) a long-term decline in resource-based employment; (2) a downward trend in the number of manufacturing jobs and a minimal increase in the quality of those jobs; and (3) a rapid increase in the number of service jobs during the decade, but an overall deterioration of earnings in those jobs.

These trends in the national economy did not affect rural and urban areas equally; instead, they resulted in increasing differences in the development paths

Figure 1.16
Net Migration of Nonmetro Population, Age 25–64, 1988–9

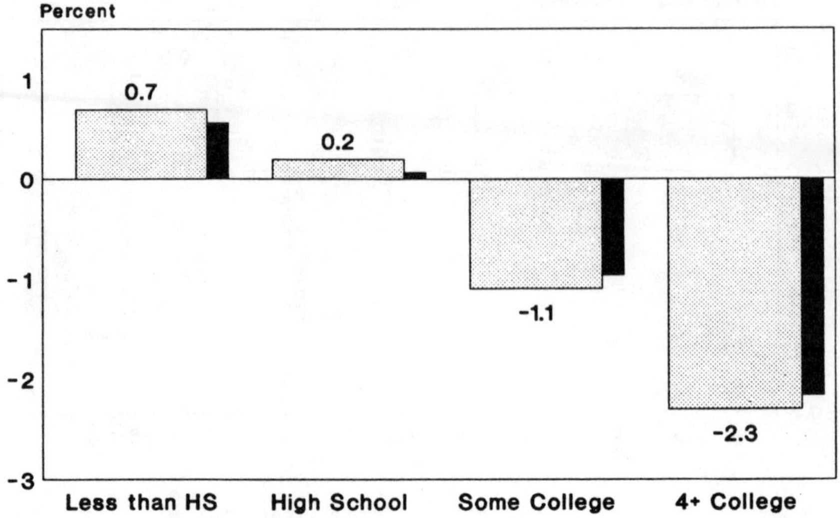

Source: U.S. Bureau of the Census, 1989a.

of rural and urban economies. Given the importance of resource-based industries for rural areas, the impacts of the long-term decline in agriculture, mining, and forestry were felt much more keenly in rural than in urban areas.

The total number of manufacturing jobs declined in both rural and urban areas, with the greatest loss in urban areas. However, the restructuring that occurred in the sector over the decade left urban areas with a smaller but stronger manufacturing sector made up of a larger share of better-paying, more competitive, complex manufacturing jobs. Meanwhile, rural areas, eventually regaining about as many manufacturing jobs as they had had in 1979, continued to rely more on low-skilled, lower-paying jobs, falling even farther behind urban areas in terms of earnings.

Steadily expanding employment in the service sector brought the most new jobs to rural areas; however, almost all of the growth in rural service jobs were the lower-paying, less desirable, consumer services. In contrast, the fastest growing jobs in urban areas were the better paying, more desirable, producer services. As a result, the quality of service jobs in rural areas deteriorated—both relatively and absolutely.

The net effect of these trends is that rural America is beginning the 1990s in a less than desirable situation. Moreover, if these restructuring trends extend into the 1990s, rural America will be at an even greater disadvantage. The new jobs in rural areas will likely be either routine manufacturing (if the value of the U.S. dollar stays down) or consumer services. Furthermore, to the extent that the uneven growth in the quality of jobs between rural and urban areas persists, we can expect a continuation of the ''rural brain drain,'' where the best and the brightest from rural areas move to the cities in search of better job opportunities.

A final important caveat to this somewhat gloomy assessment of what the 1990s will bring to rural America: There is considerable diversity among nonmetro areas in the United States. The impact of these cyclical and structural trends will vary a great deal, depending on the types of local industries, the specific types of local human capital resources, and an area's proximity to metropolitan centers.

NOTES

1. This chapter draws heavily on ongoing research being carried out by analysts in the Agriculture and Rural Economy Division of the Economic Research Service in USDA. Particularly important has been the work by David McGranahan, Leslie Whitener, Tim Parker, and Linda Ghelfi.

2. All earnings data are in constant 1987 dollars.

3. See Stam et al. (forthcoming) for an analysis of farm financial stress and farm exits in the 1980s.

4. This section draws heavily on a study by Weber, Castle, and Shriver (1988).

5. The classification of manufacturing used in this analysis was developed by McGranahan (1988a and 1988b).

6. See McGranahan (1988a and 1988b) for the definitions of consumer and producer services used here.

7. The more elite producer services, such as those offered by accountants, computer specialists, lawyers, and bankers, performed very well in both rural and urban areas. See Porterfield (1990) for a detailed treatment of this sector.

8. This section relies on the data reported in the two population sections in the first issue of *Rural Conditions and Trends* (Mazie, 1990a, 1990b).

9. Preliminary 1990 Census data suggest that earlier estimates of nonmetro growth and outmigration, while correct overall, understate the strength of the trend toward slower rural growth during the 1980s.

10. See McGranahan and Ghelfi (forthcoming) for a more detailed analysis of the relationships between the education, earnings, and migration patterns of rural and urban workers.

2. Transitions in Rural Areas of the Midwest and Nation

Andrew J. Sofranko

Ten years ago, the future looked bright for rural areas in the Midwest. Earlier trends of high unemployment and rural outmigration had been reversed and it appeared that prosperity would continue, lessening the gap between rural and urban quality of life. However, in the 1980s, rural areas returned to their earlier trends. Although urban areas in the Midwest fared somewhat better, even they lag behind the growth of the nation.

It is becoming increasingly apparent that the Midwest is a troubled region, characterized by slow growth and extensive outmigration. The 1970s, it now appears, represented an anomaly. The increased importance placed on quality-of-life considerations in residential relocations, and the expansion of manufacturing employment, combined with other factors, led to rural growth and development in many parts of the Midwest.

However, since the 1980s, other areas of the nation have gained preference due to such diverse factors as climate, recreational opportunities, limited labor unionization, and a shift to trade and professional services (Beale, 1985). This, combined with the Midwest's strong dependence on agriculture, relatively large elderly population, and dependence on local resources for economic development, has diminished the attractiveness of the rural Midwest as a place to live and work.

This chapter documents several demographic and socioeconomic trends during the past two decades in the Midwest and the nation, with specific attention to rural areas. To provide a backdrop for examining regional and rural trends, the chapter first provides a brief overview of several national trends that will be revealed in the 1990 census. Attention then shifts to national, regional, and subregional growth patterns during the past two decades. This is followed by a closer examination of the 1970s population "turnaround," with some implications of its reversal in the 1980s. Particular attention is given to rural–urban quality-of-life trends over the past two decades. The chapter concludes with a discussion of these trends.

NATIONAL SETTING

Demographic trends have significant socioeconomic impacts on the nation and region, particularly on rural areas. National population growth has declined over the past several decades to about 1 percent per year in the 1980s. This slowdown is attributable to a lower birthrate, delayed marriage and childbearing, labor force participation of women, and lower levels of immigration. Population growth also has become more regional. The nation's growth occurred mainly in the West and South, with California, Texas, and Florida representing more than half of that growth in the 1980s.

With the exception of these fast growth areas, changing population characteristics are perhaps more meaningful than numbers. These compositional changes, and their attendant social trends, set the context for understanding regional changes during recent decades. The following section draws heavily on Waldrop and Exter (1990).

An Aging Nation

The senior population (65 and over) has grown throughout this century, and has increased faster than the population because of increases in human longevity, immigration at the turn of the century, and lower birthrates. The proportion of senior citizens has increased from 4 percent in 1900 to 9.2 percent in 1960 to over 12 percent today, with the largest recent increases occurring in the population over 75 years of age. Aging is also reflected in the median age of the population, which increased from 31 years in 1980 to 33 in 1990, and is projected at 35 in the year 2000. The implications of an aging population are already apparent in the redirection of public expenditures, occupational trends, voting patterns, and attitudes toward taxing, social services, and residential satisfaction.

An Educated Population

In 1980, for the first time in the nation's history, a majority of the population in every state had completed high school, and 16 percent had 4 years or more of college. In 1990, one in five persons will have completed 4 years of college, with close to 80 percent having graduated from high school. Moreover, the educational gap between men and women is narrowing.

Women in the Labor Force

The 1970s saw a dramatic increase in women working, a trend that continued through the 1980s. Almost three out of five women are in the labor force, compared with two out of five in 1970. More than half of all families have two or more workers; half of the women with preschool children and two-thirds of those with school-age children are employed. These trends reflect family strategies for maintaining middle class lifestyles and improved educational and employment opportunities for women.

Household Formation and Composition

Household formation was slower in the 1980s than in the 1970s, but still nearly 17 percent for the decade. The slowdown has been attributed to a smaller 20–34 age cohort, stabilization of divorce rates, and changed attitudes toward establishing separate households among the young. Still, nonfamily households have grown faster than family households, with a sizeable increase in persons living alone, in single parent families, or with unrelated individuals. The convergence of household and employment trends has resulted in children growing up in smaller households, where both or the only parent works, or where only one parent is present.

Ethnic and Racial Diversity

Whereas population growth has been about 1 percent annually, the Black population has grown at 1.6 percent, the Hispanic 4.5 percent, and the Asian 7.1 percent. Through middecade, more than a quarter of the nation's growth was due to immigration, although this has tapered off since the influx of Asian refugees in the early 1980s. These trends have not been especially pronounced in rural areas of the Midwest.

Population Reversal

Although the 1970s are viewed as the decade of the rural "turnaround" or even "rural renaissance," the 1980s reestablished the predominant pre–1970 trend of urban and suburban growth. In a reversal of the 1970s, urban areas have grown faster than rural areas, and rural outmigration exceeded inmigration during the 1980s. Popular media have gone from writing about "America's Small Town Boom" to "Small Town Blues." Recently released population estimates, by residence, have once again detected a slightly higher rate of rural growth across the nation, but still well below the 1970s.

These trends have not affected all areas equally, but many of them are clearly felt in both rural and urban areas. Rural areas have generally been characterized by older populations, lower levels of female employment, fewer minorities, more family households, and somewhat lower levels of education. Although, some of these differences have become negligible over time, most pervade the nation, requiring many rural schools and communities to adjust to household and labor force trends, as well as to attitudes of an older population.

Figure 2.1
Average Annual Population Growth for the United States and the Midwest, 1950–88

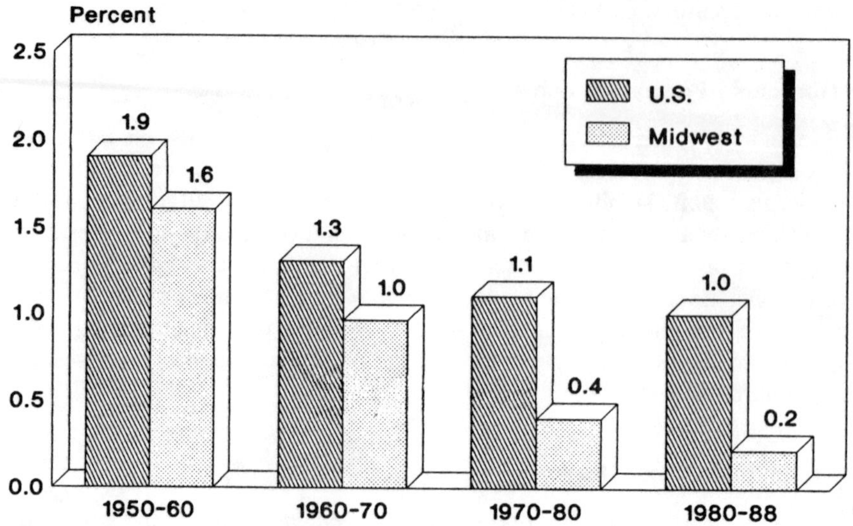

Source: U.S. Bureau of the Census, 1990c.

REGIONAL GROWTH TRENDS

The rate of population growth in the Midwest has declined even more sharply than the nation, because the economic recovery from the recession has been slow (Barringer, 1990, p. A10). Census figures for the 1980s show four states with population losses; two (Iowa and North Dakota) are in the Midwest. The resulting change in congressional seats is expected to cost the Midwest eight representatives. With its high level of outmigration, the Midwest currently accounts for a very small percent of the nation's growth. It has declined as a proportion of the U.S. population; in 1980, 26 percent of Americans lived in the Midwest, compared with 24 percent in 1990. In addition, the Midwest has "captured" only 12 percent of the immigration growth, the lowest of any region.

At no point in the past four decades has the Midwest equaled the national rate of population growth (Figure 2.1). Moreover, the gap in growth rates has increased dramatically; the region went from about 84 percent of the national growth rate during the 1950s and 1960s to 22 percent between 1980 and 1988. This disparity resulted from persistent outmigration during past decades. The Midwest has been the "traditional migration loser" with slowing population growth during a transition from manufacturing and heavy industry employment to services.

Figure 2.2
Five-Year Net Migration Trends for U.S. Regions, by Period

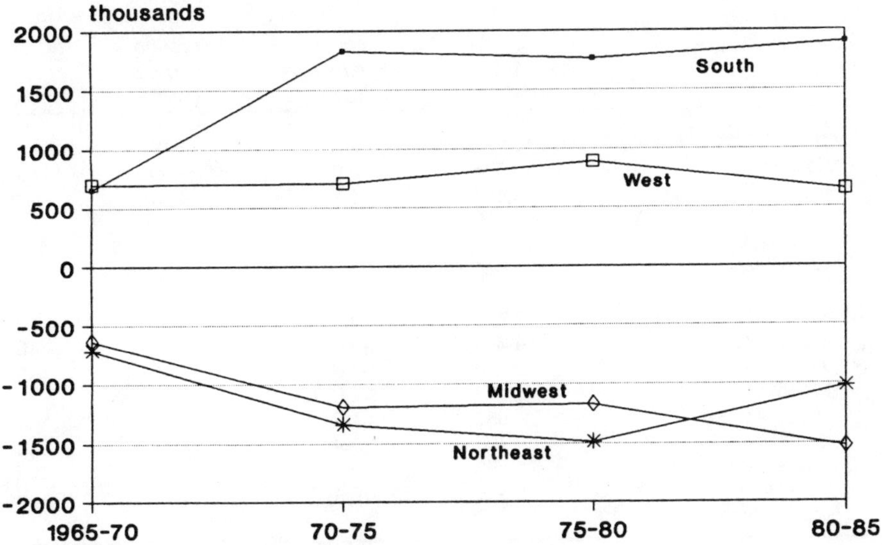

Source: U.S. Bureau of the Census, 1990c.

Net outmigration from the Midwest exceeds every other region, surpassing even the large outmigration from the Northeast (Figure 2.2). The South and West continued their traditional pattern, gaining 8.9 million persons through net inmigration in the 1980s. During the first half of the 1980s, migration from the Midwest to the South constituted the largest *interregional* flow (1.2 million, 1983–5). Throughout the decade, there was virtually no benefit to the Midwest from immigration from abroad, and little from new industry or growth of retirement communities.

During the first half of the 1980s, every midwestern state, except for Missouri, experienced net outmigration. Consequently, any growth in the region has occurred through natural increase. During the first half of the 1980s, three of the states with the largest net outmigration in the nation were in the Midwest: Michigan (−496,000), Ohio (−401,000), and Illinois (−320,000).

Most recent data (1989) show that the Midwest lost 2.23 million persons through net outmigration, with the highest rates occurring in Michigan, Illinois, Ohio, Iowa, and North Dakota (Table 2.1). The first four of these states represented nearly 80 percent of the regional net outmigration, and East North Central states (Illinois, Indiana, Michigan, Ohio, and Wisconsin) accounted for 83 percent. To illustrate the depth of outmigration, Illinois lost 420,000 persons between 1980 and 1987, exceeding the outmigration of the entire previous decade

Table 2.1
Midwest Population Growth and Net Migration, by Subregion and State, 1980–9

	Population 1989 (1000)	Percent Change 1980-89	Net Migration 1980-89 (1000)	Percent
EAST NORTH CENTRAL	42,231	1.5	-1,849	-4.4
Ohio	10,895	1.0	-469	-4.3
Indiana	5,587	1.9	-203	-3.7
Illinois	11,622	2.0	-495	-4.3
Michigan	9,263	.1	-538	-5.8
Wisconsin	4,865	3.4	-123	-2.6
WEST NORTH CENTRAL	17,777	3.9	-370	-2.2
Minnesota	4,351	6.8	-24	-.6
Iowa	2,839	-2.6	-205	-7.0
Missouri	5,143	5.0	2	--
North Dakota	650	1.2	-47	-7.3
South Dakota	708	3.4	-27	-4.0
Nebraska	1,598	2.6	-58	-3.7
Kansas	2,488	6.4	-12	-.5

Source: U.S. Bureau of the Census, 1990c.

by 40,000. Since 1960, Illinois has experienced a net loss in every decade, with the loss in each decade larger than the preceding one (Roseman, 1984).

Rural–Urban Growth Differentials

During the 1970s, rural (nonmetropolitan) areas across the United States grew slightly faster than urban (metropolitan) areas as the level of urban-to-rural migration exceeded the rural-to-urban. This reversal in a long-term trend of outmigration from rural areas had been identified in various states in the region, and across the nation. A variety of terms arose to describe this phenomenon, such as the "rural turnaround," "rural renaissance," or the "rebirth of rural America." Beale (1975) summarized the stimulus behind this reversal nicely: "In the eyes of many Americans, the appeal of major urban areas has diminished in recent years and the attractiveness of rural and small town communities has increased." Rural population growth in 1970s was a function of both a greater propensity of rural residents to remain in rural areas, and a reversal in the age-old rural-to-urban movement of people. In the first half of the 1970s, every region recorded a net gain of migrants in rural areas, and between 1975 and 1980, the Midwest recorded a net gain of 275,000 migrants to rural areas.

Figure 2.3
Average Annual Population Growth in Urban and Rural Areas of the United States and the Midwest, 1960–70 Through 1980–9

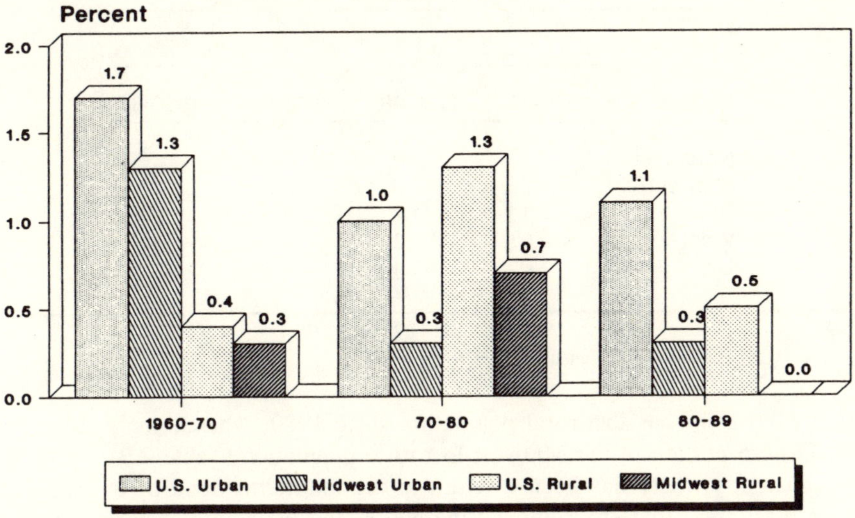

Sources: Beale, 1975; Beale and Fuguitt, 1985; U.S. Bureau of the Census, 1990b.

Rural areas demonstrated a vitality in attracting newcomers, even while many states in the region experienced outmigration. This vitality was not an outcome of population dispersal from large urban centers into neighboring rural counties—an "extended suburbanization" phenomenon. All categories of rural counties shifted from net outmigration to net inmigration. Even rural counties not adjacent to an urban area grew. In fact, much of the rural inmigration occurred in these counties. There appeared to be an inverse relationship between the magnitude of the migration turnaround and the level of "urbanization" of the rural counties.

In the Midwest, rural growth went from 0.28 percent annually in the 1960s to 0.7 percent in the 1970s, thus giving rise to optimism associated with a "rural turnaround." This trend also gave rise to renewed hope that problems of rural decline would give way to problems of growth. However, nationally, the rural growth rate has fallen to 0.5 percent per year since 1980. An element of hope continues to exist, however, insofar as the natural rural growth rate in the 1980s is still higher than it was in the 1960s. Midwestern growth rates, however, have been lower than the national rate for each period covered in Figure 2.3, and there was essentially no rural growth during the 1980s. The Midwest generally has mirrored national patterns, although at much lower rates.

In every state, rural growth is lower in the 1980s than in the 1970s. In the more rural, agricultural states of the West North Central subregion, every state

Table 2.2
Urban and Rural Population Change, 1970–88

	Average Annual Percent Change			
	Urban		Rural	
Region	1970-80	1980-88	1970-80	1980-88
Northeast	-.1	.3	.9	.5
Midwest	.3	.3	.7	0
South	2.1	1.7	1.5	.7
West	2.0	2.1	2.7	1.4
U.S.	1.0	1.1	1.3	.5

Source: U.S. Bureau of the Census, 1990c.

except Missouri has lost rural population since 1980, whereas only Illinois in the Eastern portion of the Midwest lost rural population (Table 2.2)

Apparently, there has been a return to the long-term trend of outmigration from rural areas that characterized the nation and the Midwest during most of this century. For the nation, Beale describes the recent reversal of the turnaround well:

> the demographic trend in rural and small town communities in the 1980s has proven to be as unexpectedly different from that of the 1970s as that decade was different from the 1960s. We learned in the 1970s that there are indeed conditions under which small-scale areas can retain their natural increase and also attract new residents. But we now see that major recessions in production industries can still have widespread and disproportionate effects on the population-supporting capacity of nonmetro counties (Beale, 1988, p. 6).

Illinois as a Case Study

When studying the Midwest, it is easy to overlook the region's diversity, as well as intrastate variations in many of the trends described before. Some states have lost population, whereas others have had sizeable gains. Rural areas of some states have grown at or near the rate for rural areas in the nation, whereas others have lost population. The separate treatment of states within the East North Central and West North Central portions of the region represented an attempt to show the regions' diversity by delineating the more densely populated, industrial eastern portion from the more rural, agricultural, sparsely populated western area. This section goes a step further and examines a single state, Illinois, to more specifically detail what has occurred during the past two decades and to illustrate the unevenness of change even within one state.

Rural Illinois is, like rural portions of many other highly urbanized and industrialized states, heterogeneous to the point of defying a simple characterization. Illinois is one of the nation's largest agricultural states in the nation's largest agricultural region. It is also, along with California and New York, a leader in the number of rural communities, many of which are thriving. Many rural counties are densely populated, whereas many have sparse populations and are becoming even more sparsely populated.

Illinois During the 1970s and Beyond

During the 1970s, rural Illinois counties grew by nearly 6 percent, almost three times the rate of urbanized counties. Even more revealing, urban counties had a net outmigration of 437,928 persons. Rural counties, exhibited the opposite trend, a net inmigration of 58,139 persons. Thus, whereas the state experienced very modest population growth and net outmigration, rural areas attracted newcomers.

Rural areas in Illinois, and particularly those in the southern third, were good examples of the 1970s reversal. Several predominantly rural southern Illinois counties, not near large urban centers, reported dramatic population increases, some by more than 25 percent in the decade. In fact, most counties in southern Illinois grew at rates much higher than the state as a whole. This represented a dramatic turnaround, because these counties historically had experienced population decline and outmigration.

Accompanying this rural reversal, however, were also areas in the state exhibiting a continuation of past growth patterns through the 1970s and well into the 1980s. The "collar," suburban counties around Chicago are one such example: DuPage County had a 35 percent population increase between 1970 and 1980, Kendall County a 41 percent increase, Will County a 31 percent increase, and McHenry County a 32 percent increase. For these counties, the 1970–80 decade was merely a continuation of trends begun years ago. In the past 30 years, DuPage County, for example, has grown from 154,599 to 658,177, an increase of 325 percent; Kendall County went from 12,115 to 37,202 persons in 30 years, an increase of 207 percent. These counties represent persistent, continuous, high-growth areas in Illinois.

Ninety percent of the total state population growth from 1980 through the mid–1980s was in three long-term-growth suburban counties: Lake, Kane, and DuPage. DuPage County alone had half the growth. A few other large urban counties showed modest population gains in the early 1980s, after losing population during the 1970s, whereas the rural areas of the state had the sharpest population losses, −4 percent (through 1989) (Table 2.3). The latter is especially surprising because rural counties had the highest growth and net inmigration during the 1970s.

Rural Communities

Rural community trends provide another example of how rural areas have fared over the past several decades. Again, the pattern observed in Illinois mirrors what has happened across the region. Small, rural communities are liberally

Table 2.3
United States, Regional, Subregional and State Population Growth, by Residence, 1970–88

	Average Annual Percent Change			
	Urban		Rural	
Region/State	1970-80	1980-88	1970-80	1980-88
U.S.	1.0	1.1	1.3	.5
MIDWEST	.3	.3	.7	--
EAST NORTH CENTRAL	.2	.1	.9	.1
Ohio	-.1	.1	.8	.1
Indiana	.5	.2	.7	--
Illinois	.2	.3	.5	-.4
Michigan	.2	.2	1.6	.5
Wisconsin	.4	.3	1.1	.5
WEST NORTH CENTRAL	.6	.8	.5	-.2
Minnesota	.7	1.1	.6	-.1
Iowa	.6	.1	.1	-.6
Missouri	.2	.6	1.1	.4
North Dakota	1.8	1.1	-.1	-.2
South Dakota	1.5	1.7	--	-.1
Nebraska	.9	.9	.3	-.3
Kansas	.7	1.4	.3	-.2

Source: U.S. Bureau of the Census, 1990c.

scattered across the midwestern landscape. Illinois has close to 900 communities with less than 2,500 population and the Midwest leads the nation with between 5,500 and 6,000 rural places. Rural communities arose in large measure to serve the hundreds of thousands of farmers scattered throughout the state. When small family farms dominated agriculture, it was inevitable that communities would spring up to meet the needs of farm families and farm workers. Their functions have changed dramatically over time, and their growth and development prospects are mixed. These days, rural communities tied solely to agriculture are quickly becoming extinct.

The plight of many of these rural communities is well known. Technological change in agriculture, the introduction of automobiles, and, somewhat later, a well-developed road system rendered obsolete many functions that rural communities typically performed. At the same time, cities exerted a pull on the residents of rural areas, and for most of the past 50 years, a steady stream of migrants has gone off to work or to be educated in the bigger cities within the

Figure 2.4
Growth in Urban and Rural Places, 1950–86

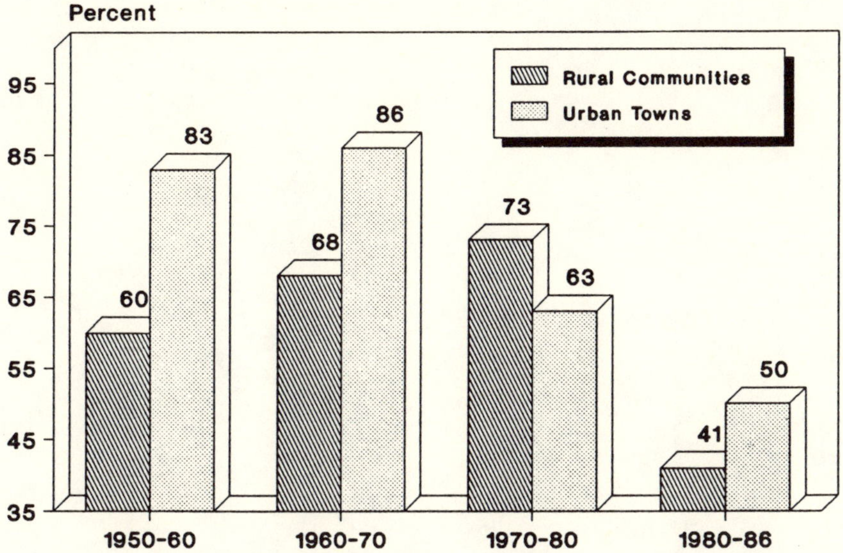

Source: U.S. Bureau of the Census, 1989d.

region. Consequently, for a large part of Illinois history, rural communities have not fared well; for many, decline has been the order of the day.

Although close to 70 percent of the incorporated places in Illinois are rural, in a dozen counties *every* community is rural (i.e., less than 2,500 population). It is not true, however, that all rural communities have declined, been depleted, or "left behind." Many have grown because of their location near a city or larger town, near good transportation, or in an attractive and scenic area. In fact, over the years, some rural communities have grown so quickly that they have become cities and larger urban towns; others have been created. Many other rural communities have held their own over the years because of state and local efforts to attract new employment and improve the types of services and facilities people have come to expect as part of everyday life. With the exception of the 1970s, rural community growth has been heavily influenced by the presence of larger towns in the same county, proximity to larger urban places, and distance to an interstate (Sofranko, Flotow, and van Es, 1985).

Rural Community Growth in the 1980s

For most of the last 40 years, urban communities in Illinois have fared better than rural communities, at least with respect to population growth (Figure 2.4).

Figure 2.5
Growth of Illinois Rural Communities by Region, 1980–6

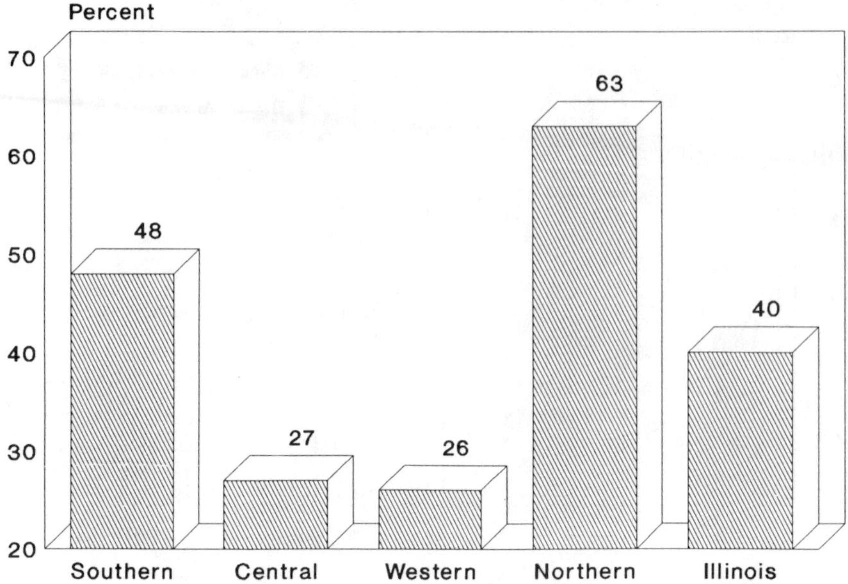

Source: U.S. Bureau of the Census, 1989d.

Between 1950 and 1980, there was a gradual increase in the proportion of rural communities that grew, and by 1980, the proportions favored rural communities. Since 1980, however, there has been a reversal to the pre–1970 pattern, but also a reduction in the growth of both rural and urban communities. Only half of all urban places are currently growing, as is 41 percent of the rural; both figures are the lowest in several decades.

A regional comparison of rural community growth within Illinois since 1980 reveals that only two of the four regions, southern and northern Illinois, exceed the overall state level (Figure 2.5), but, in both, rural community growth falls short of the 1970s level. It is quite likely that an explanation for the strength of rural communities in the South lies in the higher proportions of elderly, who are one of the least mobile segment of the population. Rural communities in northern Illinois, on the other hand, benefit from generally higher population growth in the region and the proximity to larger urban/suburban areas.

These findings are not unexpected in light of the slow growth of the state, accelerating outmigration, continued decline in farms, and a decrease in rural nonagricultural employment. Through the first half of the decade, 86 percent of Illinois counties had net outmigration. An average of 21 persons moved *out* of rural counties daily, compared with 30 moving *in* daily through the 1970s. During the first half of the 1980s, rural areas overall lost 37,000 persons, many from the state's small communities.

The evidence shows that the 1970s was a unique decade in the state. Rural areas, and particularly rural communities, grew faster than urban areas in all parts of the state. Localized growth in the suburban areas of the Chicago metropolitan area has persisted, with some letup through the last several decades. There is a tendency to overlook this suburbanization when using aggregate rural and urban growth rates. Since 1980, the suburban growth stands out more sharply against rural population loss. The agricultural financial crisis of the early 1980s, rural job losses throughout the 1980s, and outmigration from rural areas have all converged to reverse the positive growth trends of the 1970s.

BACKGROUND AND LEGACY OF THE 1970s

The onset of the widely heralded rural turnaround of the 1970s wasn't anticipated, nor was its attenuation in the 1980s. It was driven by the confluence of imprecisely known factors (Campbell and Garkovich, 1984). Among the more commonly cited antecedents were higher rates of growth in rural employment, largely in manufacturing; a shift in preferences for the attributes of rural residences; dissatisfaction with urban life; earlier retirement; and search for a better place in which to raise a family. Reversal to the more historically dominant growth pattern reflects declines in rural employment; smaller family size and a proportionally smaller number of traditional household types; shift of women into the labor force and the concomitant need for two jobs, in many cases a second job; and shifts in the relative attractiveness of more urban types of residence. The reversal was not initially due to a reduction in overall residential mobility; however, that may become a factor if the recession of the early 1990s deepens.

It is difficult to predict whether there will be a future shift of persons from urban to rural residences of the scale in the 1970s. The economic scene has changed dramatically in rural areas through the past decade. In order for rural communities in the Midwest to be competitive for residents and for the types of employment expected through the 1990s, they will have to make sizeable investments in communications, knowledge, capital availability, and attractiveness (Pulver, 1988).

Overlooked amidst the tributes to rural life in the 1970s was that rural areas, with 31 percent of the national population in 1970, gained 56 percent of the national net industrial expansion (Lonsdale, 1981, p. 132). Industry replaced agriculture as the major source of employment in rural areas, making them as industrialized as urban America.

In addition to the employment gains resulting from relocation of industry, and the location of new firms to rural areas, additional jobs were created as a result of population shifts and other development activities. For example, new employment was generated in recreation and leisure activities, in providing services to migrants, and in extractive industries following the energy shortages of the mid–1970s.

At the same time that rural areas experienced an increase in jobs, there was an attendant increase in the perceived attraction of rural life. To a large extent, the 1970s turnaround reflected improvements in levels of goods and services available in rural areas. It was widely believed that this "development of rural America" was the prerequisite change that underlay the population reversal, in many areas of the nation. This perspective has been articulated in various ways by researchers and the media alike. Beale (1975) has suggested, for example, that the reversal was mainly because the gap between urban and rural standards of living decreased. In somewhat prosaic terms, the media have suggested that there had been an expansion of the area in which urban people can live ("Americans on the Move," 1976).

Without question, there was a blurring of the differences between the city and the countryside. Rural areas were no longer perceived of as the backward, isolated places they were 30 years ago. Many developments have occurred to bring them into the mainstream of modern life and thus make them more attractive places in which to live.

Enormous improvements in transportation opened up virtually all rural areas in the country. Investments in recreational and leisure-time activities, including construction of camping areas, parks, dams, lakes, reservoirs, and the designation of state and federal forests and wilderness areas created employment and attracted visitors and permanent residents. There was an expansion of mass culture into rural areas via cable television networks, long-term improvements in the medical care available to rural residents, better access to shopping, banking, and other services, and the creation of community colleges in many smaller towns, providing employment as well as educational opportunities and cultural activities for residents.

Even though improvements occurred in many rural areas, in the mind of the public, rural communities retained and offered a unique quality of life. The public viewed rural towns as safer, friendlier, better places to raise children, as having a simpler lifestyle, cleaner environment, and as being closer to outdoor recreation. There is considerable evidence that this favorable perception of rural areas, combined with actual improvement in rural areas, is what promoted urban to rural migration in the 1970s (Sofranko, Williams, and Fliegel, 1981).

Rural–Urban Quality-of-Life Differences

Throughout the history of this nation, rural areas have typically lagged behind urban areas in what is commonly referred to as "quality of life." However, during the rural revival of the 1970s, this disparity was reduced. Improved transportation brought rural counties within the cultural and service areas of bigger towns and cities; creation of new jobs in rural areas reduced the income gaps between urban and rural people; farmers and their families improved their incomes with off-farm jobs; services improved as urban-based businesses expanded beyond their borders. In the eyes of many Americans, rural areas reflected a better quality of life, both in absolute terms, and relative to problems in cities. Some have even suggested that a *convergence* has been taking place between rural and urban areas (Fuguitt, 1985).

However, in spite of this apparent convergence, one of the major public concerns about rural America has continued to be a perceived gap between rural and urban people in terms of living standards, amenities, and access to a variety of services. Evidence of this gap is reflected in American literature, which has focused on the hardships and deprivations of rural life, and in the migration of more people out of rural areas. These concerns, although somewhat muted, still underlie many agricultural and rural development policies and programs, which have an explicit goal of redressing rural problems and narrowing the differential between rural and urban areas (Rasmussen, 1985).

At the same time, there is a parallel ideological strain romanticizing rural life, associating positive qualities with rural residences and rural people. The persistence of many of the tenets of "agrarianism" attests to the strength of the vision of rural America as the last bastion of all that is noble in society. This vision continues to provide the underpinnings for efforts to support preservation of the family farm, the revitalization of rural communities, and the preservation of natural resources. Buttressing this view are the results of numerous residential preference surveys that have consistently revealed broad based sentiment for rural places and farm life. If people could move where they wished, they have consistently indicated they would move in a more rural direction. Much of this idealization has undoubtedly come from dislocated rural persons now living in cities, but also from city people enmeshed in the types of problems typically associated with urban life.

There are, thus, two contrasting views of rural areas and people: as having unmet needs, experiencing more deprivation, fewer opportunities, and lack of financial resources; or the converse, as the natural life with unsurpassed quality-of-life amenities. These contrasting views have surfaced in various objective and subjective quality-of-life indicators. On any number of indicators, it can be demonstrated that there are rural–urban quality-of-life differences, as will be seen in what follows. What is of interest here, though, is whether there is in fact any evidence for rural–urban convergence. Was there an actual reduction in differences in quality-of-life indicators in the 1970s, and a subsequent expansion of differences in the 1980s? The following sections examine several quality-of-life dimensions during the past two decades.

Income

National data continue to show rural–urban income disparities. In 1988, farm family income was 84 percent of nonfarm family income, a higher percentage than it has been for years. However, in 1984, the per-capita income of rural people nationwide was $4,000 less than for urban areas. There was actually a convergence in income in the early 1970s, when rural income went from 69 percent of urban in 1965 to 78 percent in 1973. But between 1973 and 1984, it fell back to 75 percent (Henry, Drabenstott, and Gibson, 1987, p. 25). Although the gap narrowed somewhat in the 1970s, it increased more recently. Averaging per-capita incomes of rural and urban counties of Illinois in 1979 and 1985 reveals a similar growing gap between the two. In 1975, the average difference between rural and urban counties was $1,259, but by 1985, it had increased to $1,936.

Education

Over the last quarter century, urban residents have had more and, perhaps, a better education. In 1960, an average 1.8 years of education separated rural and urban people; this narrowed to 0.3 of a year in 1980, after the influx of urban people into rural areas, but the gap increased once more to 1.1 years by 1986. This is modest evidence of educational convergence and subsequent divergence. This is not intended to suggest that, with the exception of average levels of education, rural–urban parity has been achieved. Other indicators reveal that the school dropout rate is slightly higher overall in rural areas; rural areas have a lower proportion of persons who are college graduates and less than a third of college graduates want to live in rural areas; and rural schools have a lower proportion of teachers with advanced degrees and teaching experience.

Employment

Job growth was lower in rural than in urban areas between 1979–85, 10 percent versus 3 percent, with the reverse being the case through much of the 1970s. Over time, the mix of jobs in urban and rural areas has become more alike as the rural economy becomes more closely tied to the urban economy (Bluestone and Daberkow, 1985, p. 34). Farm and rural nonfarm women have about the same proportions in the labor force (U.S. Bureau of the Census, 1989d). However, unemployment and poverty rates have typically been higher, and there is evidence that more persons in rural areas drop out of the labor force as a result of discouragement (Beale, 1985).

Health/Medical Care

Despite improvements over time, there are still differences in availability of medical and dental care between urban and rural areas, as well as in coverage by hospitalization. Physicians per capita in rural areas are less than half that of urban areas (Ahern and Fryar, 1985), although the rate of increase was higher in rural areas during the 1970s. Rural areas have higher levels of disability in the population, and less access to public transportation. Rural elderly also have higher incidence of activity limitation due to chronic health problems, greater frequency of hospitalization, less access to physicians, and are more likely to have housing, transportation, and communication problems (Glasgow and Beale, 1985).

Poverty

There is currently a considerable gap between urban and rural areas in poverty rates (12 percent vs. 16 percent) (U.S. Bureau of the Census, 1989e). During most of the 1970s, however, the rural rate was falling while the urban was rising, thus converging. In 1979, the gap began widening once again to the point where there is now a 4 percent gap.

Poverty, one of the traditional indicators of economic well-being, has historically been higher in rural areas. As indicated before, however, the gap has been somewhat fluid, reflecting economic conditions and population composition trends in rural parts of the nation.

With the publication of *The Other America* (Harrington, 1962) and *The People Left Behind* (1967) in the 1960s, the nation suddenly became aware of the extent of rural deprivation: one in four rural persons was shown to be in poverty. The rural poverty rate in the 1960s was twice that of urban areas, and almost 8 percent higher than central cities. Farm poverty, at 29 percent, was 12 percentage points higher than the national average and 6 percent higher than rural nonfarm poverty.

Subsequent examinations of rural poverty have been framed against this backdrop, with the result that perceptions of poverty have been shaped largely by concepts of residence, farm employment, aging, and race. Research has regularly linked older persons, rural residents, farmers, central city residents, and blacks with higher levels of poverty. However, census data over the past two decades have begun to document a marked change in the composition of the poverty population, demonstrating that in some respects there is a dynamic side to poverty. This recent shift is described as a case of "floating" poverty (Hess, 1983, p. 29).

The changing profile of the contemporary poor is attributed to socioeconomic and demographic trends, which have shifted the locus of poverty away from families, to single-person families and households, from older to younger people, and from rural and farm people, to those in more highly urbanized residences. The main invariant though continues to be the relationship between poverty and race and minority status. Some of the major changes that have altered the socioeconomic and demographic context of poverty are (1) the 1970s population "turnaround" in rural areas; (2) economic improvements among the rural elderly; (3) shifts in household formation and composition; and (4) socioeconomic trends in agriculture.

Over the past few decades, there has been considerable change in poverty rates for various segments of the population. There has been a virtual convergence between rates among the elderly and families, with the overall rate, to the point where both groups are currently near the national average. In addition, all three of these figures represent 20-year declines. For the elderly, the decline has been much greater, although the rate for elderly living alone still exceeds the national average. For female-headed families, and particularly for black female-headed families, however, the rates are still three or four times higher than the figures

Figure 2.6
Poverty Rates for Selected Groups, 1989

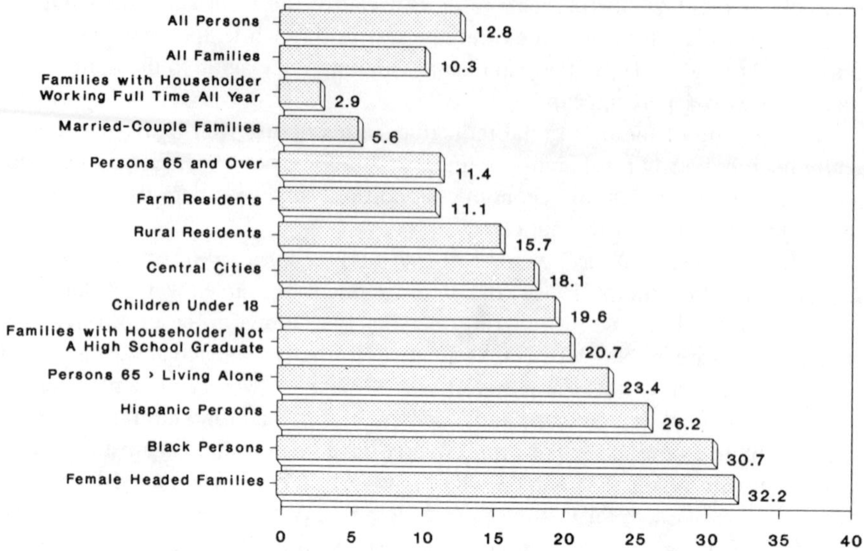

Source: U.S. Bureau of the Census, 1990c.

for the elderly and families, and rates are higher for rural whites, blacks, elderly, families, families headed by women, and unrelated individuals than for their urban counterparts (Mazie, 1990b, p. 17).

Recent (1989) poverty rate data for selected categories are presented in Figure 2.6. These reflect many of the poverty trends discussed before, and point out the importance of family structure, age, education, minority status, and multiple employment as influences on poverty. This is the "new poverty." Farm and rural residence represent the "old poverty."

These indicators provide some evidence for convergence between urban and rural quality of life. Other indicators could be added, for example, family size, birth rates, female employment, average age, and selected attitudes to support a convergence proposition. However, the strength of the convergence argument will have to be determined from the release of 1990 Census data.

Intractable and distinctive differences remain between many rural and urban areas. Most agriculture is still located in rural areas, in spite of the fact that a significant proportion of farmers and farm production resides in highly urbanized counties and farm income only accounts for a minor portion of total rural income. Rural areas are still less densely populated, and rural people are more intimately related to this nation's natural resource base for jobs and recreation. These occupational and ecological aspects of residence have helped contribute to the persistence of rural–urban differences in quality of life, as well as to differences in attitudes and values (Buttel et al., 1987).

Although the proportion of Americans reporting that they want to live in rural areas has decreased somewhat in the past decade, still nearly half of the population indicates a preference for a small town, village, or rural area, suggesting that there is still a strong attitudinal and preference base for a future shift to rural areas, similar to the one that occurred in the 1970s (Beale, 1988, p. 6). Dillman and Tremblay (1977) and others have found, for example, that in addition to a preference for rural areas, community satisfaction levels are decidedly higher in rural places. In the aggregate, these types of studies suggest that there is a prevailing favorable attitude toward many aspects of rural life, which could provide the support for rural retention of population. Unfortunately, as Johansen and Fuguitt (1990) note, whereas rural areas were once viewed as nice places to work and live, they are increasingly becoming simply nice places to live.

SUMMARY

The last two decades have been marked by major demographic and socioeconomic changes in types of employment, residential choice and mobility, household composition, and population composition and distribution. The nation is far different than it was two decades ago, and many underlying forces of change that affected rural areas in the 1970s are scarcely recognizable today. Considerably fewer urban dwellers are moving to rural areas; rural employment growth has taken a downswing in the last decade; and urban problems in many parts of the nation are not as glaring as they were two decades ago.

This is not to argue, however, that rural areas have reverted back to pre–1970 conditions. Various structural and cultural changes have maintained rural areas' attractiveness as places to live, if not necessarily work, and as places to recreate and retire. The last two decades have seen an incorporation of many rural areas into modern, urban society. Urban-based cultural influences have penetrated even remote rural areas, as rural and urban areas have become interdependent and increasingly similar. The sharp contrasts that once delineated urban and rural areas have blurred over time.

Many of the vertical linkages between rural and urban areas and the national economy have come at a "cost" to rural areas: loss of psychological identification with the community; changes in consumer preferences along with a concomitant decline in importance of many small, local businesses; expansion of labor-force participation and commuting to jobs; participation of rural residents in extra-local groups and activities. Although the character of rural economies and communities has changed, rural people and areas have benefitted from new opportunities and improvements in quality of life.

It is tempting to describe some of these recent trends in terms of cultural and structural convergence, and there is clear evidence to suggest such convergence. Many of the once reliable indicators of rural–urban differences have eroded: labor-force participation rates for women have been on a parallel and converging course; fertility levels and family size have merged; for a while, gaps in income were narrowing; the occupational structures have been moving toward a more common type; and poverty levels have narrowed across rural and urban residences.

To some extent, at least, the reduction in rural–urban differences was part and parcel of the 1970s net movement of urban residents to rural areas. Still, persistent differences between rural and urban areas suggest, at best, limited convergence, and perhaps divergence, as rural and urban areas continue to be impacted differently by many recent employment trends in agriculture, forestry, mining, and manufacturing, as well as by retirement, and recreation. McGranahan et al. (1985) go so far as to suggest that it may be outmoded thinking to focus on economic and social similarities. They propose that rural and urban areas are playing a new set of roles in American society. In order for rural areas to compete for the types of employment that will be created in the next decade, and to attract migrants from urban areas, substantial investments must be made.

In a similar vein, whereas the face of rural America has unquestionably been transformed, the appropriate focus in the future might well be on the *region*, for that is where the disparities will be most pronounced. Regional demographic differences are pronounced, as indicated throughout the early sections of the chapter, and many rural–urban differences persist, regardless of region. Rural areas are "older," experiencing a "brain drain," have lower income levels, are losing jobs, and so on. A current fear is whether, in light of these changes, rural areas will even remain a "nice place to live." In many areas of the Midwest, people have already begun to "vote with their feet." Although rural areas are clearly not back to conditions of the 1950s and 1960s, it is apparent that some of the gains of the 1970s have eroded. Halting this erosion will be difficult in a region that is not exhibiting much development potential.

3. Commercial Agriculture in Rural Economic Development

David A. Lins

INTRODUCTION

The rural economy of the United States is in a constant state of change. According to Duncan: "The agricultural sector has evolved from a relatively isolated and independent sphere of economic and cultural relationships to a sophisticated business sector that has almost fully integrated into the national and world economies" (Duncan, 1990). Commercial agricultural production both influences and is influenced by developments in the rural economy. Purchases of operating inputs and consumable durables and nondurables by farmers affect the viability of rural businesses and communities. The variety of products and price competitiveness of rural businesses influence the willingness of agricultural producers to "shop at home," as opposed to making purchases in more distant urban centers.

The symbiotic relationship between commercial agriculture and the rural nonfarm economy is clearly fragile. Changes in either environment are likely to create significant changes in the other. Distinguishing cause and effect is difficult. Consider the following scenario.

The farm machinery dealer in a small rural town has lost a considerable volume of business over the last 20 years and is about to close shop. The local dealer claims that farmers are no longer loyal to their home community and are now willing to travel up to 50 miles to make their major machinery purchases. This loss of business has made the local dealership uncompetitive. The farmers in the community complain that the local dealership is not cost-competitive and that although they used to buy locally, now they can get a much better price by shopping around. They would like to support the local dealer, but it is just too costly to do so. While this example is anecdotal, it is supported by most empirical studies of the relationships between production agriculture and rural communities.

In a 1974 study, Heady and Sonka (HS) found important trade-offs in the movement from smaller-scale to larger-scale farming operations. HS found that a shift to larger-scale farms resulted in less income in rural communities and lower farm employment. On the positive side, HS found lower food prices and higher incomes for large-farm operators resulting from an increase in farm size.

In a more recent study, Henry et al. reported that ''with the exception of the dairy sector, total nonfarm output must increase to support the same level of farm sales from medium-sized farms vis-à-vis a single large unit'' (1987, pp. 1–12). They go on to state that

> From a national perspective, the additional nonfarm output required to support the medium-sized farm may be viewed as a cost to society if resources used for this output could have been employed in alternative uses. From the regional economic perspective, rural communities would benefit from additional demand for local service and trade output.

Henry et al. (1987) found the biggest impact of a movement to large-scale farming was on the trade and service sectors of rural communities.

In a related study, Bowker and Richardson (1989) reported that reductions in agricultural production and the value of agricultural output affected agricultural services, banking and credit, and nondurable manufacturing more than other nonagricultural sectors. Household-related sectors, including retail trade and services, were also adversely affected.

The degree to which changes in farm production affect the rural nonfarm sector is clearly tied to the importance agriculture contributes in the local economy. Henry (1988), for example, found that for much of the rural South, agriculture is not the key to rural economic development. Pulver (1988) found that whereas farming remains critical to the economies of many rural communities, it is of declining importance in others. Agriculture is not the key to rural economic development in many rural communities.

Most segments of the agribusiness community have been affected by the changing nature of agricultural production. Many small-town elevators, farm supply firms, and other agribusiness firms have faced a diminished demand for their products and services. This loss of business and resulting smaller selection hurts the local community and, in turn, creates greater economic incentives to obtain products and services in larger communities.

This chapter assesses how changes in commercial agricultural production have influenced the rural nonfarm economy and explains why these changes have occurred. The chapter also addresses likely future directions in agricultural production and examines the impact of these changes on the future of rural nonfarm businesses.

FARM PRODUCTION IN THE OVERALL ECONOMY

The relative importance of agricultural production in the overall economy dropped sharply from 1940 through 1970 (Figure 3.1). However, since that time,

Figure 3.1
Farm Production as a Percent of Gross National Product

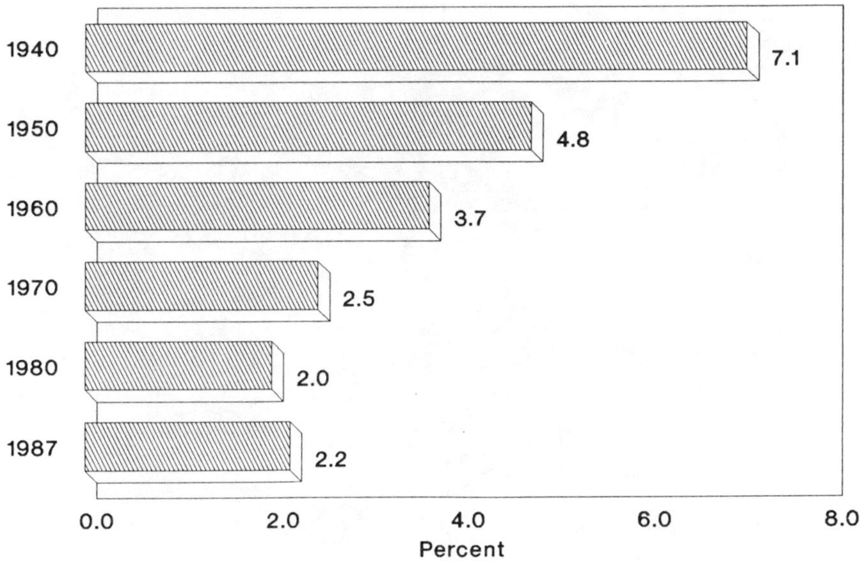

Source: U.S. Bureau of the Census, 1990c.

farm production as a percent of the Gross National Product (GNP) has remained relatively constant between 2 and 3 percent. Clearly, agricultural production in and of itself is a relatively small component of the overall economy.

A common myth is that development and prosperity of the rural nonfarm economy is inextricably tied to the health and vitality of farm production firms. This is not true from the perspective of the entire economy and the contribution of agricultural production to the GNP. However, in some areas, the linkages between agricultural production and the economic health and vitality of the rural nonfarm economy are more closely linked.

A recent study by Hady and Ross (1990) classified counties throughout the United States and included one classification for ''farming-dependent counties.'' Farming-dependent counties were defined as those counties where farming contributed a weighted annual average of 20 percent or more of total labor and proprietary income in 1981, 1982, 1984, 1985, and 1986 (see Map 2).

In 1986, they found 516 farming-dependent counties, a decline of nearly one-third from the 716 recorded in 1979. Although losses were scattered widely, higher than average losses occurred in Midwestern states such as Iowa, Illinois, Missouri, and Arkansas.

The decline in the relative importance of farming in the Midwest economy

Map 2
Nonmetro Farming-Dependent Counties, 1986

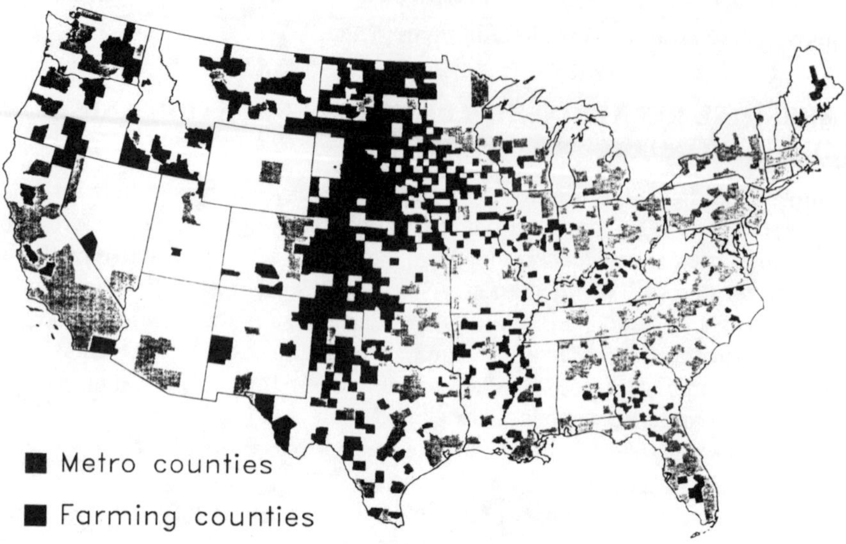

Source: Hady and Ross, 1990, p. 6.

clearly influences demand for products and services provided in rural communities. Although many areas of the Midwest are not classified as farming-dependent, many residents are part-time or small-scale farmers who rely on off-farm income. These farmers share a vital stake in maintaining strong economic activity in their local communities, because such economic activity may create the jobs they or their spouses seek.

CHANGES WITHIN THE FARM PRODUCTION SECTOR

The farm production sector has also undergone dramatic changes in form and structure and these changes have affected the economic and cultural vitality of the rural nonfarm sector. One of the most dramatic changes has been the movement to fewer and larger farms and a corresponding decrease in farm population (Figure 3.2). The number of farms in the United States grew until about 1920, reaching a maximum of 6.5 million, and has since dropped to just over 2 million. The relative change in farm numbers in the Midwest is roughly similar to that of the United States.

Farm population accounted for slightly more than 25 percent of the U.S. population in 1935. By 1987, that percentage had dropped to 2 percent (Figure 3.3). Again, the Midwest tends to reflect what has happened on a national scale.

Figure 3.2
Number of Farms in the United States

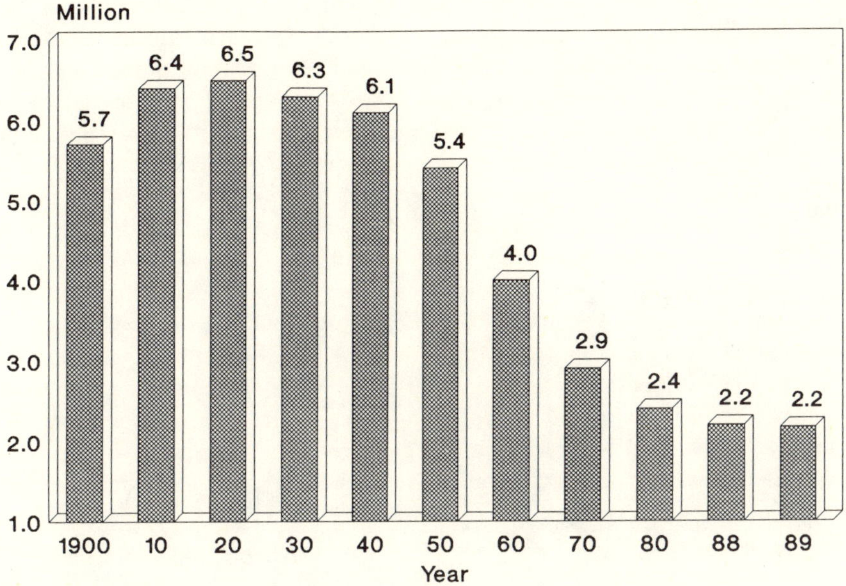

Source: U.S. Bureau of the Census, 1990c.

The decline in farms and farm population has clearly reduced the demand for personal consumption items, but the land farmed by exiting operators has been assimilated into other production units. Consequently, the decline in farm population has not resulted in a corresponding decline in demand for farm operating inputs. However, the purchasers of these inputs may be forced by competition to seek out the lowest-cost supplier, even when that reduces the viability of local supply firms.

Numerous studies have documented the effects of farm structure on socioeconomic conditions in rural communities. For example, Goldschmidt (1978) found lower socioeconomic conditions in communities dominated by large-scale industrial farms than in the family-farm communities. Rodefeld (1974) documents how a move to larger farms has been associated with a decline in local population. Wheelock (1979) found fewer or lower-quality services and decreased retail trade associated with a move to larger-scale farms. Although most research follows this view, some recent studies have found significant regional variations (Buttel and Lancelle, 1986; Flora and Flora, 1986).

Another important trend in production agriculture is a growing reliance on off-farm income, especially for smaller part-time farm operators (Figure 3.4).

Figure 3.3
Farm Population as a Percent of Total Population

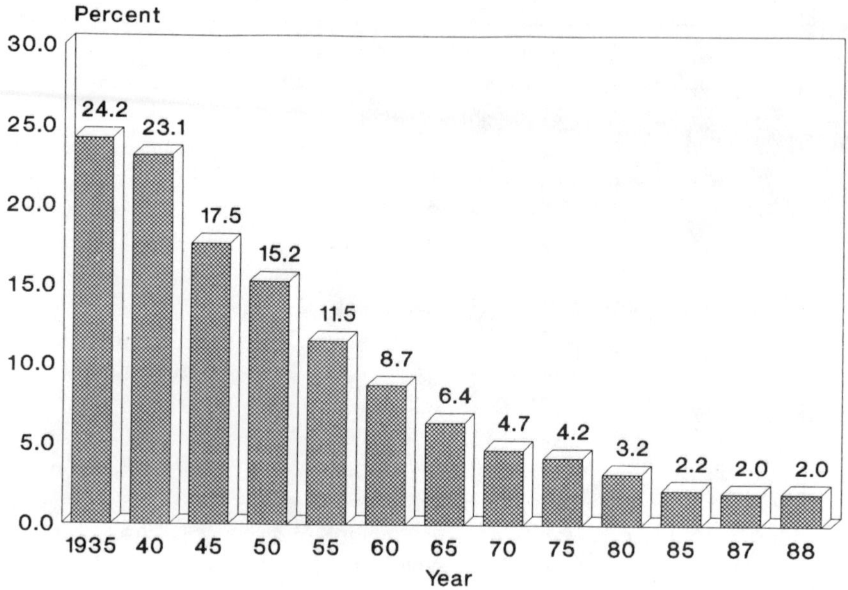

Source: U.S. Bureau of the Census, 1990c.

Farm operators now rely more heavily on off-farm income than farm income. Off-farm income is especially important to farm operators with farm sales under $40,000 per year. Studies by Deseran, Falk, and Jenkins (1984) and Godwin and Marlowe (1990) show that off-farm employment of farm wives is a major factor in the nonfarm income of farm families.

Table 3.1 identifies the distribution of farms by gross farm sales categories. The large farms, those with over $500,000 in annual gross farm sales, account for only 1.4 percent of the farms, but 31.8 percent of gross farm income and 43.3 percent of net farm income. These farms also have significant amounts of off-farm income, but their share is almost proportional to their relative importance in terms of numbers of farms.

Farms with under $40,000 in annual gross sales account for more than 70 percent of the farms, 14.5 percent of the gross income, and only 4 percent of the net farm income. In contrast, these farms account for nearly 80 percent of the off-farm income of farm operators. Clearly, these farmers rely almost totally on off-farm income and their livelihood is likely tied much more closely to jobs and businesses in the rural nonfarm economy than are the livelihoods of large-scale farmers. Unfortunately, this information is not available state by state.

Figure 3.4
Off-Farm Income as a Percent of Farm Operator's Farm Income

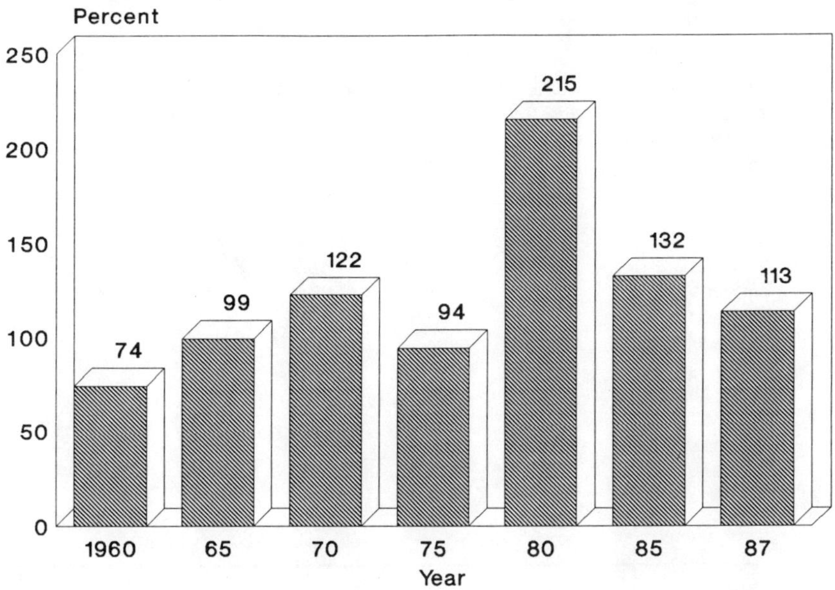

Source: U.S. Department of Agriculture, 1988.

Table 3.1
Farms by Sales Class, 1988

Gross Sales	% of Farms	% Sales	% Net Farm Income	% Off-Farm Income
$500,000 and more	1.4	31.8	43.3	1.6
250,000 - 500,000	3.5	17.2	19.9	2.4
100,000 - 250,000	9.8	21.9	21.6	7.4
40,000 - 100,000	14.6	14.6	11.2	9.1
less than 40,000	70.7	14.5	4.0	79.5
Total	100.0	100.0	100.0	100.0

Source: U.S. Department of Agriculture, 1988.

Table 3.2
Receipts from Livestock and Livestock Products as a Percent of Total Farm Receipts

Region/State	1950	1960	1970	1980	1988
Corn Belt					
Ohio	68.3	59.0	58.0	36.3	44.2
Indiana	72.2	61.6	54.0	36.9	42.5
Illinois	61.3	58.5	42.1	29.5	34.7
Iowa	81.4	78.7	72.7	54.7	55.6
Missouri	74.3	64.8	72.3	53.1	52.6
Lake States					
Michigan	60.8	53.8	53.9	41.5	45.2
Wisconsin	88.2	88.7	85.9	79.4	84.8
Minnesota	71.5	73.6	68.1	52.5	55.1
Upper Plains					
North Dakota	33.7	32.9	38.7	32.7	35.1
South Dakota	70.0	75.1	80.2	70.3	67.5
Nebraska	67.0	63.2	71.7	58.8	66.9
Kansas	55.3	50.1	68.9	57.1	64.7
U.S.	57.5	58.0	59.0	49.1	53.4

Source: U.S. Department of Agriculture, 1988.

The mix of farm production activities has also shifted over time in the Midwest. Nationally, livestock production has typically represented somewhat more than 50 percent of total agricultural production and no significant trend has occurred over time (Table 3.2). In contrast, the Midwest data clearly show a decrease in the importance of the livestock industry in Corn Belt states, especially between 1950 and 1980. In contrast, the Upper Plains states have shown little change in the relative importance of livestock production.

The decline in livestock production in the Corn Belt has created shifts in the mix of input firms and processing distribution firms. Numerous feed mills and livestock processing plants have been forced out of business as a result of this shift in production practices. In contrast, firms specializing in crop inputs or crop processing and distribution have benefitted from the shift to grain production.

Another important trend in U.S. agriculture has been a movement from self-reliant farming operations to a production system in which many inputs used in agriculture are purchased off the farm. For example, the substitution of hybrid seeds for home-grown seeds and the replacement of manure with commercial fertilizers have increased expenditures on inputs. This increased reliance on

Figure 3.5
Farm Cash Expense as a Percent of Farm Cash Income, United States

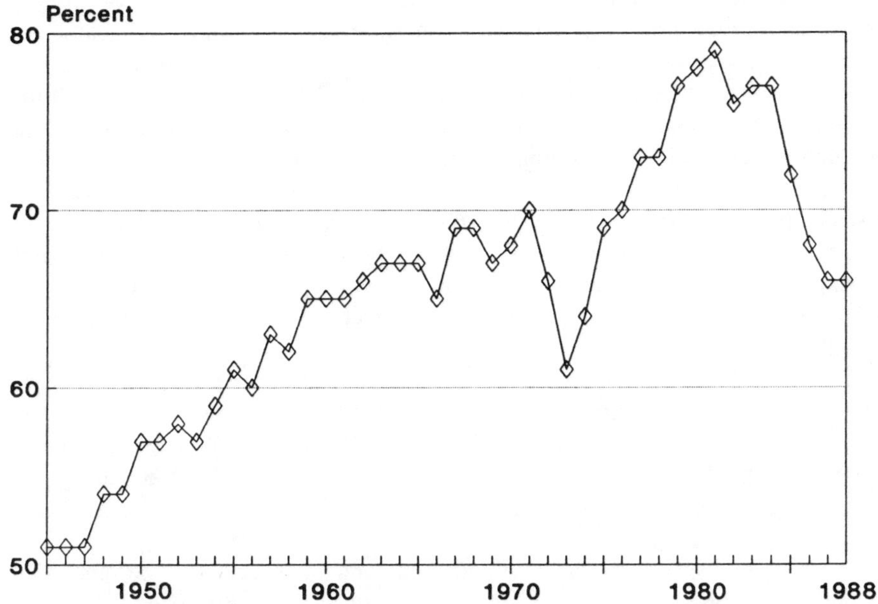

Source: U.S. Department of Agriculture, 1988.

purchased inputs seems to have waned. Cash expenditures of farmers relative to cash receipts have actually decreased in recent years (Figure 3.5). While a continuation of this downward movement is not expected, neither can the nonfarm economy expect continued growth in the relative proportion of farm inputs purchased off the farm.

IMPLICATIONS AND PROSPECTS FOR THE FUTURE

The farm production sector increasingly is becoming bimodal. Farm production is dominated by a relatively small percentage of larger-scale farms. These farms are, on average, quite profitable and profit-oriented. They are likely to demand local products and services for their farming operations, only if these are cost-competitive. Some farmers already travel great distances to urban centers to purchase the goods and services they need. Operators of small farms, in contrast, rely primarily on off-farm income for their source of livelihood.

In the Midwest, a rather significant portion of farm income in recent years has been attributable to farm commodity program payments. The 1990 Farm

Bill showed a growing uneasiness about the amount of government subsidies for agricultural production. Reduction of government farm subsidies is likely to have several adverse consequences for the rural nonfarm economy.

First, a reduction in farm subsidies is likely to lower farm incomes, at least in the short run. This will reduce the purchasing power of farmers, and the effects of this move will be felt throughout the nonfarm rural economy.

A second, and perhaps more subtle, effect of reduced subsidies is the elimination of one barrier to expansion of farm size and the consequent reduction in the number of farms. For example, producers of certain commodities now face a $50,000 payment limitation. Thus, large-scale producers often find that expansion beyond their current size may lower profits, as a result of losing program payments. If program payments are reduced or eliminated, this artificial barrier to expansion would be removed. As shown earlier, movement to larger-scale farming operations is likely to adversely affect small towns and rural communities.

The role of commercial agriculture in rural economic development will probably diminish through time. Adapting to changes in production agriculture is one component of maintaining viability in small rural communities. Although revitalization of rural communities does not seem probable from economic activity generated by production agriculture, participants in production agriculture might offer an excellent resource in promoting rural communities.

Farm leaders are astute business managers who want their local communities to thrive and prosper. Many would welcome the opportunity to become more deeply involved in community development efforts, particularly during months when agricultural production activities are slow. Employing this pool of available talent may be one of the most effective ways to incorporate commercial agriculture into the revitalization of rural communities.

4. Patterns of Employment Growth in Midwestern Metropolitan and Nonmetropolitan Counties

Bruce D. Phillips and James P. Miller

INTRODUCTION

Employment in the Midwest grew at approximately half the rate of that of the rest of the country between the mid–1970s and the mid–1980s. In the Midwest, between 1976 and 1986, the annual rate of employment growth in nonmetropolitan areas was nearly the same as that in metropolitan areas, approximately 1.9 percent. In contrast, the annual U.S. employment growth rate was 3.7 percent annually during this period.[1] The midwestern economy had not fully recovered from the 1981–2 recession by 1986. It was buffeted by environmental regulations, a rapid appreciation of the dollar, and population shifts. These factors and the general decline in manufacturing across the United States eliminated many jobs in manufacturing, agricultural-related industries, construction, and trade between the mid–1970s and the mid–1980s.

Nonmetropolitan economies are generally considered to be more vulnerable to cyclical and secular decline than metropolitan economies. Erickson (1976) and Miller (1987) observe that during a period of deep recession or retrenchment, due to foreign competition, corporations almost always phase out and close routine branch plants at rural sites before core operations at urban sites. However, with the decentralization of manufacturing and supporting services from central offices, there is evidence that nonmetropolitan industries were strengthened and became less vulnerable to corporate organizational changes than previous studies have suggested.

As indicated in the second section of this chapter, small and medium-size firms have played leading roles in creating jobs and new businesses in the Midwest, in both goods and service industries, between 1976 and 1986. Recent studies and commentary suggest that a new spatial order of production has been created by expanded world markets, improved communications and manufacturing technologies, and corporate reorganization. Firms are smaller, more efficient, and more mobile than previously. Drucker (1989), Storper and Christopherson (1987), and Carlsson (1989) have shown that many large corporations, particularly in manufacturing industries concentrated in the Midwest (e.g., metalworking), are ''vertically dis-integrating,'' and new opportunities have been presented to small firms to act as outside contractors.

A second factor contributing to the new order of production is technology. New processing and information technologies (numerically controlled manufacturing, telecommunications, and so on) rapidly increase the ability of small and medium-size firms to compete with large firms in dealing with customers, personnel, and suppliers. Our analysis shows that employment in small and medium-size firms in high-technology manufacturing industries and producer services in nonmetropolitan areas of the Midwest grew more rapidly than expected between 1976 and 1986. This is particularly true in sectors such as business services, health services, and in transportation and financial services.

The third section also evaluates how new manufacturing and information technologies have affected, and will continue to affect, the spatial distribution of industry and employment in the Midwest. Historically, manufacturing and agriculture have been dominant sectors in the nonmetropolitan Midwest. In this section, however, we question whether a growing goods-producing sector will be sufficient for complete economic recovery. Although Bender (1987) and Miller and Bluestone (1988) indicate that most service activities generally play a ''passive'' role in economic recoveries, some evidence suggests that this has not been the case in service industries of the nonmetropolitan Midwest. Jobs in higher-paying, high-growth services (e.g., producer services) and in manufacturing have rapidly expanded, but they still are not sufficient to meet employment demands.

Finally, in the fourth section, the prospects for a new industrial economy are discussed and the relative positions of nonmetropolitan and metropolitan areas during the transition to mobile industries and smaller firms are assessed.

Much of the following analysis is based on standard shift/share techniques. This technique allows researchers to compare employment growth of firms, in a given firm size and industry category, in one region, with data for the United States.[2] Firms are classified into two employment-size categories: small and medium-size firms (SMFs) having fewer than 500 employees and large firms with 500 or more employees. Firms are further classified into six industrial subcategories.[3] This analysis uses the Small Business Data Base of the U.S. Small Business Administration, a longitudinally linked microdata base with firm and establishment identification from 1976 to 1986.[4]

A positive shift component is interpreted as a shift of the firm/industry category's employment into a region or specific type of county; conversely, a negative shift is interpreted as a shift of the firm/industry category's employment away from that region or type of county.[5] Employment in a firm/industry category may be shifted from an area when (1) firms close plants and start new operations in other states; (2) production is relocated (from metropolitan to nonmetropolitan areas, or vice versa); or (3) employment at existing plants in other areas expands faster than at existing plants in the region or type of county. Previous studies by Weinstein, Gross, and Rees (1985) and Birch (1987) have documented that an interregional shift of employment occurs primarily because of (1) and (3), but seldom, if at all, because of (2).

SMALL AND MEDIUM-SIZE FIRMS (SMFs) IN THE MIDWEST

The U.S. economy vastly outperformed the Midwest between 1976 and 1986. As noted earlier, during this period, the average annual employment growth in the Midwest was just 1.9 percent, compared with 3.7 percent in the rest of the nation (Table 4.1).

The shift/share analysis reveals a pervasive shift of jobs away from the Midwest. Both SMFs and large firms lost employment shares (−2.9 and −4.6 percent, respectively) in the Midwest. Each industry group also lost jobs relative to what would have occurred if midwestern industries had grown at the respective national rates. The largest relative employment shift was out of high-technology manufacturing. The employment share of large firms decreased 7.9 percent. The results for SMFs were much the same. SMFs expanded annually by 2.5 percent in the Midwest compared with 4.0 percent annually in other regions.

It is important to note, however, that while the Midwest economy grew far less rapidly than the rest of the nation, SMFs accounted for a greater share of the growth that did occur. SMFs were responsible for 66.1 percent of net employment growth in the Midwest region, compared with 55.8 percent of net job growth in other regions.

In fact, SMFs minimized the job losses, particularly in sectors that lost substantial numbers of jobs. Thus, whereas large firms, in both high-technology and low-technology manufacturing, actually lost jobs in the Midwest (−0.8 and −1.6 percent annually, respectively), SMFs in these industries expanded employment (4.1 and 1.4 percent annually, respectively). Previous studies by Gray and Phillips (1983) and Mills and Schuman (1985) have documented the countercyclical influence of small businesses in the economy, particularly during the 1981–2 recession.

Nonmetropolitan Areas

Midwest nonmetropolitan employment growth was relatively stable during a time of general retrenchment in manufacturing and agricultural-related industries. The 1.8 percent annual employment growth rate was only 0.1 percent below the metropolitan growth rate (Table 4.2). Differences in corporate management decisions that influence the age structure of metropolitan and nonmetropolitan industries may partly explain the convergence of growth rates. Employment

Table 4.1
Employment Growth by Selected Firm Employment Size and Industry Groups for the Midwest and the United States, 1976–86

Region, Firm Employment Size and Industry Group	1976 Employees (millions)	Net Employment Growth Employees (millions)	Net Employment Growth Share %	Net Employment Growth Annual Rate %	1986 Employees (millions)	1986 Share %	Relative Share RS(ij)* %
Midwest	19.2	3.6	100.0	1.9	22.8	100.0	-3.8
Small & Medium Size Firms**	9.3	2.4	66.1	2.5	11.7	51.3	-2.9
High-Tech Manufacturing	0.3	0.1	3.0	4.1	0.4	1.8	-5.5
Low-Tech Manufacturing	1.7	0.2	6.7	1.4	1.9	8.3	-0.1
Other Goods-Producing	1.0	0.0	0.6	0.2	1.0	4.4	-5.7
Producer Services	0.6	0.4	12.4	7.1	1.0	4.4	-3.1
Business Services	0.4	0.3	8.4	8.5	0.7	3.1	-5.3
Other Services-Producing	5.3	1.2	34.9	2.3	6.5	28.5	-2.4
Large Firms***	9.9	1.2	33.9	1.2	11.1	48.7	-4.6
High-Tech Manufacturing	1.3	-0.1	-2.8	-0.8	1.2	5.3	-7.9
Low-Tech Manufacturing	3.7	-0.6	-16.3	-1.6	3.1	13.6	-2.6
Other Goods-Producing	0.2	0.0	0.1	0.2	0.2	0.9	0.1
Producer Services	0.6	0.3	8.1	4.6	0.9	3.9	-3.5
Business Services	0.3	0.3	7.6	8.2	0.6	2.6	-4.5
Other Services-Producing	3.7	1.3	37.2	3.5	5.0	21.9	-2.8
Rest of United States	49.6	18.6	100.0	3.7	68.2	100.0	3.8
Small and Medium-Size Firms**	25.8	10.4	55.8	4.0	36.2	53.1	2.9
High-Tech Manufacturing	0.8	0.5	2.9	7.0	1.3	1.9	5.5
Low-Tech Manufacturing	4.5	0.7	3.7	1.5	5.2	7.6	0.1
Other Goods-Producing	3.2	1.1	5.7	3.3	4.3	6.3	5.7
Producer Services	2.0	1.8	9.5	8.8	3.8	5.6	3.1
Business Services	1.1	1.3	7.1	11.5	2.4	3.5	5.3
Other Services-Producing	14.2	5.0	26.9	3.5	19.2	28.2	2.4
Large Firms***	23.8	8.2	44.2	3.4	32.0	46.9	4.6
High-Tech Manufacturing	3.2	1.0	5.2	3.1	4.2	6.2	7.9
Low-Tech Manufacturing	6.4	-0.3	-1.6	-0.5	6.1	8.9	2.6
Other Goods-Producing	0.9	0.0	0.1	0.1	0.9	1.3	-0.1
Producer Services	2.0	1.3	7.2	6.5	3.3	4.8	3.5
Business Services	1.0	1.1	5.9	10.7	2.1	3.1	4.5
Other Services-Producing	10.3	5.1	27.6	5.0	15.4	22.6	2.8

*Computed relative to U.S. employment in each size/industry category.
**Firms under 500 employees in 1976.
***Firms over 500 employees in 1976.

Source: U.S. Small Business Administration, Office of Advocacy, 1988.

Table 4.2
Employment Growth by Selected Firm Employment Size and Industry Groups for Metro and Nonmetro Counties in the Midwest, 1976–86

Type of County, Firm Employment Size, and Industry Group	1976 Employees (millions)	Net Employment Growth Employees (millions)	Net Employment Growth Share %	Net Employment Growth Annual Rate %	1986 Employees (millions)	1986 Share %	Relative Share RS(ij)* %
Metro Counties	15,269	2,840	100.0	1.9	18,109	100.0	0.0
Small & Medium Size Firms**	6,862	1,921	67.7	2.8	8,783	48.5	1.9
High-Tech Manufacturing	205	81	2.8	3.9	286	1.6	-1.5
Low-Tech Manufacturing	1,260	185	6.5	1.5	1,445	8.0	0.3
Other Goods-Producing	738	24	0.9	0.3	762	4.2	0.9
Producer Services	564	365	12.9	6.5	929	5.1	-5.7
Business Services	331	275	9.7	8.3	606	3.3	-1.7
Other Services-Producing	3,765	990	34.9	2.6	4,755	26.3	2.1
Large Firms***	8,407	918	32.3	1.1	9,325	51.5	-1.1
High-Tech Manufacturing	1,125	-97	-3.4	-0.9	1,028	5.7	-0.9
Low-Tech Manufacturing	2,908	-575	-20.3	-2.0	2,333	12.9	-3.2
Other Goods-Producing	149	5	0.2	0.3	154	0.9	1.2
Producer Services	605	272	9.6	4.5	877	4.8	-0.8
Business Services	317	261	9.2	8.2	578	3.2	-0.1
Other Services-Producing	3,302	1,052	37.1	3.2	4,354	24.0	-3.2
Nonmetro Counties	3,951	731	100.0	1.8	4,682	100.0	0.0
Small and Medium-Size Firms**	2,409	438	60.0	1.8	2,847	60.8	-1.9
High-Tech Manufacturing	58	28	3.8	4.8	86	1.8	1.5
Low-Tech Manufacturing	417	56	7.6	1.3	473	10.1	-0.3
Other Goods-Producing	270	-3	-0.4	-0.1	267	5.7	-0.9
Producer Services	60	78	10.7	13.0	138	2.9	5.7
Business Services	22	24	3.3	11.3	46	1.0	1.7
Other Services-Producing	1,582	255	34.9	1.6	1,837	39.2	-2.1
Large Firms***	1,542	292	40.0	1.9	1,834	39.2	1.1
High-Tech Manufacturing	202	-3	-0.4	-0.2	199	4.3	0.9
Low-Tech Manufacturing	791	-7	-0.9	-0.1	784	16.7	3.2
Other Goods-Producing	68	-1	-0.2	-0.2	67	1.4	-1.2
Producer Services	32	19	2.6	6.1	51	1.1	0.8
Business Services	10	9	1.2	8.5	19	0.4	0.1
Other Services-Producing	439	275	37.7	6.3	714	15.2	3.2

*Computed relative to U.S. employment in each size/industry category.
**Firms under 500 employees in 1976.
***Firms over 500 employees in 1976.

Source: U.S. Small Business Administration, Office of Advocacy, 1988.

growth fell below average in metropolitan areas because older, and perhaps less efficient, firms in these areas underwent major structural changes: plant closings, ownership changes, modernization of facilities, and so on.

On the other hand, nonmetropolitan employment grew faster than normal during a transitional period of slow growth, because older, urban-based firms, as part of restructuring efforts, shifted routine production from older branch plants in urban areas to newer plants in rural areas, in order to reduce labor costs.

SMFs represented 60 percent of the net employment growth in nonmetropolitan counties, although the 1.8 percent annual growth rate was a full percentage point below the annual metropolitan growth rate (Table 4.2). However, large-scale operations grew more rapidly in nonmetropolitan than metropolitan areas. Large firms grew fastest in nonmetropolitan counties not adjacent to metropolitan counties. As is discussed more fully in what follows, this is the general pattern of growth that is expected by standard location theory.

TRENDS IN THE GROWTH OF SMFs IN THE MIDWEST

Industrial location models predict that nonmetropolitan areas will attract activities that revolve around low-wage labor (low-technology manufacturing), natural resources (other goods-producing industries), or residential services. Residential services satisfy fundamental needs, such as medical care, grocery stores, or restaurants (other services-producing industries). In addition, the "product-cycle" hypothesis predicts that nonmetropolitan areas will primarily attract branch plants of large, mature companies, in low technology manufacturing. Thus, employment in larger firms in these industries is expected to grow faster in nonmetropolitan than metropolitan areas. A shift/share analysis of these firm/industry groups should, therefore, reveal a positive shift of employment into nonmetropolitan areas and a negative shift away from metropolitan areas.

Conversely, according to the product-cycle hypothesis, we can expect smaller firms in innovative industries, such as high-technology manufacturing, producer services, and business services to concentrate in urban centers, particularly in early stages of development. Thus, the normal development pattern is for employment in smaller firms in these industries to be growing faster in metropolitan than in nonmetropolitan areas. A shift/share analysis of these firm/industry groups should show a positive shift of employment into metropolitan areas and a negative shift away from nonmetropolitan areas.

Small and medium-size firms (SMFs) in the Midwest, however, reversed the normal pattern of growth predicted by the product-cycle hypothesis. Instead of a strong propensity to centralize in metropolitan areas, jobs in SMFs in high-technology manufacturing, producer services, and even business service industries are shifting away from metropolitan areas to nonmetropolitan areas. SMF employment in high-technology manufacturing, producer services, and business services shifted into nonmetropolitan areas by 1.5, 5.7, and 1.7 percent, respectively (Table 4.2). Even more surprising, the largest shift of SMF employment in high-technology manufacturing and producer service industries was into more remote nonmetropolitan counties, nonadjacent to metropolitan areas (2.7 and 3.7 percent, respectively) (Table 4.3).

Large-firm employment, on the other hand, followed a more predictable trend toward decentralization. Jobs in mature firms, with 500 or more employees, shifted away from metropolitan to nonmetropolitan areas. The largest shift was in low-technology manufacturing (3.2 percent), as predicted by the product-cycle theory.

Employment in other goods-producing industries (comprised primarily of agriculture and other natural-resource-based industries) declined in midwestern nonmetropolitan areas. Jobs declined in both SMFs and large firms. Note that SMF employment in other service-producing industries (primarily retail trade and residential services) shifted away from nonmetropolitan to metropolitan areas (−2.1 percent); conversely, large-firm employment shifted into nonmetropolitan areas (3.2 percent).

In summary, the shift/share analysis suggests that although nonmetropolitan areas in the Midwest have begun to attract new industries, the implications for long-term growth are still unknown. Clearly, some trends have been established, and other trends are just beginning to emerge and are difficult to document.

First, manufacturing employment decreased in metropolitan areas between the mid–1970s and the mid–1980s, but increased in nonmetropolitan areas. Manufacturing employment grew by 74,000 jobs, about 10 percent of the total employment growth in nonmetropolitan areas (Table 4.2). On the other hand, employment declined in other goods-producing industries, primarily in agriculture and agricultural-related industries. As Hart (1988) argues, manufacturing has replaced agriculture as the "principal driving force" in the nonmetropolitan Midwest, and has become the mainstay of many small-town economies, particularly in the eastern part of the manufacturing belt. Although urban-based firms have kept their higher-order functions (e.g., headquarters and sales offices) in metropolitan areas, they have steadily moved branch plants farther into nonmetropolitan areas. Tight urban labor markets and the work ethic of rural people have been important factors in encouraging this shift of production. In addition, the advantages of low-cost labor, cheap land, and low taxes have been reinforced in recent years, by improved communications, development of regional airline services, and deregulation of the motor carrier industry.

Second, most of the manufacturing growth in the nonmetropolitan Midwest has been in low-technology industries despite growth by some small firms in the high-tech sector. Although small and medium-size firms accounted for all of the manufacturing growth in low-technology industries between 1976 and 1986, most of the manufacturing jobs (784,000) were still primarily in branch plants of large firms by 1986. While branch plants have created many jobs, they also may have inhibited the type of local entrepreneurial climate that could lead to

Table 4.3
Employment Growth by Selected Firm Employment Size and Industry Groups for Adjacent and Nonadjacent Nonmetro Counties in the Midwest, 1976–86

Type of County, Firm Employment Size, and Industry Group	1976	Net Employment Growth			1986		Relative Share RS(ij)*
	Employees (millions)	Employees (millions)	Share %	Annual Rate %	Employees (millions)	Share %	%
Adjacent Nonmetro Counties	1,978	277	100.0	1.4	2,255	100.0	-0.5
Small & Medium Size Firms**	1,113	204	73.7	1.8	1,317	58.4	-0.9
High-Tech Manufacturing	29	9	3.2	3.0	38	1.7	-1.2
Low-Tech Manufacturing	222	38	13.7	1.7	260	11.5	0.4
Other Goods-Producing	119	-1	-0.4	-0.1	118	5.2	-0.4
Producer Services	30	34	12.2	11.2	64	2.8	2.0
Business Services	9	13	4.8	14.7	22	1.0	1.6
Other Services-Producing	704	111	40.2	1.6	815	36.1	-1.0
Large Firms***	865	73	26.3	0.8	938	41.6	-0.3
High-Tech Manufacturing	130	-18	-6.5	-1.4	112	5.0	-0.6
Low-Tech Manufacturing	468	-15	-5.3	-0.3	453	20.1	1.6
Other Goods-Producing	30	-7	-2.4	-2.3	23	1.0	-3.4
Producer Services	17	5	1.8	3.0	22	1.0	-0.4
Business Services	7	3	1.2	4.9	10	0.4	-0.7
Other Services-Producing	214	104	37.4	4.9	318	14.1	0.7
Nonadjacent nonmetro Counties	1,973	453	100.0	2.3	2,426	100.0	0.5
Small and Medium-Size Firms**	1,295	234	51.6	1.8	1,529	63.0	-1.0
High-Tech Manufacturing	29	19	4.2	6.6	48	2.0	2.7
Low-Tech Manufacturing	195	17	3.9	0.9	212	8.7	-0.6
Other Goods-Producing	151	-2	-0.5	-0.1	149	6.6	-0.5
Producer Services	30	44	9.8	14.8	74	3.1	3.7
Business Services	13	11	2.5	8.8	24	1.0	0.1
Other Services-Producing	877	144	31.7	1.6	1,021	42.1	-1.1
Large Firms***	677	220	48.4	3.2	897	37.0	1.4
High-Tech Manufacturing	73	15	3.3	2.0	88	3.6	1.5
Low-Tech Manufacturing	323	8	1.8	0.2	331	13.6	1.6
Other Goods-Producing	38	5	1.2	1.4	43	1.8	2.2
Producer Services	15	14	3.1	9.6	29	1.2	1.2
Business Services	4	5	1.2	15.2	9	0.4	0.8
Other Services-Producing	225	172	37.9	7.6	397	16.4	2.5

*Computed relative to U.S. employment in each size/industry category.
**Firms under 500 employees in 1976.
***Firms over 500 employees in 1976.

Source: U.S. Small Business Administration, 1988.

self-sustained growth within the nonmetropolitan community. Klimasewski (1978), Jacobs (1984), and Malecki (1990) observe that branch plants discourage entrepreneurial activity in small towns and rural places.

Branch plants tend to purchase a larger share of their inputs from various divisions of the parent corporation located in other areas. In addition, the low-skill labor requirements of branch plants have created a dependency on corporate jobs that weakens local initiative and self-sufficiency. Branch plants also tend to distort the occupational structure in rural areas toward lower-skilled manual workers, leaving rural workers who have technical and managerial skills to seek jobs in more prosperous urban areas.

Third, residential activities (other service-producing industries) accounted for approximately 72 percent of the total net job growth in the nonmetropolitan Midwest between 1976 and 1986 (Table 4.2). Historically, most residential activities in rural communities were locally owned. However, in recent years, large retail trade centers have proliferated throughout the nonmetropolitan Midwest (Senf, 1989). Small locally owned businesses (retail stores, restaurants, and repair shops) along the "main streets" of many rural communities are closing and are being replaced by franchises, branches, and outlets of larger firms in new centrally located shopping centers. Jobs have expanded much faster in large firms (1.6 percent annually) than small firms, particularly in more remote nonmetropolitan counties not adjacent to metropolitan areas (7.6 percent annually) (Table 4.3). Manufacturing plant closings in the industrial belt and lower farm incomes, combined with substantial losses in wealth associated with falling land values in the farming states, possibly contribute to an acceleration of this trend.

Finally, the trend among SMFs, in high-technology manufacturing, producer services, and business services, to decentralize is surprising and beneficial to midwestern nonmetropolitan areas. Many large midwestern manufacturing firms are "vertically dis-integrating," that is, they are becoming smaller, and in the process of becoming smaller, they are increasing the number of small firms by contracting out activities that are not a part of either final assembly or core management (e.g., headquarters and sales offices). With new computer-controlled equipment, telecommunications, and new information technologies, small firms are now capable of assuming more of the manufacturing and producer service functions of large firms (e.g., component manufacturing, computer services, temporary employment services, financial services, and so on).

New technological changes are rapidly reducing the effect of distance, and, thus, eliminating differences between the urban center and rural periphery. Small manufacturing subcontractors and office-based functions are relocating to nonmetropolitan areas, both adjacent and nonadjacent to metropolitan areas.

PROSPECTS FOR A NEW NONMETROPOLITAN INDUSTRIAL ECONOMY IN THE MIDWEST

The important question for midwestern nonmetropolitan areas is whether they are likely to win or lose, relative to metro areas, in the transition to smaller firms and mobile industries. Will corporate reorganization, telecommunications, and new manufacturing technologies decentralize or centralize economic activity? There are two major schools of thought.

The first position, which might be termed conventional wisdom, is that nonmetro areas will benefit substantially from new technologies. It is claimed that the new technological changes will reduce the effect of distance, and, thus, eliminate differences between the urban center and rural periphery. Office-based functions and other urban-based activities will decentralize, because the new technologies make it possible to transact business without face-to-face contact (Lesser and Hall, 1987; Coffey and Polese, 1989). Several empirical studies support this position. Phillips, Kirchoff, and Brown (forthcoming), for instance, found that small high-technology manufacturing activities have decentralized to nonmetro areas. The annual formation rate of high-technology firms with fewer than 20 employees was approximately the same (15.8 percent) in nonmetro and metro areas between 1976 and 1986. Phillips, Kirchoff, and Brown suggest that a combination of government and state university technology transfer programs may bring high technology to certain nonmetro areas at a faster rate than in the past.

According to the second school of thought, telecommunications and the new information technologies have allowed companies to concentrate higher-order administrative, "front-office," and nonroutine high-tech manufacturing functions (those with a high propensity to export) in metro areas. Administrative and control functions have been freed from the necessity of locating in proximity to the operations they direct. This has contributed to a growing centralization of key control activities. Consequently, nonmetro areas and outlying regions are left with branch plants and service outlets that perform only the most routine and standardized functions.

Although just beginning, the available empirical research, on the spatial impacts of telecommunication changes and new manufacturing technologies, generally lends strong support to the second (centralization) view. Studies show that core functions and most "front-office" activities concentrated in urban centers in the 1980s. Storper and Christopherson (1987) and Carlsson (1989), for example, report that firms in the metalworking and motion picture industries "vertically dis-integrated" in the 1980s, as they returned their "core functions" to major urban centers, and became more dependent on local networks of suppliers and service firms.

Other empirical and conceptual evidence suggests that most "tradeable" producer services (those with high propensity to export) are also unlikely to locate outside of major metro centers. Empirical work cited by Coffey and Polese (1989) shows that during the 1980s, higher-order producer services tended to concentrate in only a few major urban centers and in some smaller urban areas, serving as regional centers. In addition, Miller and Bluestone (1988) found that most two-digit SIC (standard industrial classification) producer-service industries mainly concentrated in large urban areas.

Highly specialized services, such as those provided by security and commodity brokers; large financial and insurance institutions; and specialized legal, accounting, and data processing firms, were found almost exclusively in large urban areas. Moreover, recent research on the U.S. economy by Porterfield (1990) shows that 90 percent of "advanced" producer services are located in metro areas.

Many small communities in the Midwest, particularly in counties adjacent to metropolitan areas, may benefit from the concentration and vertical disintegration of core activities. A large proportion of midwestern nonmetropolitan counties, particularly in the manufacturing belt, are within easy commuting and trucking distance to urban markets. Small subcontractors in manufacturing and support-service industries are more likely to move to adjacent or "exurban" areas than to truly rural areas. Nelson (1990) shows that in the Midwest, approximately 23 percent of manufacturing employment was exurban and only about 7 percent, truly rural, in 1985.

DRI Projections

According to Data Resources, Inc. (DRI), between 1987 and 1990, the gap in income growth between the United States and the Midwest region virtually disappeared (Data Resources, Inc., 1990). This may be compared with the early 1980s, during which time national income growth exceeded that in the Midwest by almost 2 percentage points, and employment growth lagged significantly behind. The major weakness in the region relates to the overbuilt auto industry, which has dampening secondary impacts on small suppliers. However, some reasons for optimism pervade the DRI forecasts.

On one hand, the small-firm-dominated agriculture sector in the Midwest will become a more significant contributor to growth, as farmland prices continue to rise. On the other hand, most of the major metropolitan areas in the Midwest can expect higher housing starts than during the past several years. Both of these factors should stimulate nonmetro rural economies during the 1990s.

On a state-by-state basis, the messages are mixed within nonmetropolitan regions. Wisconsin has the region's best business climate, with growing manufacturing. Partly as a result of this manufacturing growth, and partly as a result of rising population, small firms in trade, services, and finance should continue to prosper in nonmetro areas of this state. Whereas Minnesota will also share much of Wisconsin's healthy climate, the outlook in Missouri is for considerably weaker growth. Missouri will be impacted by defense cutbacks, causing its unemployment rate to be among the highest in the Midwest region. While Nebraska's economy is recovering, tight rural job markets have kept expansion below expected levels.

CONCLUSIONS AND POLICY CONSIDERATIONS

This brief review of recent employment trends in the Midwest shows that small firms have played an increasingly important role in nonmetropolitan areas. Although these firms generated a major portion of the new employment between 1976 and 1986, this expansion occurred within a declining economic base.

The expansion of small firms into high-technology manufacturing, in such areas as metalworking, computer manufacturing and business services, is a positive sign; however, the number of jobs created in nonmetropolitan areas has remained small. In addition, studies show that most of these activities are still routine manufacturing and ''back-office'' clerical functions that hire low-skilled labor and pay low wages.

The rural Midwest has also substituted jobs in service industries for disappearing jobs in manufacturing, construction, and many distributive trades. Most of these jobs are in residential services industries, and have two major disadvantages. First, they are low-pay, low-skilled jobs. Second, the growth of residential services jobs may be difficult to sustain, because of labor shortages in nonmetropolitan areas in the Midwest.

To counter these trends and encourage an influx of new businesses, the entrepreneurial climate in the Midwest will have to improve. As Booth (1986) observes, this process may have already started in the Midwest, as part of a ''longwave'' of regional growth. He found that new business formation rates were highest in the eastern industrial belt of the Midwest, where mature industries were declining. As older industries decline, more businesses are started. Capital, labor (including management), and other inputs that historically were attracted to local mature industries are already beginning to flow to new local businesses. Booth argues that the principal barrier to new business formation in older regions is not institutional (i.e., unionization, taxes, the lack of government programs, etc.), but ''simply the existence of established industries that divert potential entrepreneurs and other resources from the new business formation process (Booth, 1986, p. 459).

The challenge for state and local policy makers is to create new development strategies that will stimulate business formations in nonmetropolitan areas. Business incubator facilities, enterprise zones, and venture-capital programs are well-suited for this purpose. However, education and manpower training programs may be an even more important stimulus, as professional and skill requirements rise in new businesses.

This descriptive analysis of employment shifts in the Midwest shows that some small businesses, in high-technology manufacturing and producer service industries, are moving to nonmetro areas, primarily to the periphery or zone of influence of a metropolitan area. Thus, many nonmetropolitan areas in the Midwest have a choice. They can either provide the necessary stimulus to encourage entrepreneurship and innovative small businesses, or continue as ''repositories'' of low-wage, low-skill activities, whereas the more crucial lines of business—the administrative activities, technical support and research, and development functions—continue to concentrate in metropolitan areas.

APPENDIX 4.A. USING SHIFT/SHARE ANALYSIS TO COMPUTE RELATIVE EMPLOYMENT SHIFT COMPONENTS

The measure of employment redistribution used is this chapter is the shift component of shift/share analysis. Specifically,

$$S(ij) = Et(ij) \times USt(i)/USt - 1(i)$$

where

$S(ij)$ = employment shift for size/industry group (i) in region or county class (j)

$E(ij)$ = firm-size/industry group i's in region or county class j

$US(i)$ = United States employment size/industry group (i)

$t, t - 1$ = 1986, 1976, respectively.

To be able to make comparisons between industry groups of different sizes, a relative measure instead of an absolute measure is used, which is defined as

$$RS(ij) = S(ij)/USt - 1(i)$$

A positive shift is interpreted as a shift or relocation of the firm-size/industry class into the region or county category. Alternatively, a negative shift reflects a relative shift out of the region or county class.

APPENDIX 4.B. INDUSTRY CATEGORIES DEFINED

Industries at 2-, 3-, and 4-SIC (Standard Industrial Classification) levels are classified into six categories. Accepting the necessarily arbitrary nature of these classifications, this study selected the following definitions:

High-Technology Manufacturing: More than 8 percent of their employees were in scientific, engineering, and technical occupations, and research-and-development expenditures relative to product sales exceeded the national average (Phillips, Kirchoff, and Brown, forthcoming).

Low-Technology Manufacturing: Manufacturing industry not classified as high-technology.

Other Goods-Producing Industries: Agriculture, forestry, fisheries, and construction.

Producer Services: Finance, insurance, real estate, legal services, and miscellaneous services (engineering, architectural firms, scientific and research organizations, accounting firms, etc.).

Business Services: Advertising, mailing, reproducing, credit reporting, computer and data processing, personnel services, management consulting, etc.

Other Services-Producing: Retail and wholesale trade, residential services (local health clinics, repair shops, amusement services, restaurants, etc.), transportation, communications, and utilities.

NOTES

1. The Midwest region is the North Central census region: Illinois, Indiana, Iowa, Kansas, Michigan, Minnesota, Missouri, Nebraska, North Dakota, Ohio, South Dakota, and Wisconsin. Nonmetropolitan areas are counties not classified in 1983 (by the U.S. Office of Management and Budget) as part of Metropolitan Statistical Areas. Nonmetropolitan counties are generally sparsely populated. Most nonmetropolitan counties have urban populations of fewer than 20,000.

2. For further explanation of the shift/share technique, refer to Appendix 4.A.

3. The six categories are defined in Appendix 4.B. They are described as High-Technology Manufacturing, Low-Technology Manufacturing, Other Goods-Producing Industries, Producer Services, Business Services, and Other Services-Producing Industries.

4. For further information on the Small Business Data Base of the U.S. Small Business Administration, see *1976–1986 Linked USEEM User's Guide* (U.S. Small Business Administration, Washington, D.C., June 1988), and *The Small Business Data Base: A User's Guide* (U.S. Small Business Administration, Washington, D.C., revised, June 1990).

5. Note that a positive (negative) shift does not necessarily mean that jobs are actually moving into (away from) a region or type of county. A positive (negative) employment shift usually indicates that employment grew at a faster (slower) rate than it did nationally or regionally if the region is used as a basis for comparison. It measures an imaginary surplus (shortfall) of jobs that arises as a result of industries growing at a faster (slower) rate in the region or type of county than they did nationally (or regionally).

5. Economic Change and the Local Public Sector

Norman Walzer and Steve Deller

Earlier chapters documented the lackluster economic growth experienced by many rural midwestern counties. Population outmigration and a slowdown in business activity brought relatively slow increases, and in some case declines, in the tax base that supports local public services. The decline in population placed a greater burden of the cost of public service on remaining residents. The slowdown in business activity has been particularly important to state and local governments in the Midwest because of changes in the structure of the economic base upon which they depend.

Rural manufacturing, for example, was especially affected by the 1981–2 recession and has yet to fully recover. Many companies were marginal but still provided employment. During the 1980s, foreign competition coupled with lower wages, attracted businesses away from the rural Midwest. In addition, new business starts favored the South and Southwest, where lower energy costs and more favorable climates appealed to entrepreneurs.

Agriculture, long a dominant sector in the rural midwestern economy, experienced a strong boom–bust cycle. Plummeting agricultural land prices from record highs in the early 1980s further reduced the tax sources available for local public services. In states such as Illinois, the decrease in assessed value was so drastic that limits were placed on the percentage change. Some counties reported declines of one-third or more in the property tax base in a few years. It was not until 1987 that agriculture rebounded from the depression levels of the early 1980s, but as described by Lins in Chapter 3, even then returned with a different structure with weaker ties to the local economy. Given these weaker ties, local economies did not participate in the agricultural rebound to the level that they would have in the past.

Unstable farm income and dramatic swings in the price of farmland brought pressure from farmers for relief from the property tax. Effective property tax rates on farmland increased and taxpayers requested a revised property tax assessment procedure, swinging from ad valorem to a measure that better represented land productivity (Giertz and Chicoine, 1984; Dunford, Chicoine, and Ervin, 1986). The result of these relief efforts was a further decline in the local tax base. These declines were especially severe in rural counties where farmland is a large portion of the assessed valuation.

The declines in the rural economic base, coupled with the impacts of inflation and unemployment, rising public employment and compensation, migration patterns, structural changes in the Midwest economy, and depressed land market values, resulted in many state and local governments experiencing a budget squeeze. Although the causalities of this squeeze are wide and varying, particular attention has been paid to the status of physical and social infrastructure. Recently, Fox and Smith (1990) observed a significant slowdown in public infrastructure investment. Several studies identified a link between this slowdown in investment and the quality and quantity of the nation's stock of infrastructure (Hackett and Busson, 1986; National Council on Public Works Improvement, 1988; and Walzer and Chicoine, 1989). There is general belief that without adequate infrastructure, rural areas may encounter difficulty supporting economic development and growth. Yet, without a sufficient level of economic activity and growth, it is difficult to finance the necessary replacement and/or maintenance of the current stock of infrastructure (Doeksen and Allen, 1990).

This chapter examines the impact of economic trends, discussed in earlier chapters, on the financing of local public services, by general-purpose governments, in midwestern states. Although education, in many states, places the greatest demands on property taxes, space does not permit a detailed discussion of all services. Education is discussed only tangentially in a treatment of property taxes.

Governmental structure in midwestern states is examined first, because type of government often determines how services are financed and the efficiency with which they are provided. The discussion turns next to types of revenues collected and changes in importance during the 1980s. Special attention is paid to changes in counties classified by economic base. Finally, spending levels are compared, by type of government and economic base, during the 1980s to identify shifts in focus within the local public sector.

The data sources include the 1982 and 1987 *Censuses of Governments*. Using 1982 as a base year has disadvantages because it represents the trough of a recession. On the other hand, however, it more clearly shows the extent to which rural governments participated in the subsequent economic expansion. The final year, 1987, is the most recent year for which complete data are available.

STRUCTURE OF LOCAL GOVERNMENT

Financing patterns for local public services depend, to a large extent, on local government structure. First, state government limits and mandates differ by type of government. Special districts, for instance, typically do not have access to income taxes, sales taxes, or other broad revenue sources. Rather, they often are restricted to property taxes, benefit assessments, or similar revenues. Most midwestern states have township governments and this form of government often faces restrictive revenue limits. The greatest flexibility in revenues usually rests with general-purpose governments, such as counties and cities, that provide a wide range of services.

Second, multiple and overlapping governmental structures are criticized as duplicative and inefficient. Allegedly, these governments are not large enough to attract professionally trained staff and cannot make effective use of costly equipment (Seroka, 1989; Deller and Nelson, 1991). They are charged with promoting special interests and not having to face the more careful scrutiny required in the budgeting process of a general-purpose government. If these claims are true, and they are often disputed, a highly fragmented governmental structure fractures the tax base, creating greater difficulties in financing local public services.

Third, perceptions by residents and taxpayers about the efficiency with which local public services are financed can be important in determining the ability of local public agencies to raise revenues, especially property taxes. There are two schools of thought on how residents perceive decentralized governments. Lyons and Lowery (1989) review these two schools of thought. One, the Public Choice School, claims that more decentralized governments, within reason, are closer to voters and are, therefore, more likely to have public support for programs (DiLorenzo, 1981). In this case, one might expect more willingness to pass bond issues and referenda that provide revenues for the public sector. Whether bond issues are successful, of course, depends on marketing techniques, public information programs, and local circumstances.

Another group, which might be termed the Reform School, claims that decentralized governments overlap in service delivery, provide expensive services, and are not accountable to the public. Under these conditions, one might encounter lack of public support and difficulty obtaining sufficient resources.

Research on citizens' attitudes about public services is ambiguous because of the paucity of consistent attitude information. Two studies, Christenson and Sachs (1980) and Chicoine and Walzer (1985a), both report that governmental decentralization is not significantly correlated with higher perception of service quality. Chicoine and Walzer, in a regression analysis of Illinois local governments using 1977 data, found that counties with more decentralized governments relied more heavily on property taxes in financing services, spent more per capita on certain, but not all, services, and hired more employees per 10,000 residents (significant at 10 percent level). In addition, per-capita expenditures or employment were not correlated with citizen's perceptions. Number of taxing units or special districts per 10,000 residents, however, was significantly (negative) correlated with perception of quality. The major exceptions are parks and education, but in the case of parks, the relationship between governmental fragmentation and citizens' perceptions was significant only at 10 percent. Thus, more decentralization tends to be associated with lower perception of quality, at least based on the Illinois experience.

Comparing governmental structure in midwestern states reveals several interesting relationships. While 20 states, nationally, have the township form of government, in all of the midwestern states, except Iowa, townships provide services. The fact that states have townships, of course, does not mean that the range of services provided is the same in all states. In Illinois and Wisconsin, for instance, townships provide a broader range of services than in Minnesota, Missouri, North Dakota, South Dakota, or other states where they mainly finance transportation.

States differ widely in relative density of governments. Overall, smaller states, such as North Dakota and South Dakota, report a higher density of government, mainly because of the threshold population size to support a governmental unit. The variations are particularly noticeable in townships. In 1987, North Dakota had an average of 94.75 townships for each 100,000 residents in rural counties, and an average of 81.63 townships per 100,000 residents statewide (U.S. Bureau of the Census, 1988a, Tables 5, 6, and 7). This compares with an average of 37.67 per 100,000 thousand in Indiana and 31.42 per 100,000 in Michigan. In the latter state, townships collect revenues for roads, but hire county personnel to conduct the work. Similar findings are true of municipalities. Indiana and Ohio are lowest in number of cities per 10,000 residents and North Dakota and South Dakota are highest.

Many factors explain governmental structure, but the most commonly offered is settlement patterns. Areas settled from the South tended to have a stronger role for counties, whereas settlers from the Northeast supported the town form of government. Even within states, such as Illinois and Kansas, the same governmental structure does not exist throughout the state. Governmental structure usually does not quickly adjust to changes in transportation methods and population shifts. Thus, some governments may be vestiges of past conditions and provide limited services to relatively small population bases.

A comparison of revenues generated by government type in each state demonstrates clearly the variations in organizational structure by state (Table 5.1). Counties are especially strong in Minnesota (24.7 percent), Ohio (24.2 percent), and Wisconsin (23.8 percent), but collect a smaller proportion of local revenues in Illinois (10.8 percent) and Missouri (15.1 percent). Differences among states in the roles played by municipalities are less and all states provide educational services through school districts. Major differences are found, however, in the importance of special districts. Illinois and Nebraska lead at 17 and 13.7 percent, respectively.

REVENUE SOURCES

Many local governments, because of statutory controls and limitations, have relatively few revenue alternatives to respond to fiscal changes. State govern-

Table 5.1
Total General Revenue by Types of Government, 1986–7

State	County	Municipality	Township	School District	Special District	Total
			(percent of total revenue)			
Illinois	10.8	28.4	2.3	41.5	17.0	100.0
Indiana	22.0	25.4	1.3	46.0	5.2	100.0
Iowa	22.8	30.2	-	46.5	0.5	100.0
Kansas	20.1	36.5	0.9	40.1	2.4	100.0
Michigan	20.7	25.9	3.6	46.7	3.1	100.0
Minnesota	24.7	29.9	1.0	35.8	8.5	100.0
Missouri	15.1	29.4	0.2	46.7	8.5	100.0
Nebraska	16.2	22.8	0.4	47.0	13.7	100.0
North Dakota	19.2	24.8	2.0	48.3	5.7	100.0
Ohio	24.2	25.6	2.0	42.6	5.5	100.0
South Dakota	16.7	26.9	1.4	51.6	3.4	100.0
Wisconsin	23.8	25.4	3.1	44.3	3.4	100.0

Source: U.S. Bureau of the Census, 1988c, Table 29.

ments limit property tax rates imposed by local governments. Even when a local taxing authority could increase tax rates through referendum, residents in rural areas may be reluctant to approve them.

Local property taxes represent only one source of funds for public services. Other revenue sources, however, typically are subject to ''Dillon's Rule,'' which states that unless local governments have expressed constitutional or statutory authority to raise revenues, these powers belong to state government. When residents are seeking property tax relief, state legislators are reluctant to provide additional taxing authority to local governments. Many local governments, however, are increasing revenues by using taxing authority that previously was little used.

Charges or fees for services gained attention during the 1980s as an alternative revenue source, especially in growing urban areas. Development fees, donations of roads or transportation rights of way, and license fees are a few of the charges imposed. Rural areas, however, often have fewer fees available than urban areas. Policy makers do not wish to impose additional costs that might hinder economic development prospects. The number of residents is relatively small and even fairly substantial fees do not raise large revenues.

During the 1960s and the early 1970s, intergovernmental aid became a substantial local revenue source. In 1970, federal and state aid combined represented 34.1 percent of revenues received by local governments nationally (U.S. Bureau of the Census, 1972). With Federal General Revenue Sharing, Community Development Block Grants, and other programs, local governments' dependence on federal support mounted substantially and by 1977, intergovernmental aid had increased to 43 percent (U.S. Bureau of the Census, 1978, Table 24). In the next decade, however, the tide turned. The federal government faced mounting budget deficits, and during the Reagan Administration, state and local governments became more self-supporting.

In 1987, the General Revenue Sharing program was eliminated, causing a tighter fiscal environment for local governments. By 1988, local governments nationally received 37.5 percent of their revenues from federal and state governments (U.S. Bureau of the Census, 1989b, Table 29). The decline in intergovernmental support did not affect all governments equally and was less damaging to public agencies with economic growth. Many rural agencies, however, are not in this category, as described in earlier chapters.

State governments, a long-time source of intergovernmental support, also had fiscal problems. Following the 1981–2 recession, midwestern states experienced a substitution of high-paying manufacturing jobs for relatively low-paying consumer-service employment, slowing the growth of the income tax base. A consequence of these changes was that midwestern states were less able to replace diminishing federal support for local governments. These states now face budget deficits of their own. Of 30 states identified by the National Association of Budget Officers as facing deficits in FY1991, eight are in the Midwest.[1]

The extent to which local governments are affected by slow growth in the rural economy depends partly on public service responsibilities. Education, for certain, is one of the most costly local services, and cutbacks following population declines are difficult, because threshold levels must be met to ensure quality education. The number of teachers is not easily reduced even when class size declines. Rather, the costs must be spread over a smaller number of students. Likewise, subjects cannot be discontinued if graduates are to remain competitive in labor markets or be accepted into institutions of higher education. School districts seek alternative revenues or find ways to provide more with less. With statutory revenue controls and, in some instances, lagging state aid, the task is difficult.

Changes in tax base and intergovernmental revenues during the 1980s had a significant impact on the ability of rural local governments to finance services. The combination of cutbacks in federal revenues, fiscal stringency in state governments, and limited economic recovery clearly limited the revenues available to support desired services. This section examines changes in revenue sources of counties, cities, and townships by county economic base.

Table 5.2
Percent Changes in Metro and Nonmetro Areas, 1982–7

Revenue/ Expenditure	County		Municipality		Township	
	Metro	Nonmetro	Metro	Nonmetro	Metro	Nonmetro
			(Percent change 82-87)			
Total General Revenue	37.9	30.1	35.1	25.1	26.6	25.3
Property Taxes	41.7	34.0	23.0	20.4	32.0	32.9
Total General Expenditure	38.5	33.3	36.0	21.4	41.4	25.2
Population	1.3	-0.2	4.0	-1.8	1.7	-0.3

Source: U.S. Department of Commerce, 1982 and U.S. Department of Commerce, 1987.

Nationally, county governments received an average of 57.9 percent of total general revenues from their own sources in 1982, but, by 1987, this percentage had increased to 63.2 percent (U.S. Bureau of the Census, 1983, Table 23, and U.S. Bureau of the Census, 1988c, Table 29). Municipalities received 65.4 percent of their general revenues from own sources in 1982 and received 71 percent from these sources in 1987. Thus, the tax burden on local taxpayers increased during the postrecession period. A major factor is the Reagan Administration legacy of fiscal federalism, which reduced federal government support and placed greater responsibility for services on state and local governments.

In midwestern states, revenues in nonmetropolitan county governments increased 30.1 percent, compared with 35.1 percent in metro counties (Table 5.2).[2] Municipal revenues in nonmetropolitan counties increased 25.1 percent, compared with 37.1 percent in metro counties. There was virtually no difference in township revenue growth. Clearly, total revenues in nonmetropolitan governments did not increase nearly as rapidly as in metro areas. Likewise, property taxes collected by county governments in nonmetropolitan areas grew by 34 percent, compared with 41.7 percent in metro areas.

Midwestern local governments followed a pattern similar to national trends, except that they relied more on local revenue sources in 1982 (Table 5.3). Local revenues provided two-thirds (65.9 percent) of county general revenues in 1982 and increased only slightly to 66.7 percent five years later. The comparison of the midwestern and national experiences suggests that the relatively sluggish midwestern economy did not provide as large an increase in local revenues as

Table 5.3
Per-Capita Revenue of Nonmetro Midwest States,[1] 1982–7

	County 1982 (n=854)	County 1987 (n=854)	County % Chg 82-87	Municipality 1982 (n=5,875)	Municipality 1987 (n=5,878)	Municipality % Chg 82-87	Township 1982 (n=10,005)	Township 1987 (n=9,954)	Township % Chg 82-87
General Revenue ($) (%)	$320.08 (100.0)	$417.95 (100.0)	30.6	$255.31 (100.0)	$339.69 (100.0)	33.1	$93.34 (100.0)	$123.23 (100.0)	32.0
Intergovernmental	109.26 (34.1)	139.03 (33.3)	27.2	93.42 (36.6)	120.48 (35.5)	29.0	35.50 (38.0)	41.78 (33.9)	17.7
Federal	18.35 (5.7)	16.36 (3.9)	-10.8	30.49 (11.9)	25.58 (7.5)	-16.1	8.30 (8.9)	5.24 (4.2)	-36.9
State	83.93 (26.2)	114.30 (27.3)	36.2	57.94 (22.7)	82.23 (24.2)	41.9	24.56 (26.3)	33.53 (27.2)	36.5
Gen. Rev. fr. Own Sources	210.81 (65.9)	278.92 (66.7)	32.3	161.89 (63.4)	219.22 (64.5)	35.4	57.84 (62.0)	81.45 (66.1)	40.8
Taxes	103.87 (32.4)	155.62 (37.2)	49.8	64.76 (25.4)	91.84 (27.0)	41.8	49.05 (52.5)	65.72 (53.3)	34.0
Property	95.53 (29.8)	128.48 (30.7)	34.5	49.41 (19.3)	69.13 (20.3)	39.9	45.67 (48.9)	61.40 (49.8)	34.4
Gen & Sel. Sales	2.29 (0.7)	7.36 (1.8)	221.4	9.88 (3.9)	15.15 (4.5)	53.3	* -	.23 (0.2)	-
Income	1.34 (0.4)	2.60 (0.6)	94.0	1.90 (0.7)	2.79 (0.8)	46.8	- -	* -	-
Other	4.71 (1.5)	17.18 (4.1)	264.8	3.56 (1.4)	4.77 (1.4)	34.0	3.34 (3.6)	4.09 (3.3)	22.5
Charges	74.00 (23.1)	88.83 (21.2)	20.0	43.14 (16.9)	62.45 (18.4)	44.8	3.25 (3.5)	1.97 (1.6)	-39.4
Misc. Revenue	32.94 (10.3)	34.46 (8.2)	4.6	54.00 (21.1)	64.93 (19.1)	20.2	5.54 (5.9)	13.76 (11.2)	148.4

[1]The Midwest States are IL, IN, IA, KS, MI, MN, MO, NE, ND, OH, SD, WI.
*Negligible, less than 0.1.

Source: U.S. Department of Commerce, 1982 and U.S. Department of Commerce, 1987.

in other states. This is especially likely if counties in the Midwest contain a larger proportion of farmland in their tax base than other, more urbanized counties.

Midwestern county governments collected an average of $278.92 per capita from their own sources in 1987 compared with an average of $294.57 nationwide (U.S. Bureau of the Census, 1988c, Table 29). The increase of 32.3 percent between 1982 and 1987 outstripped the 17.7 percent increase in the Consumer Price Index during this period.

The per-capita comparisons are distorted somewhat by population changes. Rural counties, for instance, lost an average of 0.2 percent between 1982 and 1987, whereas metro counties increased by 1.3 percent. Municipalities in non-metropolitan areas declined by 1.8 percent compared with an average increase of 4.0 percent in metro counties. Population declines between 1982 and 1987 are contained in the revenue figures.

Municipalities in nonmetropolitan counties reported a growth of 35.4 percent in their own source revenues. The portion of municipal revenues paid by their own sources remained about the same—63.4 percent in 1982 compared with 64.5 percent in 1987. Cities depend slightly less on local sources for services, but they also have a broader tax base. Larger communities may have participated in the economic recovery to a larger extent than rural counties.

The main local revenue source in both county and municipal governments is local taxes, especially property taxes, which represented 46.1 percent of their own source county revenues in 1987. The importance of property taxes in the overall revenue picture did not change substantially during the 1980s, increasing only from 29.8 percent to 30.7 percent during the 5 years.

Municipalities in nonmetropolitan midwestern counties are comparable to county governments in revenue sources. Property taxes represented 19.3 percent of general revenues in 1982 and 20.3 percent 5 years later. The 39.9 percent increase clearly exceeded inflation, demonstrating that taxpayers, in real terms, paid more property taxes for public services than 5 years earlier. Detailed information is not readily available to determine whether the increases arose because of conscious tax rate changes, assessed valuation growth, or both.

A comparison of townships largely responsible for services in rural areas shows similar increases in property tax revenues. Thus, even in the most rural areas, property tax revenues increased more than inflation.

There is substantial reason to expect differences in revenue changes by economic base. Counties based mainly on agriculture, for instance, may have performed differently from those in which manufacturing is the dominant income source. Comparing the two groups of counties yields several interesting findings, and, by and large, they are contrary to a priori expectations (Appendix 5.A).

First, agricultural-based counties generated much higher per-capita revenues than manufacturing ($467.15 compared with $352.77). One explanation is the smaller population size in agricultural counties. Second, there was no substantial difference in percentage increase between the two groups: agricultural counties increased 31.1 percent compared with 30.6 percent for manufacturing counties.

Third, property taxes represent a much greater proportion of general revenues in agricultural-based counties (34.8 percent) compared with manufacturing counties (22.2 percent). This is explained by the relatively larger proportion of the tax base in farmland, which, in turn, explains the larger percentage of income generated from agriculture. In addition, local revenue sources, including property taxes, represent a much higher proportion of general revenues in agricultural counties (69.5 percent) than in manufacturing counties (62.3 percent).

Fourth, their own source revenues in manufacturing counties were stable—63 percent to 62.3 percent, whereas counties dependent on agriculture increased reliance on local revenues slightly, from 67.7 to 69.5 percent. The decrease in federal intergovernmental support in agricultural-based counties is certainly a factor explaining the difference.

Municipalities differ from counties in reliance on local revenues. Cities in agricultural-dependent counties collect 64.5 percent of general revenues from their own sources compared with 66.7 percent in manufacturing-based counties. Growth in their own source revenues in agricultural counties was 42.3 percent during the period compared with 25 percent in manufacturing counties. Property taxes increased 50.8 percent per capita in agricultural counties and only 25.1 percent in manufacturing counties.

Nationwide, much attention is paid to the growing dependence on user charges and fees for services. It is interesting that nonmetropolitan counties in the Midwest did not increase user charges substantially. In reality, reliance on this revenue source declined from 23.1 to 21.2 percent. The most plausible explanation is that county governments do not provide public services that can be sold.

Municipalities, on the other hand, are better able to price services, such as water, sewer treatment, golf courses, and recreational activities. Municipalities increased user fees by 44.8 percent, more than double that of counties. Although the dollar amount of revenue ($62.45 per capita) is not small, it represents only 18.4 percent, an increase from 16.9 percent in 1982. Thus, municipalities appear to have held the line on property taxes and to have shifted some of the burden to user charges and fees.

Townships are interesting because they decreased charges and fees 39.4 percent between 1982 and 1987. Although these charges were a small portion of the revenues in 1982 (3.5 percent), they decreased to 1.6 percent of revenues in 1987. Property taxes in counties remained about the same percentage and the difference is represented by an increase in miscellaneous revenues, including interest income and assorted other small revenue.

The main shifts in revenues affecting rural local governments involve intergovernmental aid. In each type of government, changes in federal revenues have been the largest. In county governments, for example, federal revenues declined 10.8 percent between 1982 and 1987. Cities lost more than counties (16.1

percent) and townships lost the most (36.9 percent). In each case, federal aid in 1987 represented less than 10 percent of the general revenues available for services, and for township governments, the percentage decreased from 8.9 to 4.2 percent during the 5-year period.

Changes in federal aid are even more interesting when counties are compared by economic base. County governments in manufacturing counties reported an average increase of 9.9 percent in federal aid compared with a decline of 20.7 percent in counties based on agriculture. The precise reason for the difference is unclear because the other governmental units reported a decline.

Municipalities in manufacturing-based counties lost 33.3 percent of federal revenue compared with a decline of 13.3 percent in agricultural counties. Township governments were just the reverse with a larger decline (48.7 percent) in agricultural counties compared with a 13.2 percent decline in manufacturing counties. Although one obvious explanation is elimination of General Revenue Sharing, the reasons for the differences in percentage declines between the two county types are not completely clear.

Part of the decline in federal intergovernmental aid was offset by increases in state aid. County governments received an increase of 36.2 percent compared with 36.5 percent for townships. Municipalities received the largest increase (41.9 percent). In all instances, the per-capita increases in state aid exceeded inflation and were higher than the overall revenue growth. Municipalities in agricultural-based counties reported a 32.3 percent increase in state aid compared with 42.7 percent in manufacturing counties. Townships in agriculture counties reported a 44.9 percent increase in state aid compared with 36.5 percent in manufacturing counties.

Comparisons of changes in revenue sources, by type of government, yield several important results. First, on average, rural governments in the Midwest increased revenues more than inflation. This is partly explained by the time period of the study. Because the base year, 1982, was in the depths of the recession, one would expect the recovery to bring some revenue increases to most governments.

Second, a decided shift occurred away from reliance on federal intergovernmental aid to reliance on own source revenues.

Third, user charges increased in constant dollars, but did not increase in relative importance as a revenue source for counties. Municipalities seem to have better incorporated user fees as a revenue source, but townships, especially those in agricultural-based counties, reduced reliance on user fees.

Fourth, because state aid replaced federal intergovernmental revenues to at least a limited extent, less additional burden was placed on local revenue sources.

SERVICE EXPENDITURES

Revenues support local public services and economic conditions dictate changes in the types of services required. Public programs are determined both by demand

and ability to finance them. Comparing expenditures by type of government is complicated by differences in service responsibilities and differences in state government support. In some instances, state governments fund programs directly, whereas in others, they provide intergovernmental assistance to local governments that administer the services. In other cases, notably education, services are provided by a separate unit of government, often a single-purpose government.

Although differences in responsibility must be recognized, a common set of services is provided by most local governments. Police/fire protection, highways, governmental administration, and refuse disposal/sewage treatment are provided by many governments. Perhaps the largest differences among states in the present study involve overlap between counties and townships. In most midwestern states, townships are responsible for rural highways and bridges. Service varies from collecting the revenues and contracting with another unit of government to provide highway services (Wisconsin and Ohio) to the direct provision of a broad assortment of services, as in Illinois (Walzer and Baird, 1989).

Local governments usually operate under a balanced budget requirement. This does not mean that they cannot borrow, but continued deficits are viewed by taxpayers as poor management. With this requirement, one might expect to be able to compare revenues with expenditures, to determine how well local governments have done in the postrecessionary period. The comparison is complicated, however, because governments can manage the ending balance by delaying the payment of bills. In addition, the receipt of funds, especially in intergovernmental aid for capital projects, does not always correspond with spending. A portion of the funds are received early in the project, causing an apparent surplus, but the remainder is received after the project is completed, causing an apparent deficit for an intervening year.

In spite of difficulties in data presentation and analysis, it is possible to examine shifts in local priorities. This section examines the distribution of expenditures for local public services and trends during the 1980s by type of government and county economic base. Per-capita expenditures are used to adjust for population differences. County governments in nonmetropolitan areas increased general expenditures 33.3 percent compared with an increase of 38.5 percent in metro counties. Municipalities in nonmetropolitan counties increased expenditures 21.4 percent compared with 36 percent in metro areas. The township expenditure increases were 41.4 percent in metro counties and only 25.2 percent in rural counties. Thus, although expenditures increased by more than inflation, a substantial difference is found between rural and metro counties.

The average general expenditures of county governments increased 31.9 percent in nominal terms between 1982 and 1987 (Appendix 5.B). Compared with Consumer Price Index increases of 17.7 percent during the same period, counties increased the level of real services. The same findings are true for municipalities (28.6 percent increase) and townships (33.4 percent increase).

Highways are the largest expenditures in each of the general-purpose governments and dominate township expenditures. County governments devote 29.9 percent of their expenditures to highways compared with 21 percent in municipalities and 62 percent in townships. The trends in highway expenditures between 1982 and 1987 were mixed. They were stable in county governments, increased slightly from 19.3 to 21 percent for municipalities, and decreased from 70 percent to 62 percent in township governments.

Accordingly, highway expenditures increased the most (39.9 percent) in municipalities and the least (18.1 percent) in townships. One explanation is that township governments, at least in Illinois, Minnesota, Ohio, and Wisconsin, spent a major portion of Federal General Revenue Sharing funds for roads and bridges (Chicoine and Walzer, 1984; Walzer and Chicoine, 1989). Loss of GRS funds almost certainly limited expenditure growth. Even so, townships, on average, increased per-capita highway expenditures by more than inflation during this period, but this comparison is not corrected for population loss.

General government administration is the second largest expenditure function commonly provided by most governments. In 1987, county governments spent an average of $58.40 per resident for this service and it remained at nearly the same level of importance during the 1980s—14.1 percent of expenditures in 1982 compared with 14.7 percent in 1987.

Municipalities spent less ($43.37 per capita) on general government, but this figure represents nearly the same proportion (14.3 percent) of total expenditures as counties. Expenditures in this category increased much more rapidly than did total city expenditures—45.3 percent compared with 28.6 percent.

Expenditures for governmental administration grew most rapidly in townships, with an increase of 59.2 percent during the 5-year period. Administrative expenditures represented 15.9 percent of total township expenditures in 1987. Precisely why governmental administrative expenditures increased more rapidly than overall expenditures, especially in municipalities and townships, is not clear.

Also important are expenditures for police and fire protection. Many rural governments have a part-time police force and a volunteer fire department. Detailed information on percentage of governments with full-time versus part-time police and fire departments is not available. On average, county governments spent $20.92 per capita for protective services, but they represent only 5.2 percent of the aggregate county budget. Municipalities spent an average of $35.87 per capita, representing 11.8 percent of the total, and townships spent an average of $6.08 per capita, 5.3 percent of expenditures. Expenditures for police and fire protection in county and municipal governments increased at less than the rate of total expenditures, but in townships, the increase was slightly faster than total expenditures.

Public health expenditures are among the most rapid growing services in cities and townships, but represent small proportions of overall expenditures—less than 1 percent in the case of municipalities and townships. Counties spend much more on public health, but the increase was only slightly faster than overall expenditures.

CONCLUSIONS

Revenue and expenditure trends in rural midwestern counties are somewhat unexpected. The demographics and economics of the region indicated a pattern of slow growth during the mid- and late 1980s. The revenues and expenditures of general-purpose local governments, however, seem to have responded fairly well between 1982 and 1987, outpacing inflation even though they increased less than in urban counties. The observations must be tempered by the fact that double-digit inflation during the early 1980s almost certainly brought a reduction in real resources. Thus, the better-than-expected growth in the postrecessionary period may partly compensate for earlier losses.

Local government finances exhibited several trends. First, a shift from intergovernmental aid (especially federal) is partly offset by increases in state aid and greater dependence on local revenues. Second, per-capita property taxes maintained their relative position as a revenue source for most local governments and increased in real terms. In all probability, for many governments, property taxes were one of only a few local revenues available to support services. Third, user charges increased in importance for municipalities, but not significantly for counties, and certainly not for township governments, where they declined in importance.

Local government finances also differ by economic base, with governments in agricultural-based counties receiving less of an increase in state aid than manufacturing counties, and township governments receiving a substantially larger increase. Property taxes are much more important as a revenue source in agricultural-based counties than in manufacturing counties. The property tax increases in municipalities and townships in agriculture counties were much higher than in manufacturing counties.

Population characteristics and economic conditions continue to change in rural areas. These changes will surely cause adjustments in financing patterns. Based on the comparisons between 1982 and 1987, rural areas have participated in the economic growth process and have been able to maintain their expenditures. They have done so, however, with a real increase in property taxes. A looming recession could, once again, adversely affect local revenues and trigger higher expenditures for social services.

APPENDIX 5.A

Table 5.A. Per-Capita Revenue of Nonmetro Midwest States[1] by Type, 1982–7

	County 1982 (n=368)	County 1987 (n=368)	County % Chg 82-87	Municipality 1982 (n=2,467)	Municipality 1987 (n=2,469)	Municipality % Chg 82-87	Township 1982 (n=4,147)	Township 1987 (n=4,109)	Township % Chg 82-87
Agriculture									
General Revenue ($)	$356.31	$467.15	31.1	$243.14	$327.57	34.7	$103.46	$138.27	33.6
(%)	(100.0)	(100.0)		(100.0)	(100.0)		(100.0)	(100.0)	
Intergovernmental	115.02	142.25	23.7	94.72	116.29	22.8	34.59	38.33	10.8
	(32.3)	(30.4)		(39.0)	(35.5)		(33.4)	(27.7)	
Federal	21.85	17.32	-20.7	29.47	25.55	-13.3	11.02	5.65	-48.7
	(6.1)	(3.7)		(12.1)	(7.8)		(10.6)	(4.1)	
State	86.04	116.36	35.2	61.05	80.80	32.3	20.16	29.21	44.9
	(24.1)	(24.9)		(25.1)	(24.7)		(19.5)	(21.1)	
Gen. Rev. fr. Own Sources	241.29	324.91	34.7	148.42	211.28	42.3	68.87	99.94	45.1
	(67.7)	(69.5)		(61.0)	(64.5)		(66.6)	(72.3)	
Taxes	130.91	205.35	56.9	61.78	93.48	51.3	60.67	82.45	35.9
	(36.7)	(44.0)		(25.4)	(28.5)		(58.6)	(59.6)	
Property	121.90	162.79	33.5	50.26	75.77	50.8	57.52	77.99	35.6
	(34.2)	(34.8)		(20.7)	(23.1)		(55.6)	(56.4)	
Gen & Sel. Sales	1.22	5.79	374.6	7.56	12.60	66.7	*	*	-
	(0.3)	(1.2)		(3.1)	(3.8)		-	-	
Income	1.12	2.01	79.5	-	*	-	-	-	-
	(0.3)	(0.4)		-	-		-	-	
Other	6.66	34.75	421.8	3.96	5.10	28.8	3.14	4.42	40.8
	(1.9)	(7.4)		(1.6)	(1.6)		(3.0)	(3.2)	
Charges	72.23	79.39	9.9	39.31	65.65	67.0	2.44	1.64	-32.8
	(20.2)	(17.0)		(16.2)	(20.0)		(2.3)	(1.2)	
Misc. Revenue	38.15	40.17	5.3	47.32	52.15	10.2	5.76	15.85	175.2
	(10.7)	(8.6)		(19.5)	(15.9)		(5.6)	(11.5)	

continue..

Table 5.A. Cont'd.

	County 1982 (n=187)	County 1987 (n=187)	County % Chg 82-87	Municipality 1982 (n=1,421)	Municipality 1987 (n=1,420)	Municipality % Chg 82-87	Township 1982 (n=2,306)	Township 1987 (n=2,306)	Township % Chg 82-87
Manufacturing									
General Revenue ($) (%)	$270.13 (100.0)	$352.77 (100.0)	30.6	$282.74 (100.0)	$348.52 (100.0)	23.3	$73.29 (100.0)	$94.62 (100.0)	29.1
Intergovernmental	99.91 (37.0)	132.84 (37.7)	33.0	96.76 (34.2)	116.13 (33.3)	20.0	32.83 (44.8)	41.15 (43.5)	25.3
Federal	13.00 (4.8)	14.29 (4.0)	9.9	30.25 (10.7)	20.20 (5.8)	-33.2	4.92 (6.7)	4.27 (4.5)	-13.2
State	80.21 (29.7)	110.35 (31.3)	37.6	61.34 (21.7)	87.54 (25.1)	42.7	26.62 (36.3)	34.84 (36.8)	30.9
Local	6.70 (2.5)	8.20 (2.3)	22.4	5.17 (1.8)	8.38 (2.4)	62.1	1.29 (1.8)	2.03 (2.1)	57.4
Gen. Rev. fr. Own Sources	170.22 (63.0)	219.93 (62.3)	29.2	185.97 (65.8)	232.39 (66.7)	25.0	40.46 (55.2)	53.47 (56.5)	32.2
Taxes	68.20 (25.2)	95.96 (27.2)	40.7	68.51 (24.2)	87.37 (25.1)	27.5	29.07 (40.0)	38.07 (40.2)	31.0
Property	58.78 (21.8)	78.46 (22.2)	33.5	50.25 (17.8)	62.88 (18.0)	25.1	27.54 (37.6)	35.74 (37.8)	29.8
Gen & Sel. Sales	3.15 (1.2)	7.32 (2.1)	132.4	8.55 (3.0)	10.63 (3.0)	24.3	* -	.74 (0.8)	-
Income	3.91 (1.4)	7.49 (2.1)	91.6	7.02 (2.5)	10.16 (2.9)	44.7	- -	* -	-
Other	2.36 (0.9)	2.69 (0.8)	14.0	2.69 (0.9)	3.69 (1.1)	37.2	1.44 (2.0)	1.56 (1.6)	8.3
Charges	77.28 (28.6)	97.25 (27.6)	25.8	51.91 (18.4)	68.71 (19.7)	32.4	4.54 (6.2)	2.19 (2.3)	48.2
Misc. Revenue	24.74 (9.2)	26.72 (7.6)	8.0	65.57 (23.2)	76.31 (21.9)	16.4	6.85 (9.3)	13.21 (14.0)	92.8

[1]The Midwest States are IL, IN, IA, KS, MI, MN, MO, NE, ND, OH, SD, WI
* Negligible - Less than 0.1

Source: U.S. Department of Commerce, 1982 and U.S. Department of Commerce, 1987.

APPENDIX 5.B

Table 5.B. Per-Capita Expenditure of Rural Midwest States,[1] 1982–7

	County 1982 (n=854)	County 1987 (n=854)	County % Chg 82-87	Municipality 1982 (n=5,875)	Municipality 1987 (n=5,878)	Municipality % Chg 82-87	Township 1982 (n=10,005)	Township 1987 (n=9,954)	Township % Chg 82-87
General Expenditure ($)	$301.81	$398.22	31.9	$235.58	$303.01	28.6	$85.90	$114.63	33.4
(%)	(100.0)	(100.0)		(100.0)	(100.0)		(100.0)	(100.0)	
Education	.48	2.32	383.3	-	.37	-	-	.11	-
	(0.2)	(0.6)		-	(0.1)		-	(0.1)	
Highways	92.15	119.19	29.3	45.50	63.67	39.9	60.15	71.03	18.1
	(30.5)	(29.9)		(19.3)	(21.0)		(70.0)	(62.0)	
Police/Fire	16.29	20.92	28.4	30.08	35.87	19.2	4.48	6.08	35.7
	(5.4)	(5.2)		(12.8)	(11.8)		(5.2)	(5.3)	
Welfare	20.80	47.55	128.6	3.00	6.09	103.0	.39	.57	46.1
	(6.9)	(11.9)		(1.3)	(2.0)		(0.4)	(0.5)	
Hospital	58.10	63.88	9.9	13.22	11.33	-14.3	*	*	-
	(19.2)	(16.0)		(5.6)	(3.7)		-	-	
Health	16.64	22.98	38.1	.96	2.85	196.9	.22	.50	127.3
	(5.5)	(5.8)		(0.4)	(0.9)		(0.3)	(0.4)	
Sanitation/Sewer	2.33	3.24	39.1	36.30	54.26	49.5	1.89	1.61	-14.8
	(0.8)	(0.8)		(15.4)	(17.9)		(2.2)	(1.4)	
Govt. Admin.	42.47	58.40	37.5	29.85	43.37	45.3	11.46	18.24	59.2
	(14.1)	(14.7)		(12.7)	(14.3)		(13.3)	(15.9)	
Int. On Debt	6.42	8.41	31.0	15.89	22.88	44.0	1.01	1.25	23.8
	(2.1)	(2.1)		(6.7)	(7.5)		(1.2)	(1.1)	
Others	46.13	51.33	11.3	60.78	62.32	2.5	6.30	15.24	141.9
	(15.3)	(12.9)		(25.8)	(20.6)		(7.3)	(13.3)	

[1]The Midwest States are IL, IN, IA, KS, MI, MN, MO, NE, ND, OH, SD, WI
* Negligible - Less than 0.1

Source: U.S. Department of Commerce, 1982 and U.S. Department of Commerce, 1987.

NOTES

1. Survey released at a press conference January 1, 1991, National Governor's Association of State Budget Officers, Washington, D.C.
2. U.S. Department of Commerce, Survey of Governments, Annual Finance Statistics, computer tapes for respective years.

6. Education and Rural Development: Lessons for the Rural Midwest

John B. Crihfield

Education is sometimes viewed as a panacea for problems in economic development. If local workers in depressed communities were only better trained, it is claimed, then businesses would be attracted to these places. A more diverse industrial base would then increase opportunities for workers and reduce incentives to leave the communities for more prosperous towns and states. It is but a short step to a policy statement that more be spent on primary and secondary schools, or community colleges and state universities, especially in regions with slow growth or economic decline.

This chapter assesses these and other arguments within the context of recent research in the economics of education and rural economic change. The first section considers arguments for public spending on education and reviews recent literature regarding the effectiveness of public educational expenditures on student performance. The next section examines the empirical relationships between school spending and student achievement, and local economic behavior. Data from Illinois are used for purposes of illustration. These data are likely to be typical of rural midwestern states, however, and the findings are consistent with other research as noted. Implications for development policy in rural areas are presented next.

PUBLIC SPENDING ON EDUCATION: JUSTIFICATION AND EFFECTIVENESS

Many reasons are advanced to justify public support for education. Although some of these justifications are valid, most do not fit well into a strategy for rural economic development. One rationale is the "public good" argument. Basic education bestows benefits on more than students. It benefits other people throughout society, in addition to the private gains to the students receiving the education. Without public support, students (or their parents) would underinvest in their learning because they do not directly gain from the benefits their training bestows elsewhere in society. Similarly, local governments—as opposed to higher levels of government—may also underinvest in basic education because some students who receive training in their schools migrate to other regions after graduation. This is the "brain-drain" problem: training costs are incurred locally, but benefits from training are received elsewhere. These arguments are general. They apply as much to education in urban areas as they do to education in rural areas. In principle, the public good argument with regard to primary and secondary education is valid. Contrary to the impression given, there is no evidence in the literature, however, that the "positive externalities" from schooling are greater in rural areas than in urban areas.[1] Indeed, at current levels of school spending, public good externalities for public school spending may be exhausted. In other words, additional spending on public schools may contribute little to "society," above and beyond private gains received by each student.

A good example of education as a public good, and how it relates to development, concerns public support for basic research in universities. The cost of basic research can be very high, whereas the cost of dissemination of knowledge from research is low, leading private institutions to underinvest in research and development when they cannot control dissemination of their work. Because they are not dependent on selling their research, public universities (or publicly supported research at private universities) allow free use of their findings and are less likely to underinvest in basic research.

Public support for basic research, however, is not practical as a *rural* development strategy, although some aspects of basic research promote rural activities. For years, Agricultural Experiment Stations throughout the Unitied States conducted research into agricultural activities that directly benefit the farm sector. More recently, research into agricultural "value-added" activities have sought new uses for farm products, for example, the development of corn-based sweeteners and biodegradable plastic bags, and soybean meal that can be fed directly to animals. However, in general, basic research can lead to improved productivity in any industrial sector, rural or otherwise, and is ill-suited for promotion of particular areas.

A third argument is that public support to education benefits the local economy because it makes a community a desirable place to live and work, attracts new business, and helps retain existing business. This argument has less to do with education per se than with amenity values associated with public school spending. There are difficulties with this argument as a development strategy, however. There is no clear evidence that the local provision of educational services affects interregional (or intermetropolitan) locational choices of firms or workers.[2] In a city with many neighborhoods, one may observe that families choose where to live *within* the city on the basis of educational (and many other) characteristics. These location decisions, however, do not affect the resource base for the whole metropolitan area.

There is also a question of ability to control local spending for schools. The level of educational services in a community reflects the local demand for education. This means that the level of local educational services is endogenous and may not be easily controlled by policy makers. In particular, affluent communities may provide relatively high levels of educational services for their students, but this spending is mainly an income effect of the demand for public schools. In other words, schools do not create the affluence. Households in these communities are already well off, and they choose to spend their income on education for their children. When it is also recognized that relatively high levels of local services (such as public schools) are often financed by relatively high local taxes, it becomes clear that schools (or any other public service) come at a cost to the community, and are not a magic lever to stimulate local economic growth.

Another argument stresses the importance of rural schools in local development, due to the large share of community employment attributable to public schools. Indeed, it may be true that public schools are the largest employers in many rural towns, and that through their spending, the employees of these schools support local retail and service-sector employment. Such considerations, however, are irrelevant to the rational use of educational and other resources. If a school closes because of consolidation, local businesses may also suffer, but, over time, resources in these supporting activities will relocate to places of new growth.

The preceding arguments deal directly or indirectly with the question of efficiency, that is, getting the highest return from a given amount of resources devoted to education. There are also arguments for publicly supporting education for reasons of "fairness" and "equal opportunity." Although these arguments are difficult to define, they pertain to the belief that everyone has a right to at least a minimal level of financial support for education, regardless of personal resources or individual attributes. In many communities choosing the appropriate level of educational service is a local decision, because many school districts set school expenditures and then raise revenues necessary to meet these spending levels (typically through property taxes). States often impose spending floors on districts, but allow localities to spend more than the minimum if they choose. Recently, California has attempted to enforce spending caps as well (Dynarski, Schwab, and Zampelli, 1989). A crucial concern by anyone's definition of "equal opportunity" in education is establishing a minimally acceptable level of support. Once established, the relevant questions are those of efficiency, which are the central focus of this chapter.

Most arguments for publicly supporting primary and secondary education presuppose that public educational expenditures positively affect a student's performance in school. Arguments linking public schools to local economic activity implicitly make the same assumption, because improvements in student achievement presumably represent increases in human capital. Most discussions on financing public education take as given the ability to affect school outcomes by increasing public support to primary and secondary schools. For example, Nowlan and Hickrod recently wrote that students in Illinois school districts with relatively low expenditures per pupil are being "shortchanged educationally," and "are at grave risk of becoming left out when it comes to good jobs and fulfilling lives."[3] This argument implies that higher public expenditures per pupil in these school districts would lead to higher levels of student achievement. Deavers (1990, p. 4) writes that "current rural economic underperformance is a result of 'market failure,' " and that "the education of rural children seems to be a good example [of such market failure]." His argument implies that higher spending on rural education would improve the performance of rural schools, and, thereby, improve rural economic performance generally. A related view is voiced by Ward: "More money in many districts can make a difference because more money can mean a better and richer curriculum, more appropriate facilities and equipment, and higher quality teachers and administrators."[4] One could surely find similar sentiments expressed in newspapers and magazines in virtually every state.

To many people, these arguments are intuitively obvious. It may come as a surprise that a preponderance of research finds very little correlation between expenditures per pupil and student performance. Hanushek (1981, 1986) has compiled two of the most comprehensive surveys of this literature. His findings should be sobering to anyone inclined to throw additional money at public schools.

In 75 percent of studies (49 of 65), expenditures per pupil were not systematically related to student performance. In 79 percent of studies (89 of 112), teacher/pupil ratios were not systematically related to performance. In 89 percent of studies (95 of 109), teacher education was not systematically related to performance, and in 83 percent of studies (50 of 60), teacher salary was not systematically related to performance.

The studies represent a wide range of school experiences that differ considerably in terms of scope, methodology, and analytical rigor. Because output measures differ, as do variables introduced as controls, comparisons are difficult. However, despite these limitations, there is a consistent theme regarding the impact of additional expenditures, leading Hanushek (1986, pp. 1162, 1163) to conclude: "There appears to be no strong systematic relationship between school expenditures and student performance" and that "expenditure parameters are unrelated to student performance after family backgrounds and other educational inputs are considered." There are, of course, important determinants of student achievement, including parental education and wealth, family size and structure, and inborn aptitude. However, these are only remotely affected by a state's policy toward education.

The implications of these findings are far-reaching. If "marginal changes" in educational inputs do not affect student performance, that is, changes that are small relative to existing levels of spending and inputs, and that typify most contemplated changes, then they are also unlikely to affect long-run measures of labor productivity, economic growth, and poverty. There is some evidence that employment growth has been stronger in places where educational attainment levels are higher (Schaeffer and Sander, 1987; Crihfield, 1989). However, the literature indicates that changes in educational spending, given the current structure of public schools, do little or nothing to alter levels of student achievement.

EMPIRICAL RELATIONSHIPS BETWEEN EDUCATION AND LOCAL ECONOMIC ACTIVITY

Although the preceding discussion reports no clear relationship between additional school resources and school output, this section examines empirical relationships between education and local economic activity. Data from Illinois are used for purposes of illustration. Aside from Chicago and its collar counties, most counties in Illinois are rural; therefore, the results for Illinois are likely to be similar to those in other midwestern states with relatively large rural areas. Indeed, the findings described in what follows for Illinois are similar to those for North Carolina, a Sunbelt state experiencing a different economic climate than midwestern states and that places greater reliance on state (as opposed to local) support for public education (Crihfield, 1990).

Employment growth and unemployment rates are useful, if not always unambiguous, measures of economic performance. Average county employment in Illinois declined by about 3 percent from 1980 to 1985 (Tables 6.1 and 6.2).[5] Employment growth, however, varied widely across the state. Using 1988 Illinois Cooperative Extension System regions, employment in the Chicago area grew by almost 14 percent during this period, whereas the southern counties had employment growth of about 2 percent, and the northern and central counties experienced employment declines.[6] Average employment decline was somewhat higher in rural counties than in urban counties (−3.6 percent compared to −1.5 percent).[7] Most employment gains were concentrated in the Chicago area and in the Illinois counties surrounding St. Louis. Within the northern and central counties, declines were evenly distributed in urban and rural areas, with 8 percent declines in the northern counties and 6 percent declines in central counties.

Patterns of unemployment around the state are loosely related to patterns of employment growth. In general, rural unemployment was higher than urban unemployment (12 percent vs. 8 percent). The average 1986 unemployment rate across all counties was 11 percent. The average in the Chicago counties was lowest at 5.9 percent, and highest in the southern counties at about 14 percent.

Rough measures of educational attainment are provided by high school and college completion rates for residents 25 years old or older. In 1980 (the most recent year for which data are available), roughly 62 percent of people over 25 in Illinois had completed high school, and 11 percent had completed college. Both measures are highest in the Chicago counties, and lowest in the southern counties. Comparing rural to urban areas, high school completion rates were about 9 percent lower in rural counties (60 percent compared to 69 percent),

Table 6.1
Economic and Educational Averages for Illinois Regions[a]

Region	FREQ	ENR8086	12+	16+	LGXPP	TLRPP	TSRPP	FDREVPP	TNLRPP	REVPP	ENR86	TRANPP	EG8085	UNEMP
Illinois	102	-12.4	62.3	10.7	2570.51	1664.44	1160.60	121.86	1282.46	2946.90	17807.4	906.07	-3.1	11.0
Central	33	-13.1	65.5	11.8	2517.25	1789.67	1028.02	118.99	1147.01	2936.68	8149.4	727.59	-8.1	9.3
Chicago	3	-9.1	75.0	23.7	2946.36	2826.53	885.58	153.26	1038.83	3865.36	314841.7	119.82	13.9	5.9
North	27	-14.7	67.4	11.4	2614.05	2000.67	984.42	94.36	1078.78	3079.45	13893.9	613.38	-5.7	9.3
South	39	-10.6	55.0	8.3	2556.51	1236.31	1415.91	140.92	1556.82	2793.13	5840.1	1320.20	1.7	14.0
Rural	76	-13.6	60.1	9.3	2613.15	1609.49	1202.67	121.87	1324.54	2934.03	4528.2	1003.66	-3.6	12.0
Urban	26	-9.0	68.7	14.8	2445.86	1825.07	1037.62	121.84	1159.46	2984.53	56623.6	620.79	-1.5	8.2
Rural:														
Central	25	-15.4	63.5	10.0	2574.47	1776.21	1053.27	115.40	1168.67	2944.88	4476.1	798.25	-8.0	10.0
North	17	-18.6	66.3	10.6	2735.40	2110.89	962.97	92.96	1055.93	3166.82	6198.7	624.51	-5.2	9.7
South	34	-9.8	54.4	8.2	2580.47	1236.20	1432.38	141.08	1573.46	2809.66	3731.2	1344.27	0.5	14.5
Urban:														
Central	8	-5.9	71.7	17.3	2338.45	1831.70	949.11	130.21	1079.32	2911.02	19628.4	506.75	-8.5	7.3
Chicago	3	-9.1	75.0	23.7	2946.36	2826.53	885.58	153.26	1038.83	3865.36	314841.7	119.82	13.9	5.9
North	10	-8.1	69.2	12.9	2407.76	1813.30	1020.89	96.74	1117.63	2930.93	26975.7	594.46	-6.5	8.6
South	5	-15.7	59.3	9.0	2393.61	1237.12	1303.94	139.77	1443.71	2680.83	20180.8	1156.49	10.3	10.1

[a] All dollars are expressed in 1982 dollars. See Table 6.2 for definitions and sources.

Table 6.2
Definition of Terms and Sources of Data

Variable *	Definition
MET	Metropolitan status (0 = rural, 1 = urban)
ENR86	Public school enrollment , 1986-87
ENR8086	Percentage change in public school enrollment, 1980-1986
12+	Percentage of the population 25 years old or older with a high school degree (1980)
16+	Percentage of the population 25 years old or older with a college degree (1980)
LGXPP	Local government expenditures for elementary and secondary education per pupil. Includes all expenditures of local school systems other than for interest, duplicative intergovernmental payments, and retirement benefits paid to former education employees. Expenditure data are for 1982, and enrollment data are for 1986-87.
TLRPP	Local taxes and payments in lieu of taxes, and other local revenues per pupil, 1986-87.
TSRPP	General state aid, and other state revenues per pupil, 1986-87.
FDREVPP	Federal revenues per pupil, 1986-87
TNLRPP	Total nonlocal revenue per pupil (TSRPP plus FDREVPP)
REVPP	Revenue per pupil (TLRPP + TNLRPP)
TRANPP	LGXPP minus TLRPP
EG8085	Percentage change in employment, 1980-85
UNEMP	Unemployment rate, 1986

**Note:* Variables for TLRRP, TSRPP, FDREVPP, see *Illinois Public Schools Financial Statistics*, 1988. For 1980 employment, see U.S. Bureau of the Census, 1980. For all other data, see U.S. Bureau of the Census, 1988b.

and college completion rates were about 6 percent lower in rural counties (9 percent compared to 15 percent).

Between 1980 and 1986, primary and secondary public school enrollment declined throughout Illinois. The average county experienced a decline of about 12.5 percent over this period. Declines varied between 9 and 15 percent around the state, but were highest, on average, in rural counties (−13.6 percent in rural counties compared with −9.0 percent in urban counties).

The county average per-pupil expenditure for primary and secondary public schools in Illinois (1982 dollars) was $2,571 in 1982. Expenditures were highest in Chicago ($2,946) and lowest in central Illinois ($2,517), but the difference in these averages is only 17 percent. It is surprising, perhaps, that rural per-capita expenditures exceeded those in urban counties ($2,613 vs. $2,446). In the 1986–7 school year, rural counties provided less support per pupil from local revenue sources than did urban counties ($1,609 versus $1,825), and received more state and federal support per pupil than did urban counties ($1,325 versus $1,159). Indeed, rural students in southern Illinois received more state and federal support per pupil than any other region in the state.[8]

These figures provide an overview of general conditions in education and the state economy by location and rural status. The relationships among these variables are illustrated through an array of two-way Pearson correlation coefficients (Table 6.3). The correlation coefficient is constructed by calculating an index ranging from -1 to 1 to test for a positive or negative correlation between two variables. An index value near zero indicates no correlation. Values near 1 indicate positive association, whereas values near -1 indicate negative association. Each coefficient is tested against a null hypothesis of no correlation.

The most pertinent correlations are those between metropolitan status (0 = rural, 1 = urban) and economic and educational characteristics. These coefficients are a convenient way to examine and summarize strong correlations in the data, even though they are less revealing than multivariate analysis.

A significantly positive correlation exists between unemployment and rural status, although no significant relationship between employment growth and rural status was found. There are also significantly negative correlations between rural status and high school and college completion rates. The positive association between local government expenditures per pupil and rural status also is significant, as is the positive correlation between state and federal financial support per pupil and rural status. The public spending bias favoring rural counties results from the state component of spending, rather than the federal component.

Table 6.3 also shows the relationships between education, student achievement, and local economic activity. High school and college completion rates are not significantly correlated with per-pupil expenditures, nor are they significantly correlated with employment growth.[9] Similarly, per-pupil expenditures are not significantly correlated with either employment growth or county unemployment rates.

Several conclusions are possible from these findings:

1. Recent employment decline has been slightly larger (in percentage terms) in rural Illinois counties than in urban counties. Counties in southern rural Illinois actually experienced small employment gains for the years studied. Unemployment rates tend to be about 4 percentage points higher in rural counties than in urban counties.
2. Educational attainment levels are higher in urban than rural counties.
3. Average per-pupil expenditures in public primary and secondary schools are somewhat higher in rural than in urban counties. Moreover, rural counties receive more state

Table 6.3
Pearson Correlation Coefficients[a]

	MET	ENR8086	12+	16+	LGXPP	TLRPP	TSRPP	FEDREVPP	TNLRPP	ENR86	TRANPP	EG8085	UNEMP
MET	1.00 0.00												
ENR8086	0.20 0.04	1.00 0.00											
12+	0.47 0.00	0.06 0.54	1.00 0.00										
16+	0.48 0.00	0.25 0.01	0.78 0.00	1.00 0.00									
LGXPP	-0.18 0.07	-0.28 0.00	-0.09 0.37	-0.01 0.89	1.00 0.00								
TLRPP	0.13 0.18	-0.09 0.36	0.54 0.00	0.40 0.00	0.31 0.00	1.00 0.00							
TSRPP	-0.20 0.05	-0.03 0.80	-0.68 0.00	-0.38 0.00	0.10 0.30	-0.72 0.00	1.00 0.00						
FEDREVPP	0.00 1.00	0.03 0.75	-0.36 0.00	-0.02 0.85	0.33 0.00	-0.33 0.00	0.64 0.00	1.00 0.00					
TNLRPP	-0.18 0.07	-0.02 0.85	-0.66 0.00	-0.34 0.00	0.14 0.17	-0.70 0.00	0.99 0.00	0.72 0.00	1.00 0.00				
ENR86	0.30 0.00	0.04 0.67	0.14 0.16	0.27 0.01	0.13 0.18	0.16 0.11	-0.01 0.94	0.29 0.00	0.03 0.74	1.00 0.00			
TRANPP	-0.24 0.02	-0.07 0.49	-0.60 0.00	-0.41 0.00	0.27 0.01	-0.83 0.00	0.79 0.00	0.52 0.00	0.79 0.00	-0.09 0.39	1.00 0.00		
EG8085	0.06 0.54	0.11 0.26	-0.03 0.79	0.12 0.22	-0.14 0.17	0.00 0.98	-0.04 0.70	-0.09 0.36	-0.05 0.64	0.02 0.84	-0.08 0.41	1.00 0.00	
UNEMP	-0.45 0.00	-0.03 0.75	-0.75 0.00	-0.60 0.00	0.12 0.23	-0.47 0.00	0.58 0.00	0.35 0.00	0.57 0.00	-0.18 0.08	0.55 0.00	-0.05 0.58	1.00 0.00

Prob > R under Ho: Rho=0 / N = 102

[a]See Table 6.2 for definitions of variables.

support per pupil than urban counties. Federal support per pupil is about the same, on average, for rural and urban counties.

4. Correlation analysis confirms that rural status is significantly related to higher levels of per-pupil expenditures and higher levels of state funding per pupil. In other words, rural counties receive more state aid, and spend more, than urban counties, based on per-pupil measures. Correlation analysis also indicates that local spending on education is not significantly related to high school or college completion rates, or to rates of employment growth or unemployment. Similarly, high school and college completion rates are not significantly correlated with recent employment changes.

Findings for other midwestern states may vary, of course. For example, without further study, one cannot say that expenditures per pupil in rural areas tend to equal or exceed those for urban areas throughout the Midwest. However, based on findings for Illinois and North Carolina, and the wide body of literature cited earlier, it is likely that the weak and ambiguous relationships between school resources, school output, and local economic activity are widespread throughout the Midwest and the United States.

POLICY IMPLICATIONS

It is difficult to build a case for increased spending for rural schools in order to promote rural development on the grounds of either empirical data or efficiency. Substantial empirical evidence indicates that increased spending on rural schools would not improve student performance, and consequently would not necessarily increase rural labor productivity. From an efficiency point of view, there is no compelling case that externalities are greater for rural schools than for urban schools.

Primary and secondary school education in rural and urban areas is dominated by de facto public school monopolies that restrict choice and limit incentives for cost containment. This organizational structure and its incentives facing school administrators, teachers, and parents may help explain public school performance in recent decades. Total expenditures per student and instructional expenditures per student in the United States have risen substantially in real terms since 1960, while average class size has decreased.[10] During the same period, however, there has been little overall improvement in student performance. Increased costs may be attributable, in part, to changes in student mix and teacher quality. At the same time an important reason for increasing costs may be greater influence of teachers' unions in contract negotiations, and lack of incentives for school administrators and school boards to contain costs. Parents have not been effective in preventing these higher costs, and an important reason may be that they have had limited options in choosing schools. In short, "the incentives existing within schools appear to provide a compelling explanation of public school inefficiencies" (Hanushek, 1981, p. 33).

The argument for rural schools, in particular, is sometimes presented as a mechanism to improve the allocation of workers in rural labor markets. That such a strategy is unlikely to succeed is due, in part, to the limited relationship between school expenditures and student achievement. More fundamentally, as long as workers exploit real wage differentials across areas, labor markets provide this allocative function and there is no reason to expect schools to carry out this function. In fact, increased training in rural areas, as a method to make rural labor more attractive to would-be employers, may exacerbate conditions of rural surplus. In North Carolina, for example, spending more on rural public schools may increase labor-market imbalances, because most rural areas in the state already have projected surpluses at all skill levels (Crihfield, 1990). Given current population growth rates, high school and college completion rates, and forecasts of occupational demand by skill level, it is likely that many rural areas in the Midwest may also experience future labor surpluses. In general, public and private primary and secondary schools are awkward tools for fine-tuning labor markets.[11]

This discussion leads to several rather specific implications regarding economic development and education policy in the rural Midwest. Using public schools as explicit instruments in attracting or retaining employers or employees in community development strategies may misdirect educational policy. The business of the schools is to educate students, not to lure business or entice employees. Many factors affect business location decisions, and it is not clear what effect, if any, schools have on them. An efficient and equitable policy in education would allow each pupil an acceptable level of financial support, while seeking a cost-effective mechanism of providing educational services. In general, such a policy is not place-specific and does not have a meaningful rural–urban dimension.

Nor does it seem appropriate to give policy relevance to the importance of rural schools as local employers. Local businesses will always be attracted to consumer demands generated from sources of outside income, such as income generated from manufacturing plants or income received from local and state governments for public schools. When plants (or schools) close, these businesses will go elsewhere in the long run.

Third, an underlying goal in promoting education in depressed rural areas (or impoverished urban areas) is to break the grip of poverty on youth. This is a laudable goal; unfortunately, two decades of research show that we have been unable to affect systematically learning in the aggregate (for example, as measured by test scores) with available policy tools (for example, increased spending per pupil, lower teacher–pupil ratios, higher teacher salaries, and degree requirements for teachers). This does not mean that schools are irrelevant, but it does suggest that at current levels of school resources, incremental changes in school inputs—the type usually contemplated in policy—are unlikely to have much impact on school output.

Finally, most primary and secondary education is publicly funded and publicly provided. Although parents choose where to live, and thereby choose a school district, they have little choice in school selection once their residence has been determined. Such arrangements give local public schools effective monopolies in their respective school districts. Allowing parents greater choice in school selection could increase the accountability and efficiency of public schools.

One way to offer parents more choice is to devise a system of voucher payments that parents use at the school of their choice, public or private, to fund a child's education. Vouchers need not be equal for all students. Premiums could be allowed for transportation, special problems (mental or physical handicaps), type of school (elementary, middle, or high school), and so on. Premiums could also be allowed for rural school districts that experience high fixed costs per pupil. Schools that have difficulty attracting students would either curtail operations or close, because revenues come from students with vouchers and not directly from local and state governments. Schools that attract students would prosper and serve as models for new schools. In general, the intent of a voucher system is to bring market incentives and accountability to schools. There are valid reasons for publicly funding primary and secondary school students, but it is much more difficult to justify local public school monopolies in providing the service itself.

It may be that rural areas have less to gain from a voucher plan, due to their lower population densities and inability to support competition among several primary or secondary schools.[12] Consequently, rural schools may face at least two cost disadvantages: diseconomies from small size, and inefficiencies from less competition among schools for students. Diseconomies of scale is an issue for rural schools regardless of whether parents have more choice in school selection. If enrollment declines, such as have been experienced in Illinois (Table 6.1), are in the future for the rural Midwest, then shrinking rural school districts will experience rising average costs. Edelman and Knudsens' (1990) findings indicate that average expenditures per pupil (including transportation costs) in very small school districts (less than 250 students) are about 17 percent higher than for districts with about 1,000 students. Thus, consolidation of small rural school districts will continue to be an important restructuring tool, regardless of other changes in public school policies.

CONCLUSIONS

This chapter argues that local public schools in rural areas are not the solution to problems of rural development. The linkages between increases in educational inputs, improvements in student performance, and changes in economic growth are complicated and are not easily manipulated by policy. In the coming years, enrollment declines in small rural school districts are likely to cause an increase in average costs per pupil and to give continued impetus to consolidations, which achieve scale economies in providing primary and secondary school services.

Everyone has a stake in how well public schools perform and how they are funded. Evidence indicates that additional spending on public schools in rural areas is not likely to improve student performance or to cause economic growth.

At the same time, existing educational resources could be more efficiently organized by opening local public school districts to market incentives and accountability—to the advantage of students and economy alike.

NOTES

I wish to thank Norman Walzer for detailed comments and suggestions, and Martin Panggabean and Alexander Amuah for help in collecting and organizing the data used in this chapter.

1. For example, Deavers (1990) stresses alleged underinvestment in rural education without indicating that investment in education is as much an urban issue as a rural one.

2. There is evidence that local public spending in general (controlling for taxes) exerts a positive impact on such choices, however. See Crihfield (1989).

3. James D. Nowlan and G. Alan Hickrod, "State Tax Boost Key to School Equity," *The Champaign-Urbana News-Gazette*, Sunday, January 14, 1990, p. B–3.

4. James G. Ward, "Lawsuit Not Answer for Education Funding," *The Champaign-Urbana News-Gazette*, Tuesday, February 27, 1990, p. A–5.

5. All averages reported in Table 6.1 represent county averages, where counties are weighted equally.

6. The Cooperative Extension regions split the state into thirds. "North" is regions 1 and 2, "Central" is 4 and 5, and "South" is 6 and 7. "Chicago" is region 3 and is the three-county area defined by Cook, DuPage, and Lake counties.

7. "Urban" counties are defined as those that belong to Metropolitan Statistical Areas. By this definition, 26 Illinois counties are urban and 76 are rural.

8. An alternative measure of resources per pupil is total revenue per pupil (REVPP), which is based on more recent data (1986–7) from the Illinois State Board of Higher Education (see Table 6.2). These revenue data include revenue for retirement benefits and interest payments, and are not directly comparable to expenditure data from the *1988 County and City Data Book*. However, patterns in REVPP are similar to those for LGXPP.

9. High school and college completion rates are negatively and significantly correlated with the unemployment rate. However, it is clear that an omitted third variable—rural status—is responsible.

10. Expenditures per student in the United States (1983 dollars) rose steadily in real terms from $1,262 in 1960 to $2,960 in 1983. Over the same period, the average pupil–teacher ratio fell steadily from 25.8 to 19.0. Relative to other workers, teacher salaries also rose almost steadily over these years. See Hanushek (1986, pp. 1147–9).

11. Coming from an institutionalist perspective on growth, Smith (1988, 1989) arrives at a similar conclusion regarding the role of education in fostering development. He finds that in economically depressed counties in rural Kentucky, there is adequate funding for schools and other infrastructure, and reasonable balance in the supply and demand for low-skilled jobs. What is intractable is an apparent inability for the region to grow out of poverty and to become less dependent on a low-skilled work force.

12. A recent study suggests that scale economies are achieved at roughly 800 to 900 students per school district in Iowa, a predominantly rural state (Edelman and Knudsen, 1990). Some rural areas may be unable to achieve these economies with even a single elementary, middle, or high school, and would be unable to support competition among several schools.

7. Local Economic Development: Perceptions and Actions of Small City Officials in Illinois

Norman Walzer and John Gruidl

Economic changes in the 1980s threatened the viability of many small rural communities throughout the United States. Researchers have documented a growing disparity between rural and urban America and have suggested policies to improve the economies of small rural communities (U.S. Congress, 1989). Some have examined common characteristics of rural counties or communities with high economic growth during the 1980s in an attempt to determine factors contributing to that growth (John, Batie, and Norris, 1989).

Sustained local economic development activity is one common characteristic of high-growth communities. In most successful small communities, public officials are vital participants in development activities. At the same time, however, a systematic profile of the issues and concerns of local government officials and of the development activities of local governments is not fully incorporated into rural development studies.

This chapter examines three issues. First, the study documents issues and concerns of mayors in small Illinois cities about the local economy. Second, the study examines the response of local economic development agencies to the perceived need for economic development activities. Third, factors affecting the presence of economic development activities in small communities are examined statistically. The presence or absence of an economic development plan is related to community characteristics, mayoral perceptions, and fiscal pressures on local government. The study is based on a sample of 299 Illinois cities smaller than 25,000 population.

The study finds that mayors consider economic issues a high priority.[1] Yet economic development activities are minimal, particularly in the smallest communities. It appears that many small communities lack the capacity to undertake sustained economic development efforts. However, the evidence does suggest that those communities with more apparent problems are more likely to be active.

Table 7.1
Size Distribution by Sample, State, and Midwest Region, 1987

Population	Sample			Illinois			Midwest		
	Population (000)	(N)	Pct	Population (000)	(N)	Pct	Population (000)	(N)	Pct
Less than 2,500	165	(182)	62.8	663	(871)	71.9	4,342	(6,507)	79.5
2,500 - 5,000	160	(45)	15.5	459	(127)	10.5	2,563	(721)	8.8
5,000 - 24,999	675	(63)	21.7	2,504	(214)	17.6	10,856	(957)	11.7
Total	1,000	(290)	100.0	3,626	(1,212)	100.0	17,761	(8,185)	100.0

Sources: Survey of Municipal Officials, 1987 and U.S. Bureau of the Census, 1988a, Table 6.

PERCEIVED CONDITIONS IN SMALL RURAL COMMUNITIES

This study is based on a 1987–8 mail survey of mayors in Illinois cities of less than 25,000 population (Walzer and Kapper, 1989). Mayors were asked to evaluate the local economy and to describe current development activities and policies. A total of 299 usable questionnaires were received, for a response rate of approximately 25 percent of Illinois cities less than 25,000 and 30 percent of those between 2,500 and 25,000.

The size distribution of cities responding to the survey differs little from the overall size distribution within Illinois (Table 7.1). Cities described in this report slightly underrepresent the smallest size category (under 2,500 population) and may overrepresent those cities between 2,500 and 5,000. Response rates are lower in the smallest cities, because of limited staff available to complete the questionnaire and minor involvement in many economic development activities on which information was requested.

Cities in 87 counties responded to the survey with 130 of the cities located in metropolitan counties and 169 cities located in nonmetropolitan (rural) counties. Many cities are county seats and are the driving force for surrounding rural unincorporated areas. Although the findings are based on one state, it is reasonable to believe that they are representative of other midwestern states and, in fact, are consistent with a recent study of Nebraska (Reed and Paulsen, 1990).

A minority of responding mayors (37.1 percent) reported improvements in the city economy in the previous 3 years. Their perceptions vary with city size. In communities smaller than 2,500 population, 26.4 percent reported improvements compared with 65.2 percent in cities greater than 5,000. Small communities clearly did not do as well in attracting manufacturing or retail businesses.

Table 7.2
Perceived Conditions in Small Communities

			Population					
	Statewide		Less than 2,500		2,500-5,000		More than 5,000	
Issue	Pct.	(n)	Pct.	(n)	Pct.	(n)	Pct.	(n)
Satisfied with the performance of the city economy?								
Yes	28.4	(85)	25.8	(47)	33.3	(15)	31.7	(20)
No	67.6	(202)	69.8	(127)	62.2	(28)	65.1	(41)
No response	4.0	(12)	4.4	(8)	4.4	(2)	3.2	(2)
	100.0	(299)	100.0	(182)	99.9	(45)	100.0	(63)
Major factors contributing to economic decline in the community:								
Competition from neighboring larger retail centers	43.5	(130)	45.2	(82)	51.1	(23)	31.7	(20)
Closing of large retailers in town	2.7	(8)	3.3	(6)	-	-	3.2	(2)
Loss of manufacturing in area	25.4	(76)	26.9	(49)	20.0	(9)	28.6	(18)
Loss of city population	11.4	(34)	12.6	(23)	11.1	(5)	6.3	(4)
Business closings because of retirements	4.3	(13)	6.0	(11)	2.2	(1)	-	-
No response	12.7	(38)	6.0	(11)	15.6	(7)	30.2	(19)
	100.0	(299)	100.0	(182)	100.0	(45)	100.0	(63)
Overall Condition of retail establishments:								
Prosperous and expanding in sales	11.4	(34)	6.0	(11)	13.3	(6)	25.4	(16)
Stable and reasonably prosperous but not expanding	45.5	(136)	44.0	(80)	53.3	(24)	46.0	(29)
Declining but not seriously dilapidated	20.7	(62)	24.2	(44)	13.3	(6)	14.3	(9)
Major declines and empty storefronts	15.4	(46)	17.0	(31)	17.8	(8)	7.9	(5)
No response	7.0	(21)	8.8	(16)	2.2	(1)	6.3	(4)
	100.0	(299)	100.0	(182)	99.9	(45)	99.9	(63)

Source: Survey of Municipal Officials, 1987.

Approximately two-thirds of responding mayors are dissatisfied with the performance of the local economy, suggesting that economic development efforts may be needed in most communities. Statewide, only 28.4 percent reported satisfaction (Table 7.2), a lower percentage than those reporting an improving economy. It is surprising that satisfaction does not vary significantly with city size, as does economic performance.

Mayors in cities facing economic decline said the main factor was competition from neighboring larger retail centers. Statewide, 43.5 percent of respondents reported this factor as most important (Table 7.2). The response pattern was not systematic by city size. It reached a high of 51.1 percent in the middle-size group, but slightly less than one-third (31.7 percent) of responding mayors in communities larger than 5,000 reported competition from larger centers as most important. The lack of a systematic pattern is not surprising, given the importance of physical location. In an analysis of similar size cities in Illinois, Walzer and Stablein (1981) demonstrated the importance of distance as well as the drawing power of larger cities in retail trade patterns.

Loss of manufacturing was another significant factor reported by approximately one-quarter of responding mayors (Table 7.2). Responses differ by size, with 28.6 percent of mayors in cities larger than 5,000 reporting this factor compared with 20 percent in cities between 2,500 and 5,000.

Both the 1981–2 recession and foreign competition for manufacturing products severely hurt economies in small communities. Statewide, 16.7 percent of mayors reported that at least one large employer had closed in the previous 3 years, and 15.6 percent reported that at least one large employer had started up during the same period. A comparison by size shows that 14.3 percent of the communities smaller than 2,500 had closings, whereas only 8.2 percent of communities of this size reported startups. In communities larger than 5,000, on the other hand, 27 percent of mayors reported closings compared with 34.9 percent reporting startups. The sizes of those businesses starting or closing are not available.

Mayors also described the condition of the retail sector, a particularly important component of small-town economies. Statewide, 56.9 percent of the mayors described the retail sector as "prosperous and expanding" or "stable and reasonably prosperous" (Table 7.2), but retail conditions differ with city size. In cities with populations below 2,500, approximately 40 percent of mayors reported declining retail economies, whereas in the largest communities, only 22.2 percent reported declining retail conditions.

The mayors' evaluation of city economies raises several issues.[1] First, mayors from all city sizes are dissatisfied with the performance of the local economy. Second, both retail trade and manufacturing are of concern. Third, mayors perceive weaknesses in the retail sector as primarily due to competition from neighboring retail centers. Fourth, the economic performance of the smallest communities (less than 2,500 population) has been especially weak. Retail trade has been damaged in these communities, with approximately 40 percent reporting retail decline. Manufacturing losses in these communities seem to be due more to a lack of startups than to abnormally frequent closings. Clearly, the economic future of the smallest communities is being threatened.

ECONOMIC DEVELOPMENT RESPONSES

Community leaders determine the economic development policies adopted by cities. Local decision makers determine the extent to which cities take advantage of the many federal and state assistance programs available. Local involvement is difficult to predict and often is a response to a crisis, such as loss of a major employer.

The extent to which small communities can respond to the need for economic development actions varies with the community infrastructure and leadership available. Some communities have aggressively moved to entice industry, and others have been reluctant to engage in economic development efforts. Quite often, the availability of a retired or semiretired resident who is willing to make business contacts makes all the difference. The interest and willingness of community leaders to support such endeavors, of course, is paramount in successful economic development efforts (Walzer, 1990).

Reed and Paulsen (1990) found that almost half of the small Nebraska towns in a recent survey engaged in some type of economic development activity. Their efforts depended on community size, with the smallest cities engaging in the fewest projects. The study also reported that development activities depended heavily on volunteers. Communities had little regular interaction with external agencies, such as the state economic development department, utility companies, universities, and others offering development assistance.

In small Illinois communities, mayors often have primary responsibility for economic development activities. This is especially true in very small communities, where 29.7 percent of respondents reported that primary responsibility rests with the mayor (Table 7.3). Larger cities have a more formal development organization. In cities larger than 5,000, for instance, economic development committee responsibility was reported by 22.2 percent. Managers and city administrators also are a popular option in these cities, as reported by 17.5 percent.

Only 2.0 percent of respondents reported that regional councils of public officials had primary responsibility. This may be explained partly because these councils play a supporting role, for example, helping local officials organize, assisting in developing a work plan, grant preparation, and related tasks. Mayors may not see regional councils as having primary responsibility, but rather as key players in organizing the economic development process.

Chambers of commerce are also reported to be relatively unimportant in economic development activities. Again, the fact that they do not have primary responsibility does not mean they are ineffective; rather, they may focus more on retaining existing businesses. Chamber of commerce members may serve on an economic development committee as well. It is difficult to discern overlapping activities of personnel from a mail questionnaire.

Because mayors are dissatisfied with the economy, and often have primary responsibility for initiating development, one might expect a high percentage of communities to actively engage in economic development. The findings, however, do not support this view. Nearly one-fifth of the mayors (18.4 percent) reported no economic development efforts underway (Table 7.3). A comparison of cities by size indicates, as expected, that cities under 2,500 are least likely to engage in development activities and those larger than 5,000 are most involved. A major explanation for the lack of involvement in the smallest communities is shortage of trained staff and dependence on volunteers.

Statewide, only 21.1 percent of respondents said their city had an economic development plan and, formal plans are much more common in communities larger than 5,000. Even in the larger cities, however, only slightly more than

Table 7.3
Economic Development Activities

Issue	Statewide Pct.	(n)	Less than 2,500 Pct.	(n)	2,500-5,000 Pct.	(n)	More than 5,000 Pct.	(n)
			Population					
Primary responsibility for economic development:								
Mayor	23.7	(71)	29.7	(54)	17.8	(8)	12.7	(8)
Member of city council	4.7	(14)	5.5	(10)	2.2	(1)	1.6	(1)
Economic development committee	14.4	(43)	11.0	(20)	17.8	(8)	22.2	(14)
Chamber of commerce	5.7	(17)	3.3	(6)	11.1	(5)	9.5	(6)
Manager or city administrator	5.7	(17)	0.5	(1)	4.4	(2)	17.5	(11)
Regional council of officials	2.0	(6)	1.1	(2)	2.2	(1)	4.8	(3)
Other	5.0	(15)	3.8	(7)	2.2	(1)	11.1	(7)
No economic development efforts	*18.4*	*(55)*	*24.7*	*(45)*	*15.6*	*(7)*	*3.2*	*(2)*
Have a formal economic development plan:	21.1	(63)	12.6	(23)	33.3	(15)	38.1	(24)
Hired an economic development consultant:	13.0	(39)	7.1	(13)	22.2	(10)	23.8	(15)
City works with state agency on economic development projects:	58.5	(175)	47.8	(87)	66.7	(30)	82.5	(52)
If city does not work with state agency, what is the major reason:								
City not interested in economic development	5.7	(17)	7.1	(13)	4.4	(2)	3.2	(2)
Do not know about programs	13.4	(40)	19.2	(35)	8.9	(4)	1.6	(1)
Marketing rep. not available	4.0	(12)	4.4	(8)	4.4	(2)	1.6	(1)
Too much paperwork	5.4	(16)	6.6	(12)	4.4	(2)	1.6	(1)

Source: Survey of Municipal Officials, 1987.

one-third (38.1 percent) have plans in place. However, the lack of a written economic development plan is no guarantee that economic development activities are not underway. What it probably does mean is that the efforts are not well-organized and several groups may be involved in diverse activities. Strong leadership and coordinated leadership are important in these efforts and are more likely to be found when community leaders have prepared an organized plan.

Small communities could rely on economic development consultants to assist in industry attraction or business development. Contracting can replace the need for in-house staff and can offset the inability of state agencies to work individually with many communities that, collectively, represent a relatively small number of jobs.

On average, only 13 percent of the communities responding to the survey hired an economic development consultant. Larger communities can more effectively use these resources, for two reasons. First, cities larger than 5,000 have more resources to pay a consultant and the likelihood of successful development projects is greater. Second, the number of jobs to be created in the smallest communities is likely to be small and the paperwork needed may be relatively uncomplicated, making it possible for these communities to achieve their goals without the use of a consultant. They can perhaps work with regional councils of public officials, especially those with a staff committed to these activities.

In Illinois, as in most states, a state economic development agency has primary responsibility for working with businesses and local governments on economic development issues. The services range from general planning to obtaining low-cost loans for remodeling or starting a business (Illinois Department of Commerce and Community Affairs, 1989). State agency representatives typically serve at least two roles. First, they help local governments set objectives and develop an organizational structure to pursue economic development. Second, they serve as an information clearinghouse and contact point for industries seeking to locate in their state.

Most state services are provided at no cost to local governments or, in the case of financial packages, involve relatively small proportions of local participation. Therefore, one might expect widespread local involvement in state economic development programs. Such is not the case (Table 7.3). A slim majority (58.5 percent) of responding communities reported working with the state on economic development projects. As expected, however, the proportion of cities involved in these programs increases with city size. In cities larger than 5,000, most respondents (82.5 percent) were involved.

When asked directly about reasons for noninvolvement, some mayors (13.4 percent of all respondents) reported no knowledge of the programs. This lack of information was more common among smaller communities. None of the other reasons suggested in the questionnaire elicited much response (Table 7.3).

Small communities, at least in a state such as Illinois, have access to a multitude of economic development tools, some federally funded and others provided by the state. Mayors were asked about the use of nine common economic development programs and incentives (Table 7.4). Generally, these programs are designed to attract or retain businesses by improving the profitability of locating in the city. The incentives usually reduce costs to businesses.

Overall, communities reported infrequent use of incentives. Most commonly used are industrial revenue bonds (IRBs) (30.1 percent). IRBs are public issues for the purpose of lending funds to businesses wishing to locate in the city. The attraction of the IRBs is that they are relatively cost-free to the city, but can

Table 7.4
Economic Development Incentives

Economic development tools	Statewide	Population: Less than 2,500	Population: 2,500-5,000	Population: More than 5,000
	(Percent)			
Industrial revenue bonds	30.1	14.8	44.5	63.5
Job Training Partnership Act	27.1	17.0	26.6	53.9
Property tax abatement	21.8	9.8	24.4	52.3
Small business assistance	21.1	11.0	24.4	46.0
Free or low cost city services	17.4	14.3	17.7	27.0
Subsidized wages or training	12.3	4.9	15.5	30.2
Low cost loans from city funds	10.0	3.2	8.9	28.6
Tax increment financing district	9.7	2.7	13.3	28.6
Subsidized rent	7.0	3.8	13.3	12.7

Source: Survey of Municipal Officials, 1987.

represent a substantial cost saving to capital-intensive businesses. Although the city lends its name to the issue, it is obligated to repay the loan only to the extent of the proceeds for the specific project.

The second most commonly cited economic development inducement is subsidized training and wages via the Job Training Partnership Act. This program was used by 27.1 percent of respondents. The subsidized training and wages program is attractive for cities because a major portion of the funding is from federal and state governments.

Based on earlier discussions, larger cities are expected to use economic development tools more frequently than smaller communities. This, indeed, is the finding. In every instance, communities larger than 5,000 reported more common usage than cities smaller than 2,500.

Several reasons may explain the infrequent use of development incentives. First, many small communities are without an economic development plan, which may reflect inactivity on this issue. Second, in the smallest communities, the size of operations may be so small that they do not qualify for certain state-funded programs or the staff may be too small to permit active involvement. Third, local public officials may simply be unaware that their city qualifies for programs or how such programs might benefit local economic development.

In spite of this apparent inactivity in economic development programs, innovative programs can be found. A recent set of case studies in small Illinois communities revealed clear examples of community leaders who had effectively turned their communities around (Walzer, 1990). One community of 2,100, after facing considerable frustration in attracting business, formed a for-profit corporation, raised capital locally, purchased a manufacturing business, and relocated it to their town. The business is now showing a profit and the economic development organization is seeking another business to purchase.

In a completely different approach, community leaders in another city, concerned about preserving their school system, provide property tax relief to people willing to build or purchase a home. This community attracted widespread attention because it does not provide typical property tax relief for incoming businesses. Rather it focuses on attracting homeowners. The program has stimulated new investment and has stabilized the property tax base. School enrollments are now stable and the community has experienced substantial new investment, some of which involves new businesses as well.

Another small community organized its residents in an effort to attract a prison that the state was seeking to locate. Community leaders conducted letter writing campaigns, attended public hearings, worked with their state-elected officials and organized a media campaign to convince state officials of their interest. The group was successful and the prison has added significant employment in the community.

Although other examples of creative economic development programs can be identified in small communities, such is not the norm. Human, financial, and physical resources often are not sufficient to afford an extensive development effort. Remote rural communities face additional limitations when they have little access to modern transportation systems.

An important question arises regarding the characteristics of communities that have undertaken economic development activities. Additional research on characteristics of communities that have been successful in economic development projects is reported by Flora and Flora (Chapter 10). How community characteristics affect the role that economic development plays in a community is examined in the next section.

FACTORS AFFECTING ECONOMIC DEVELOPMENT ACTIVITIES

Better insights into the adoption of economic development activities can be gained from a more sophisticated analysis of development actions and community characteristics. In particular, an econometric analysis relates economic development activity to community characteristics, mayoral perceptions, and fiscal pressures on local government.

Economic development activity is difficult to quantify. In this analysis, the presence or absence of an economic development plan is used as an indication of an active economic development program. In fact, economic development activity is more appropriately measured on a continuum. Unfortunately, information on the type of plan or its effectiveness is not available. Also, some communities may have an effective economic development program, but not a formal plan. Nevertheless, an economic development plan in place is one indication of activity.

Table 7.5
Variable Definitions

Dependent Variable	
PLAN	The city has a formal economic development plan, Yes = 1, No = 0
Independent Variables	
SIZE	The population of the city (in thousands)
MANUFACT	The percentage of working residents who are employed in manufacturing
RETAIL	The percentage of working residents who are employed in retail trade
SATISFACTION	Is the mayor satisfied with the performance of the city economy?, Yes = 1, No = 0
ATTRACTION	Is the ability to attract industry a very pressing problem?, Yes = 1, No = 0
PROPTAXES	Do you expect higher property tax rates in the next fiscal year?, Yes = 1, No = 0

Because the dependent variable, presence or absence of an economic development plan (PLAN), is binary, a probit model is estimated. A complete data set from the survey is available for 139 cities and observations with missing values are excluded. The dependent variable is modeled as a function of community characteristics, mayoral perceptions, and fiscal pressure. The variables are defined in Table 7.5.

Community Characteristics

City population size (SIZE) should be positively correlated with the presence of an economic development plan, according to previous discussions. Larger cities are more likely to have a development plan, mainly because of more organizational and financial resources.

A priori, strength of the local economy might affect the adoption of an economic development plan. However, in their study of small Nebraska towns, Reed and Paulsen (1990) found that measures of economic vitality such as per-capita income, population growth, community wealth, and location did *not* affect the number of development projects. Reed and Paulsen used the number of development projects as a measure of economic development activity.

Unfortunately, secondary data for small Illinois cities that would permit an evaluation of local economic performance are not readily available. However, cities with a strong export base, that is, industries engaged in export of goods to other regions, are likely to perform better. The percentage of workers employed in manufacturing (MANUFACT) is used as a proxy for the strength of the export base. A higher percentage in manufacturing is expected to be negatively associated with the adoption of an economic development plan. Conversely, a higher percentage of workers employed in retail trade (RETAIL) suggests the need to bolster the economic base and is expected to be positively associated with adoption of an economic development plan.

Mayoral Perceptions

Perceptions of mayors affect the likelihood of adoption of an economic development plan. Those mayors satisfied with local economic performance (SATISFACTION) are less likely to propose economic development plans. Unfortunately, without secondary data to control for actual performance, it is not possible to distinguish between objective performance of the economy and subjective evaluation by mayors.

Another relevant factor is the extent of concern about attracting industry to a community. Mayors were asked to rank a series of problems, one of which was the ability to attract industry. Cities in which the ability to attract industry is considered a more pressing problem (ATTRACTION) are more likely to have an economic development plan in place.

Fiscal Pressures

Cities provide many local public services. The financing of services depends on having an adequate tax base, which, in turn, depends on a healthy economy. Growing fiscal pressures may cause local public officials to undertake more economic development programs to stimulate higher tax collections. Therefore, those communities in which mayors expected property tax rate increases in the next fiscal year (PROPTAXES) are more likely to have a formal economic development plan.

Results

Results from the probit estimation are shown in Table 7.6. Some evidence is found that all three factors, community characteristics, mayoral perceptions, and fiscal pressures, affect the probability of adopting an economic development plan. In particular, the coefficient on SIZE is positive and statistically significant, indicating that larger cities are more likely to adopt economic development plans. Size is an index for many factors that affect the capacity to conduct active economic development projects, including the depth of the leadership pool and access to financial resources.

The coefficient on MANUFACT is negative, as expected, although not statistically significant. The coefficient on RETAIL is small compared to its standard

Table 7.6
Results of Probit Estimation

Explanatory Variables	Dependent Variable: PLAN
SIZE	.71* (.25)
MANUFACT	-.71 (.56)
RETAIL	-.17 (.92)
SATISFACTION	-.59* (.30)
ATTRACTION	-.34 (.24)
PROPTAXES	.51* (.26)
Intercept	-.78* (.39)
Sample size(n)	139
Cases correctly predicted	100
Chi-square (d.f)	13.3 (6)

Note: Numbers in parentheses are standard errors. An asterisk indicates significance at the 0.05 level.

error. Possibly, neither of these measures is adequate to assess the strength of a city's economic performance.

Perceptions of the mayor regarding recent economic performance are statistically related to the adoption of an economic development plan. In particular, if a mayor is satisfied with economic performance, adoption of a plan is less likely. This finding is consistent with the relative importance of mayors in the economic development process, as noted earlier. One might expect also that mayors' concerns about economic development trends are communicated to other groups in the community and can cause a predisposition to action.

Contrary to expectations, the coefficient of ATTRACTION is negative, although not statistically significant. Because this variable is an attitudinal scale, there is considerable room for ambiguity in response. Detailed information was not collected on the number of years the community had been trying to attract business, the success rate, or the involvement of the mayor in these activities.

Finally, fiscal pressures affect the adoption of a plan. Shrinking tax bases because of loss of business activity places more of the burden on residential property owners. In small communities, the viability of schools often is a major community issue that can spur residents to action. The coefficient on PROP-TAXES is positive and statistically significant, as expected, suggesting that as concern over property taxes rises, so does the likelihood of an economic development plan. A reasonable interpretation of this finding is that residents are concerned that to maintain existing services, the property tax base has to be increased. This approach is evident in the case studies cited before (Walzer, 1990).

The overall statistical findings in this chapter suggest that lack of capacity constrains many communities from active economic development efforts. However, those communities with more apparent problems, either as perceived by the mayor and/or as affecting local government finances, are more likely to be active. Community leaders who have identified severe problems are responding to the extent that local capacity allows.

SUMMARY AND CONCLUSIONS

This chapter has examined local development activities and perceptions of mayors in small rural communities. Nearly two-thirds of the mayors responding to the survey are dissatisfied with the performance of the city economy. They are concerned about the viability of both retail and manufacturing businesses. Certainly, not all communities are in a state of decline, although the smallest communities are most at risk. The negative scenario is, at least partly, caused by competition from large urban centers in the surrounding area encroaching on what traditionally had been the main market for small communities.

It is common for mayors to have primary responsibility for economic development activities in small communities. With limited staff, they may have had to contract with economic development professionals on development projects, but most of the cities in the sample do not hire these professionals, and only one city in five (21.1 percent) had a formal economic development plan in place in 1987. Therefore, there is a wide disparity between interest in economic development and the capacity to undertake it, particularly in the smallest communities.

Active participation in economic development, as measured by a formal plan, was positively related to city size, dissatisfaction with the local economy, and pressure on property taxes. These relationships, at least, suggest that those mayors who have identified economic development as a problem are acting to remedy the situation.

The rural "crisis" is far from over. Many adverse economic trends will continue. It is the task of policy makers to find remedies for these concerns and to manage the change in the best possible way. However, this analysis has revealed the incapacity or unwillingness of many small rural communities to undertake development efforts. Sustained and coordinated help is needed for these small communities to manage change and to find solutions.

NOTE

1. Rural residents, in general, have similar concerns about the local economy. In 1989, the Institute for Rural Affairs surveyed 2,800 rural residents who participate in the Illinois Rural Life Panel to determine their overall perception of rural conditions and what might lie ahead (Thistlethwaite, Wendland, and Conrad, 1990). Several issues emerged frequently; unemployment, job opportunities and entertainment for youth, loss of manufacturing, and loss of retail trade. The survey results reflect a deep concern on the part of rural residents toward the economic vitality of their communities.

8. Developing Leadership to Address Rural Problems

Ronald J. Hustedde

Many social scientists and policy makers believe that the key to addressing rural problems lies in the "capacity building" of local leaders and citizens. Capacity building is concerned with enhancing the potential of local people to solve problems. It means engaging leaders, organizations, and citizens to identify needs, resources, and opportunities through the mobilization and organization of groups within and outside the community in order to pursue community goals (Garkovich, 1989). Leaders play important roles in capacity building. Yet, their roles and those of followers are often hard to pinpoint. It is difficult to define leadership, and even more difficult to practice it or teach it.

The purpose of this chapter is to investigate persistent questions about rural leaders and their involvement in change. What special challenges are faced by rural leaders? What defines a leader and a follower? How is the effectiveness of followers and leaders measured? Are there different leadership models that might be appropriate in rural settings? How are leaders recruited? What kinds of rural leadership-training approaches are being used in rural America today? This chapter examines these and other questions.

SPECIAL CHALLENGES FOR RURAL LEADERS

In contrast to their urban counterparts, rural leaders face three major limitations in assembling the knowledge and resources for effective community capacity building.

First, leaders are often limited by organizational size. Typically, rural organizations draw upon a smaller population base than urban groups. So, there may be fewer individuals who are available for community projects.

Second, although larger urban institutions can hire regular staff and a range of specialists for assistance, smaller-sized rural organizations and communities rely more on volunteers. These volunteer leaders may lack the technical or organizational skills necessary to deal with complex leadership challenges. Hence, they have to rely on time-consuming and often ineffective trial-and-error methods.

Third, many rural communities are geographically or socially isolated from major knowledge bases, such as universities and colleges, or specialists from the outside. Rural leaders may rely on traditional sources of information because they may be unaware of or unable to access these outside resources. In other cases, educational institutions, with useful knowledge to share, are constrained from involvement in rural settings by mission statements or limited financial resources.

These three major limitations are especially severe in more remote or less populated rural communities. Intervention strategies may be needed if rural people are to move into capacity building. Typically, capacity-building programs involve recruiting new leaders and working with outside agencies to address the new challenges and opportunities faced by the community.

Definitions of Rural Leadership

Because leadership means different things to different people, a brief overview of leadership definitions is presented in this section.

For the most part, theorists have not made a distinction between rural leadership and urban leadership. One of the most prominent theorists on this subject, Max Weber (1947), identified the leader as one who influences others. Weber argued that the leader's authority does not come from the leader alone, but that it rests in the social structure of both the leader and the follower. Weber's definition set the stage for viewing the leader as an individual rather than as a group of individuals, or an organization, or community.

Later studies focused on the identification of leaders through personal traits, such as intelligence, values, and appearance (Jenkins, 1947; Gibb, 1954; Mann, 1959). Findings from these studies indicate that leadership traits are specific to certain situations, rather than universal.

Although many studies have identified business managers as leaders, others have distinguished between managers and leaders on a behavioral basis. Zaleznik (1977) argues that managers have practical responsibilities that are so deeply embedded within the structure of an organization that their imaginative capacity and ability to generate new values are reduced. On the other hand, he perceives leaders as individuals who take risks in order to propose new alliances and in order to find new solutions to old problems. Leaders, according to Zaleznik, are less concerned with maintaining existing structures than managers. Others have questioned such definitional boundaries (Gardner, 1989), reporting that managers and leaders draw on skills that overlap. Managers often have to provide vision and creativity to changing organizations, and leaders often need to draw upon management skills, such as delegating, providing incentives, supervising, and evaluating.

Still other researchers have moved beyond the focus on the individual as leader to leadership as a collective endeavor. Miller, Rossing, and Steele (1990) in their work with rural-based Wisconsin Cooperative Extension Agents suggest that leadership is often a collective endeavor rather than a solo act. A core group of partners may attempt to influence or motivate others in relation to a specific program.

So what is the most appropriate definition of a leader? Because this chapter focuses on "capacity building" in rural areas, this definitional discussion excludes leaders who wish to defend the status quo. Those who rely exclusively on autocratic relationships with their followers can also be excluded, because such methods will not build the capacity of rural citizens to address and solve problems. Hence, rural leaders are defined in this chapter as individuals or groups of individuals who attempt to influence or motivate others, to build problem-solving capabilities, in order to bring about social or economic change in a democratic environment. This definition assumes that most rural leaders operate within a democratic framework.

Followers

Organizations and communities may rise or fall because of their leadership, however, leaders cannot operate without followers. Effective followers are not necessarily docile sheep who do what they are told. Such followers can inhibit creativity and openness in the community.

Kelley (1989) identifies four qualities of effective followers. These are (1) self-management capability; (2) commitment to the community or organization and to persons, principles, or purposes outside themselves; (3) commitment to competence; and (4) courage, honesty, and credibility.

Effective followers are also self-managers who think for themselves. They can work without close supervision and can anticipate problems and needs. According to Kelley, effective followers see themselves as equal to their leaders. They are likely to openly question their leaders and are less likely to be intimidated by organizational structure or hierarchy, whereas ineffective followers might see themselves as subservient or powerless. Self-managed followers are particularly important in rural areas, where many leaders are volunteers who do not have the time to supervise followers.

Effective followers are committed to a cause or crusade outside themselves. This commitment is not necessarily to the leader as an individual. The effective follower sees the leader as part of the crusade. This kind of commitment to a common cause builds morale in a community and generates more enthusiasm from those who were previously uninvolved. Ineffective followers are those who are committed to goals other than the community project or the community's interest. Such followers may obstruct a leader's control and impede progress toward a community goal.

Effective followers are eager to learn more, in order to improve their competence, and less effective followers expect training to come to them. Good followers acknowledge problems and seek ways to solve them. Rural community leaders can enhance their own competence and that of their followers through a variety of adult education tools, such as seminars, workshops, publications, and educational videos and tapes.

Courage and honesty also are qualities of an effective follower. They can establish themselves as independent, critical thinkers whose opinions can be trusted. With their insights and candor, they can keep both leaders and colleagues informed. Rural leaders who get defensive or dismiss such followers are likely to weaken their own influence.

Leaders are not necessarily superior to followers, rather their activities are equal but different. The same qualities of effectiveness in followers are also desirable for leaders. Unfortunately, not all leaders appreciate effective followers. Kelley (1989) found that some followers were rewarded for effective qualities such as self-management, commitment to the cause, competence, and courage. Yet, he reported that about half of the time, leaders punished their followers for exercising judgment and taking risks. In order to retain effective followers, leaders must find ways to reward them in order to create an energetic, creative, and enthusiastic community.

Leadership Models

Three major models of the process of democratic leadership have emerged in recent years. James MacGregor Burns (1978) developed two of the models, transactional and transformational leadership. The third model, community-based leadership, may be on "the cutting edge of leadership theory" (Vonder, 1989, p. 7), and cannot be attributed to any single author. The transactional and transformational models are highly individualistic. Both of these approaches assume that leaders are relatively permanent and do not change places with followers. However, the community-based approach views leaders as a group of people who frequently change roles with followers.

Transactional Leadership: The Businessperson's Approach

Transactional leadership can be viewed as the businessperson's approach to being a leader. It has much in common with the definition of leader as manager. James MacGregor Burns views transactional leadership as a contractual arrangement in which individuals exchange valued things that may have an economic, political, or psychological quality. The exchange takes place in the form of favors, support, or negotiated power. The long-range motives and purposes of the transactional leaders and followers are not necessarily the same. Their contractual arrangement ends when the followers have completed their agreed-upon goals. This relationship may be relatively short-lived, because neither follower nor leader can repeat the identical exchange and will, therefore, move on to new gratifications.

The transactional leadership model focuses on an ethic of utilitarian values. That is, it emphasizes efficiency, cost–benefit analysis, short-term profits, fairness, and the honoring of commitments. Followers base their decision to join the transactional relationship based on the same values (Vonder, 1989). The transactional approach is commonly practiced in everyday rural life, especially among managers in business and government. Rural communities need transactional leaders, who can keep parts of the economic, political, and social infrastructure running smoothly.

The transactional approach has limitations in rural settings. Citizens may feel frustrated because this leadership model tends to limit creativity and input from a variety of groups, especially those with scarce resources to exchange. Typically, transactional leaders approach problems with the quick-fix mentality of the marketplace. They tend to ignore some of the more critical questions about community that do not yield short-range results. Followers enter a contractual arrangement with the leader. Yet, their role is relatively limited in terms of how leadership is implemented. They often lack the resources to directly influence change. This passivity is not productively helpful in building the capacity of a community to solve its own problems.

Transformational Leaders: Visionary Leaders for Special Groups

The transformational approach can be viewed as the visionary's approach to leadership. In the typical case, the visionary in this model frequently works with special groups, not necessarily with the entire community. Burns draws on diverse work in leadership theory for his perspective on transformational leadership. "Such leadership occurs when one or more persons engage with others in such a way that leaders and followers raise one another to higher levels of motivation and morality. Their purposes, which might have started out as separate but related . . . become fused. Power bases are linked not as counterweights but as mutual support for common purpose" (Burns, 1978, p. 20). In contrast to transactional leadership, the bond between transformational leaders and followers is strictly voluntary. Mutually held goals and purposes, rather than payoffs, bind the group together. Generally, transformational leaders operate with the intent to improve conditions for the group. Followers are more involved in this model than in the transactional approach. Both leaders and followers have a "transforming effect" on each other (Burns, 1978, p. 20). Although the followers strongly influence the leader in this model, they do not necessarily implement policy.

The transformational model contains a set of ethics that is associated with long-term values such as liberty, justice, and equality. In many cases the model focuses on the concerns of groups within the community, rather than on the community as a whole.

Transformational leadership occurs in a variety of rural settings. For example, agricultural producers may establish a cooperative. Hospitality leaders, who are interested in diverse aspects of tourism development, may work together to achieve their desired end, or a downtown merchant might motivate his colleagues to revitalize a deteriorating business section.

Although this approach has merits, there are obvious limitations. Transformational leaders may minimize transactional concerns, such as cost–benefit analysis or profit maximization, in order to reach long-term goals. This may lead to problems with those who place a high value on transactional ethics. Furthermore, some people may believe that this model limits the capacity building of followers. The followers influence or "transform" the leader, but they often assume a less visible role, and the leader carries out their action agenda.

Others are concerned that the transformational approach may neglect the common good. Essentially, transformational leaders inspire groups to improve their situations and to develop and carry out an action plan. For example, a coalition of tourism and environmental groups may nobly attempt to stop all pollution in its region. The efforts may be so effective that several polluting firms are forced to close down and many blue-collar jobs are lost. In this example, the transformational approach results in a healthier environment, but neglects the even bigger question of what is best for the community as a whole.[1]

In spite of these limitations, the transformational approach has merits. A transformational leader can help disadvantaged people articulate their needs and can develop a vision to encourage and inspire their change.

Community-Based Leaders: Blurry Distinctions Between Leaders and Followers

The community-based leadership model bears some similarity to the transformational approach. Both approaches rely on higher methods of motivation rather than on mutual payoffs. However, whereas the transformational model assumes that leaders are relatively permanent, the community-based model assumes followers and leaders exchange roles frequently, based on the best interests of the community. The leader responds to encouragement of the community in order to help clear paths to meet a desired goal. He or she may then step back to let someone more appropriate carry out the next step of the community's mission (Vonder, 1989). The community-based model is "a consensual task, a sharing of ideas and a sharing of responsibilities, where a leader is a leader for the moment only, where the leadership exerted must be validated by the consent of the followers, and where leadership lies in the struggles of a community to find meaning for itself" (Foster, 1989, p. 61).

In the community-based model, followers do not wait for enlightened leaders to speak, but they often show their leaders where to move. Whereas the transformational model oftens focuses on the interests of certain groups, the community-based model recognizes that the "tension between private interest and the public good is never completely resolved in any society. But in a free republic, it is the task of the citizen, whether ruler or ruled, to cultivate civic virtue in order to mitigate the tension and render it manageable" (Bellah et al., 1985, p. 270).

Proponents of the community-based model tend to view the transactional and transformational models as too limited because of the focus on individual leaders, rather than on the leadership–followership relationship. Community-based leadership advocates view the transactional approach as too limited because of its focus on "economic man." The transformational model comes closer to the community-based approach because of the emphasis on creating a new vision of social reality. However, some community-based critics see the transformational model as too limiting, because of its frequent focus on the needs of special groups, rather than on the entire community.

The ethics of community-based leadership involve the well-being of everyone in the community at large, including future generations who will be affected by leadership activities. The purposes of leaders and followers must be consistent with the values of the affected community (Vonder, 1989).

Like the other two models, the community-based model has limitations. When the community problem is highly technical, the transactional model may be more effective than the community-based approach. In other situations, a particular group in a community may feel that the focus on the common good neglects its needs or that it reinforces the status quo. In such cases, the transformational approach is most suitable. Others might argue that the assumptions of the community-based leadership approach are naive and ineffective. Such critics might contend that community-based leadership is a vision that is rarely realized. Cynics may believe "we the people," despite our democratic visions, are caught up in a transactional exchange among self-centered individuals or, perhaps, in a competition of special interest groups that are trying to control information and resources.

Each of these leadership models, with its own ethics and assumptions, has applications to rural communities. Of course, real life is much more complex than these sharply differentiated models. These three models often overlap or blend. For example, communities may employ researchers (transactional leaders) to help them conduct a needs assessment survey. Some transformational leaders may use survey results to inspire a group of teenagers to take some action that would benefit all teenagers in the community. In contrast to the transformational model, the community-based leadership model would use the same information to mobilize all groups in the community.

Recruiting New Rural Leaders

The recruitment strategies chosen by a community depend on the type of leadership strategy desired by the community. A group or community must determine its need, in order to strengthen or build its capacity for problem solving. It may use combinations of transactional, transformational, and community-based models, or it may rely on one model exclusively.

Transactional leaders are typically recruited through promises of better pay, higher status, or increased influence. A community needing transactional leaders may advertise through professional journals and organizations or through individual mentoring in a community setting. Many communities need transactional leaders for short periods of time. For example, a city may hire a planner for a 6-month effort to get an historic preservation effort underway. In other cases, groups or communities pool their resources to hire a permanent transactional leader. Some communities may cooperate, through the creation of commissions, agencies, or special boards, to offer transactional leaders the opportunity to shape public policy. Groups or communities that have meager resources or power to exchange may be unable to recruit transactional leaders and will have to rely on transformational or community-based leadership approaches.

Luther and Wall (1989) synthesize theory and experience in small towns throughout the United States to propose ten suggestions for finding leaders. Their recruitment strategies are applicable to both transformational and community-based leadership models.

1. Ask "who's not here?" To answer this question, communities need to understand the composition of their community and which groups are missing. Through this understanding, they can target certain segments of the community's potential leadership pool.
2. Look for skills, not names. Some groups rely on the same people over and over again, resulting in leader burnout. By listing the skills required for each task, new leaders can be identified.
3. Try involvement by degrees. Start by asking for help on small tasks to boost confidence levels and get the individual involved, then move gradually on to larger and more complex tasks.
4. Appeal to the intellectual, altruistic, or social self-interests of individuals. Some may wish to repay a debt to the community or to get approval from friends or neighbors. Essentially, this personal drive allows the individual to take a risk and accomplish something. Recruitment efforts can be tailored to such motives.
5. Recognize that leadership potential takes many forms. Small accomplishments such as planting flowers or mass mailings may seem modest, but they contribute to the whole picture of a vibrant community. Recognizing and encouraging these contributions may lead to increased involvement.
6. Define the task. Recruiting new leaders is easier when the task is clearly defined. This definition should include skill and time requirements, as well as an indication of how the task fits into the larger picture.
7. Encourage current leaders to recruit new leaders. Highly visible leaders are in an excellent position to recruit new leaders, through media, public meetings, and existing committee structures. By sharing responsibilities, existing leaders can recruit newcomers to the leadership pool and provide mentoring for them.

8. Create a history of using people's time efficiently. Meetings should be focused and productive. If members are convinced that their effort is well-managed, they are more likely to assume a leadership position.
9. Offer membership "premiums" such as trips to conventions, workshops, or a letter of recognition to an employer, highlighting the employee's community efforts. These rewards can help the potential leader to overcome some hesitancy to get involved.
10. Make sure the community is aware of local efforts. Through word of mouth and effective use of the media, the community can learn what has been accomplished and what projects are underway. This technique can also attract potential leaders. These recruitment strategies may not always be effective. Potential leaders may have to be nourished and developed through leadership training program.

Innovative Projects for Training Rural Leaders

Rural leadership is often learned "on the job." But the trial-and-error method and frequent lack of current information can be frustrating for rural leaders who wish to build their people's capacity to identify and solve problems. Indeed, rural leadership training is a difficult undertaking. What should these programs teach and to whom should they be directed? The answers to these questions depend on one's ethics and assumptions about leadership, as well as on the leadership skills that are needed in the rural group or community.

Some insights can be gained by examining several rural leadership programs. These innovative programs are roughly categorized within the transactional, transformational, and community-based frameworks discussed earlier.

Transactional leadership training usually involves business and government leaders who are in paid and/or elected positions. Training is relatively short, because of the contractlike arrangement between followers and leaders.

Michigan's Center for Local Economic Competitiveness (CLEC) was created by the state's Department of Commerce, because of the enthusiasm of many communities for economic development. CLEC was organized to provide informational leadership to regional areas within the state by analyzing their economies and furnishing economic competitiveness strategies that could later be implemented by community leaders and officials in that area.

CLEC's personnel services were provided free of charge, but clients were expected to provide funding for a local half-time staff liaison and to pay for mailing and other incidentals. The client pool included groups of local governments that were organized into "Community Growth Alliances"—areawide economic development organizations. CLEC examined each region's economic performance over a certain time period and compared that performance to the nation, state, and other areas. They conducted surveys of businesses in the area and used tools, such as location quotients and shift/share analysis. The analysis and subsequent discussions lasted about 6 months.

Although this training program is too new to accurately evaluate, this transactional approach has had mixed preliminary results. It sparked creative discussions in the community about economic development prospects and problems that were based on factual information. As a result, communities could strengthen their capacity-building capabilities and "build their economic development strategies on facts rather than myths and misperceptions."

Some community members were disappointed that the analysis did not offer any "magic bullets." The state was reluctant to make strategic recommendations to the communities, because it believed it was inappropriate and politically dangerous to do so. The economic development committees were intended to reflect community interests, "but, perhaps, inevitably were dominated by businessmen, government officials, and, behind the scene, local economic development professionals." Organized labor and the minority community participated little. Business elites dominated because they could see the payoff of the study and discussions on their businesses more readily than other elements in the community (Wolman and Voytek, 1990). This definitional problem of community may be one of the weaknesses of the transactional approach.

Unlike the transactional model, *transformational* leadership training attempts to focus on creating long-term visions among potential leaders, who will eventually influence followers. There are a variety of *transformational* approaches to rural leadership training. Most of these programs have an operational assumption that leaders are individuals who can motivate and influence others to bring about change. For the most part, transformational training does not involve followers. It assumes that potential transformational leaders will eventually move into permanent leadership positions.

The Wisconsin Rural Leadership Program is designed for men and women who are in the early stages of their leadership careers, between ages 25 and 45. The program exposes rural leaders to a broad range of people, ideas, and issues they might not otherwise encounter. It broadens participants' understanding of U.S. and international economic, political, and social systems through eight seminars and two field trips over a 2-year period. Participants spend 2 weeks in an international seminar to enhance understanding of international trade, and a week in Washington, D.C.

The program brochures do not emphasize the ethics of transactional leadership (contractual arrangements, profits, etc.), but, rather, clearly focus on creating new visionaries in rural places. According to the program literature, many of the graduates of the program have become effective leaders in private and public organizations in both rural and metropolitan settings.

The Michigan Agricultural Leadership Program is similar to the Wisconsin program. However, it is designed to strengthen the leadership capabilities of individuals in farming or food systems occupations. The program has three main objectives: (1) to build self-understanding and an understanding of others; (2) to understand the social, political, and economic systems in which people function; and (3) to use this framework to analyze the complex problems faced by people, agricultural systems, and the rural community. The leadership experience extends over a 2-year period and includes travel seminars.

These transformational approaches to leadership training are highly individualistic. They expand the vision and perspective of emerging rural leaders. However, it is difficult to determine how or whether these trained leaders have influenced the vision of followers or the larger community from which they come.

Whereas transformational training builds rural leaders through exposure to new people and travel outside local confines, *community-based leadership* usually occurs within the community. It is a type of capacity building with an experiential focus. It assumes that community people learn best by doing and that local people learn from each other. Outsiders may provide the structure for such training. However, they minimize their role, because excessive output could hinder local capacity building.

As noted earlier, followers and leaders change places frequently in this model, allowing educational experiences to be offered to a wider audience. An Iowa State University Extension program, ''Tomorrow's Leaders Today'' (TLT), is a community-based approach that treats a cluster of towns, villages, and countryside areas as a spatial unit. Clusters range in size from three to eight communities. About twenty-five participants are involved in each cluster.

TLT's program objectives are to provide an educational program for emerging community leaders through improving leadership skills; expanding visions of the possibilities for rural community development; and identifying and mobilizing resources to address community issues. Now in its third year of operation, the program includes ten sessions during a period of 9 months.

Because rural communities have limited resources for development, TLT systematically explores multicommunity development by emphasizing interpersonal ties and a new group identity. For example, in the first session, participants use slides of each other's communities in order to create a ''cluster'' slide show. Through this exercise, they not only learn about their ''cluster,'' but also they learn to work with each other and build a new group identity. In another session, they are asked to conduct an informal needs inventory in the community. Eventually, participants identify potential cluster projects and work together to carry them out. Because the program is still being evaluated, it is difficult to determine its impact at this time (Almquist, Foley and Wells, 1990; Wells, 1990).

Although the TLT program was implemented by a university, community-based leadership training can be nourished through individuals or grass-roots organizations. Ivanhoe is an unincorporated town in the Appalachian mountains of Virginia. It had a 200-year history in which the economy was dominated by single industries, including lead, iron, carbide, and zinc. At its peak in the 1940s, the town had 4,500 residents, with a school, railroad, theater, doctor, and stores. As industry moved elsewhere, the town lost these services. In 1981, the closing of its last plant, New Jersey Zinc, resulted in despair, apathy, and outmigration. The community's industrial land lay in two counties, which Ivanhoe straddled. Because this land had stood vacant for years, the counties decided, in 1986, to sell. This action irritated an individual who didn't want to let the town die. The land became a symbol of the town's last chance to survive. This individual attended the next county board meeting and convinced county authorities to give Ivanhoe citizens 2 years to find an industry to occupy the land.

The citizens formed the Ivanhoe Civic League and the League sponsored a "Hands Across Ivanhoe" in November 1986 in order to raise funds. Three thousand people paid $3 each to link hands over a 2-mile course that spanned the two counties.

As the Civic League worked with industrial development authorities, they eventually challenged these economic development spokesmen and concluded it was unrealistic to recruit a manufacturing plant onto the industrial land.

The League built and organized its own economic development classes to determine who benefitted the most from different economic development strategies and came to the conclusion that the workers had made very little to make the factory owners rich.

The group did a survey of every household in the community. The survey challenged regional assumptions that Ivanhoe residents just wanted to be on welfare or were lazy. "Nobody said they wanted to be rich. They said they wanted jobs and they wanted education. But we don't want just jobs, we want better jobs. So, we started with education. Out of 175 houses, 16 people wanted to learn to read and 37 people wanted GED" (Thomas, 1988, p. 138). This information was used by Ivanhoe people to build local self-esteem, which had been shattered by economic hard times.

As a result of their community-designed learning experiences, League participants constructed new definitions of their social and economic life. The Ivanhoe program is clearly a capacity-building program that fits within the community-based leadership model. Followers and leaders change roles frequently. Its ethical concerns involve the well-being of everyone. "We are dealing with something entirely different from what has been done before. We have been so creative . . . we will be a role model in economic development" (Waller et al., 1990, p. 28).

Transactional leaders might criticize Ivanhoe people as naive or not paying enough attention to the bottom line. After all, Ivanhoe residents did not reach their original goal of recruiting a manufacturing plant on the industrial land. Instead, they have turned the land into a community-owned enterprise. It is a park with a convenience store, camping, bike and raft rentals, which provide jobs and recreation for the community and attract tourists (Waller et al., 1990).

Some transformational leaders might argue that Ivanhoe's approach is too broad and unfocused. They might contend that the focus should be on women or minority groups or the needs of teenagers in the community. A transformational training program would have drawn a clearer distinction between potential leaders and followers than did the Ivanhoe Civic League.

As the case studies indicate, the most appropriate leadership training program for a community depends on how one defines community and leadership, concerns about followers, one's values about leadership, and the kinds of leadership skills that are required and available. In many cases, rural communities may wish to draw upon each of the three leadership models.

SUMMARY

This chapter examined several aspects of the rural leadership puzzle. Three leadership models were discussed: transactional, transformational, and community-based. Each of these three approaches has its strengths and weaknesses when applied to the special problems of rural leaders.

This chapter examined innovative rural leadership programs in the United States; however, no universal answers were offered for the leadership problems that face rural communities. Nevertheless, readers will find some useful ideas that can be applied in building a successful rural leadership program.

NOTE

1. For more thorough discussions about the limitations of transformational leadership, see *Leadership in the Twenty-First Century* by Joseph C. Rost (New York: Praeger, 1991).

9. State and Federal Policy Initiatives in Rural Development

Tom Unruh

Earlier chapters demonstrated that rural areas in many states lagged behind most of the country during the economic expansion of the 1980s (Reid et al., 1988). At approximately the same time, state governments were developing new and innovative policies to promote economic development through building the capacities of their work forces and encouraging the small and medium-sized firms that drove most job growth across the United States (National Governors Association, 1987; Osborne, 1988). In the interest of broadening the positive effects of economic expansion to all areas of their states, governors and legislators began to seek ways to improve rural economies in order to narrow the gap between urban and rural economic growth. Nearly every state has undertaken a rural initiative in the past 3 years.

The 1980s were also a decade of retrenchment for federal programs that had addressed infrastructure and economic development needs of rural areas. Funding levels for nearly all Farmers Home Administration programs were cut, as were programs such as the Small Cities Community Development Block Grant. Farm programs also saw steady reductions throughout the 1980s.

The trend of shifting responsibility for development policy and assistance from the federal government to state and local governments continues. States have increased their assistance to local units of government over the past several years,[1] while both states and local governments are raising concerns about federally mandated activities that are no longer funded.

Finally, current economic conditions severely limit the ability of states to assume new responsibilities, especially new and expensive social obligations, such as funding for Medicaid. According to the January 1991 National Association of State Budget Officers (NASBO) and the National Governors Association survey, twenty-eight states reported that "they would have a negative ending balance if they did not cut spending or increase revenues before the end of the fiscal year."[2] NASBO also reported that the trend is worsening and improvement is unlikely in FY1992.

In the NASBO survey, six Midwestern states indicated serious shortfalls in FY1991 budgets. As a percent of general fund appropriations, Minnesota, Iowa, Missouri, Indiana, Ohio, and Michigan all expect budget shortfalls; most were in the 0 to 3 percent range, with Michigan expecting more than a 5 percent gap. Because states are required to balance their budgets (with one exception), governors and legislatures must make difficult adjustments in spending and revenues to solve the problems. With this level of fiscal pressure, large new spending initiatives in support of rural development may be difficult to achieve this year.

It is also important to note that state economic development policy initiatives face a relatively volatile political context. At this writing, nineteen new governors have taken office and are in the process of preparing their first budgets, which often become the hallmark policy documents of their administrations. Nebraska, Kansas, Minnesota, Illinois, Michigan, and Ohio have new administrations. Under these new administrations, some programs and policy initiatives described in this chapter may be significantly changed or even eliminated for political or fiscal reasons.

In spite of the current fiscal difficulties, new policy directions for rural areas are being discussed. Although these approaches will not solve the difficult infrastructure problems in some rural areas, they are designed to enhance the ability of communities to undertake and direct their own development strategies.

The changing emphasis in statewide rural economic development policy, away from a heavy reliance on industrial recruitment to improving the performance of existing firms and supporting the growth of new enterprise, is also extending to rural economic development policy. States and communities are discovering that the costs of attracting businesses to relocate may not equal the benefits to the community. In fact, because of the competition in industrial attraction, most rural communities have found that their economic development resources are better spent assisting new and existing businesses.

State development officials are recognizing the importance of rural leadership, community involvement and commitment, and local capacity to conduct economic development activities. During fiscal constraints, governors and legislatures are questioning the appropriateness of top–down strategies for rural areas. The vast diversity of rural communities, in terms of development assets and capabilities, requires governmental responses that are based on flexibility, improved access, and communication between local actors (both public and private) and state government. Making changes in organizational attitudes and program structures to improve service delivery can improve the effectiveness of economic development efforts, without significantly increasing public costs.

States, and now federal agencies as well, are looking for ways to create and implement rural economic development policy in partnership with local and private-sector interests. In this alternative approach toward economic development, the government's role is as a catalyst for development activities, rather than as an exclusive provider of development assistance. Doug Ross and Robert Friedman of the Corporation For Enterprise Development describe a "Third Wave" of economic development policy. "The role of government is changing. Operating less as mass suppliers of particular goods or services, these public agencies are discovering the need to act more as facilitators, brokers and seed capitalists" (Ross and Friedman, 1990).

The "Third Wave" indicates a direction for development policy. The initiatives described in this chapter contain elements of that approach that emphasize involving the private sector in policy development and implementation, and giving strategy and priority-setting responsibility to policy actors nearer the grass roots of economic development.

This chapter describes a number of recent state and federal rural development policy initiatives, beginning with the State Rural Development Academy, conducted by the Council of Governors' Policy Advisors. Several other approaches will then be described that address certain parts of the rural policy spectrum or certain points in the policy development process. Two recent federal initiatives, one in the executive branch and the second in the 1990 farm bill, will be examined. Finally, possible future developments are noted and some conclusions are presented about state and federal rural development policy.

STATE RURAL DEVELOPMENT POLICY

A pervasive characteristic of rural America is diversity—diversity in demographic makeup, economic bases, political attitudes. The recognition of this diversity by state policy makers results in many different constructions, both formal (legal), and informal, of what is rural. The makeup of the state helps to determine how state government addresses rural policy. In states with few urban areas, rural development policy is really statewide economic development policy. In more populous states, rural development policy may be seen as a substate component of statewide economic development policy.

State activities to promote rural development have varied widely. The most comprehensive rural development policy activity has been in the states participating in the Council of Governors' Policy Advisors (CGPA) Rural Policy Academy.[3]

The CGPA State Policy Academy

One of the most significant developments in state economic development policy regarding rural areas is the application of the Council of Governors' Policy Advisors' (CGPA, formerly the Council of State Policy and Planning Agencies, CSPA) policy academy model. In 1990, CGPA selected ten states, through a competitive process, for the intensive policy development laboratory.

The policy academy model has been refined over the past 7 years, during which time CGPA has conducted six academies on issues including self-sufficiency for the developmentally disabled and for older workers, teenage pregnancy, illiteracy, high school dropout prevention, and families and children at risk. The policy academy combines three crucial elements with a strategic planning process: the right people with the resources and authority to affect outcomes, isolation from distraction, and team time in an environment and process "designed to produce proposals that are likely to be both politically acceptable and effective in addressing the policy issue" (Colgan, 1990).

The policy academy takes the state teams through a six-step strategic planning process. The first step is an *environmental scan* to determine the current situation by examining factors that describe and affect the policy issue. Because of the great diversity in rural areas, the scan is particularly important to rural policy development. Step two is a *problem and opportunity diagnosis* that takes into account the various factors affecting the issue, the range of opinions and perspectives about causes and trends, and a complete a range of possible policy interventions. The diagnosis results in an objective problem statement that does not presume any particular solution. Step three is *goal and objective setting*. In this step, teams are asked to set broad, yet clearly defined goals and then begin the process of refining them into specific policy objectives. Whereas earlier steps emphasized broad analysis, this step begins the prioritization process and team members are encouraged, and indeed pushed by facilitators, to get conflicting views on the table for discussion and resolution. Step four is *strategy identification*. Policy brainstorming is the first step in designing methods for achieving the objectives.

The second session of the academy continues the work on strategies, and then moves on to steps five and six, *recommendations for policy selection* and *an action plan*. Based on the information and knowledge gathered in the preceding steps, the teams select priority strategies and design programs. Teams are instructed to use the outcome-oriented objectives developed in step three as the basis for evaluation. The action plan brings in elements from the environmental scan to identify the important players in the political system and their interests. It details a strategy for the team and the governor to follow in implementing the new policy and includes a statewide analysis and a communications plan. The final outcome of the academy process is a policy document that contains analyses, objectives, program proposals, accountability measures, and an action plan for implementing the policy.

It is important to note that while CGPA's academy process is a detailed, linear process on paper, in operation, the policy academy process is kept very flexible so as to respond to the specific needs of the teams themselves. The needs and capacities of each state are carefully monitored by academy staff, and individualized support is available, both during and after academy sessions.

The Rural Academy

CGPA's rural policy academy included several Midwestern states: Arkansas, California, Iowa, Maine, Michigan, Mississippi, Missouri, North Dakota, Pennsylvania, and Wyoming. The participants from each state were selected by the governors and were encouraged to make a significant commitment of their time, including nearly 2 weeks over the two academy sessions to the development of their state's rural development policy. CGPA provided facilities, a structured program, with expert faculty on hand for both presentations and on-site consultation with teams, as requested, and trained facilitators for each team.

Rural academy sessions were held in May and July 1990. The timing of the sessions was set to mesh with state budget and policy processes, with the goal of having completed proposals and legislative strategies ready for the 1991 legislative sessions. Of the ten states in the Academy, four will have new rural development legislation up for discussion in the coming session. North Dakota and Iowa are among those that have made the most progress.

North Dakota

The report and recommendations of North Dakota's Academy Team, in conjunction with the report of a blue ribbon commission called North Dakota 2000, resulted in the governor's appointment of a broad-based committee. This committee was charged with creating and implementing a comprehensive economic development legislative program for 1991. The so-called "Committee of 34" (1990) issued recommendations in a report called *Growing North Dakota* (see Figure 9.1). The report's eleven recommendations essentially outline a comprehensive statewide economic development strategy. Each general recommendation is accompanied by specific program recommendations, proposed legislation, and spending targets.

The *Growing North Dakota* plan calls for the use of over $20 million in profits of the Bank of North Dakota to fund its initiatives and would not tap general revenue funds. It suggests reorganization of the current state economic development agency in order to consolidate functions and add a number of programs aimed at addressing specific needs of rural communities.

North Dakota's situation may be unique; as a very rural state, its statewide economic development strategy must be tailored to promote rural development. Although many of the specific policy initiatives have been undertaken in other states, the *Growing North Dakota* proposals are contained in one piece of legislation. This comprehensive approach may ease the initial passage of the legislation, and simplify administration, monitoring, and adjustment of the policy in the future.

Iowa

The Iowa policy academy team prepared a policy proposal that makes recommendations for business development, retention, and capital access; community development and organizational capacity; agriculture; health care; governmental services and infrastructure; and rural telecommunications. These recommendations were offered within an overall state rural policy framework. The policy framework consists of four major points (see Figure 9.2).

Figure 9.1
***Growing North Dakota* Recommendations**

1. Maximize the use of Bank of North Dakota Profits.
2. Enhance the capabilities of the North Dakota Economic Development Commission.
3. Create a primary sector development fund that would be used to expand the economy in value-added agriculture, manufacturing, energy by-product development, and exported services.
4. Develop a science and technology corporation to tap the resources of higher education and link it to the state economic development delivery system.
5. Revitalize our agriculture industry through diversification.
6. Develop capacity building for economic development at the local level.
7. Deliver a strong community economic development education program.
8. Targeted recruitment program.
9. Enhance minority business.
10. Business development for women.
11. Develop entrepreneurship awareness programs for bankers.

Source: Committee of 34, 1990.

The Iowa academy team also recommended several new programs and changes to existing programs. Among the new initiatives are the following:

Expansion of the Rural Community Leadership Program. Iowa's independent colleges, community colleges, and extension service will contract with the state department of development to deliver the program to ten cluster or county groups, which could cover 50 to 100 communities.

Rural Health Services Development Program. The goal of this program is to support the development and implementation of community-based health care delivery systems, given existing resources and changing technologies and markets. Demonstration grant money would be available, along with technical assistance. A local match would be required for grants.

Civic Laboratories and Government Service Coordination. This initiative would fund demonstration projects—''civic laboratories''—to encourage experimentation in the provision of local services; establish a state-level entity to focus on intergovernmental relations; and conduct research on effective practices in governmental service-sharing arrangements.

Livestock Initiative. This educational program would provide one-on-one technical assistance to increase the competitiveness and profitability of livestock producers.

Competitive Livestock Facilities Demonstration Project. This project would address two environ-

Figure 9.2
Rural Policy Framework

---

* Rural development is important for all of Iowa, not just rural Iowa. For example, the incomes of rural Iowans are spent at least partially on goods and services within metropolitan areas. It is important for all Iowans to understand that a strong rural Iowa is a stronger Iowa.

* The process of rural development must occur from the bottom up, rather than from the top down. The state or federal government cannot lead change and define the future for rural Iowa; only citizens can. The future will probably be different, but it will be locally determined. The state's primary role should be as <u>facilitator</u> for local decision-making processes.

* Partnerships and cooperative arrangements among like entities will be critical for the future quality and viability of rural communities, farms, businesses, and institutions. The state's role should be to encourage, but not force such arrangements.

* State government's role should become more and more that of a facilitator and a catalyst for action by others who have a vested interest in rural development, rather than to serve necessarily as the direct and sole provider of a given service.

Source: Iowa Academy Team, 1990.

mental issues, odor control and water quality, through the demonstration of new technologies for dealing with animal waste.

Credit School for Commercial/Business Lending. A joint venture of the Iowa State University Extension Service, the Iowa Bankers Association, and Iowa Department of Economic Development would develop and offer a curriculum for managers of small rural banks on agricultural lending.

Other states that were not involved in the rural policy academy are also undertaking rural policy development activities. Most of these activities are not as comprehensive or as intense as the academy, but represent significant interest in rural issues and can be seen as the first steps toward more comprehensive rural policies.

Rural Policy Conferences

Access to state government is often cited as a problem for rural communities. Local leaders often are unaware of programs that may be appropriate to assist them with a particular issue. They also may be unsatisfied with the level and quality of service delivery to their community. Conferences provide a way to identify and communicate with rural leaders, to market existing state services, and to identify and prioritize policy issues for administrative and legislative consideration. Finally, conferences offer rural leaders an opportunity to hear from their colleagues about what works in their communities.

Universities and extension services in many states have been the moving forces behind educational conferences, providing information about the state's rural areas and their economies. State departments of development are also becoming involved in sponsoring or cooperating with universities and extensions to co-sponsor such conferences. Statewide rural development policy conferences bring together a broad range of people with rural interests and can begin to build a constituency for statewide rural development policy.

The Mississippi Department of Economic Development sponsored a rural development conference in conjunction with the state extension service. The conference brought together over 300 state, local, and private representatives of rural interests. The conference participants heard from state political leaders as well as university experts and state development officials, who described the social and economic situation in rural Mississippi. Conference participants discussed the presentations and the issues raised, and used a prioritization process to identify key issues for rural communities in the state.

Oklahoma used a conference to kick off a strategy development process, resulting in recommended priorities for state actions. A primary recommendation was the creation of a statewide rural leadership development program to build local economic development capacity. The Oklahoma Department of Commerce, Oklahoma State University, and the University of Oklahoma are working together to design this training program.

Michigan has undertaken a broad-based approach to rural community development. State officials held public meetings in more than seventy communities to discuss local perceptions of state development programs. The comments and suggestions received in these meetings were used as part of the environmental scan prepared by the Michigan academy team. The academy team's report has been presented to the state's Rural Partnership Advisory Committee, which passed a resolution urging consideration of the report's initiative by the new governor.[4]

Local planning and economic development capacity building are key elements of more comprehensive state rural development efforts. Michigan, through its rural partnership grants program, has been working with communities to create and implement local economic development plans. The program emphasizes locally driven economic development efforts, by supporting local planning efforts with small "rural economic strategy grants." Additional funds are available to implement strategies selected through the planning process. The program attempts to catalyze the provision of local planning assistance by allowing localities to choose among competing service providers, rather than using state agency staff exclusively.

Rural Partners, the Illinois coalition for rural community development, is sponsoring a twelve-county local leadership and economic development training program. Citizens will work through self-help guides, called Community Action Models, that use case studies and "learn-by-doing" exercises that address local issues. Authors of the guides will provide technical assistance. The program has a broad base of funding that will help in sustaining its activities beyond its initial 3-year horizon.[5]

Kansas, Inc., the state's economic development policy agency, is implementing legislation that authorized a local economic development planning program. Kansas counties will be offered financial assistance to support initial economic development planning efforts. The program will also coordinate the county-level plans with a regional and a state-level rural economic development plan.

South Dakota provides community development assistance through the Guide to Opportunities for Local Development (GOLD) program. The GOLD program gives communities a framework to establish their own goals and work plans through the efforts of local volunteers. The self-help program is available to all South Dakota communities. To participate, a community undertakes an assessment of its economic and social resources, including work force, utilities, income, taxes, and available land and buildings. Each community is also required to survey its citizens to determine their assessment of community strengths and weaknesses. Based on the self-assessment process, the community establishes goals to address the weaknesses that were identified and then builds on its strengths. The final portion of the program helps communities develop a strategic plan to reach their goals. The plans are submitted, along with the data gathered by the communities, to the Governor's Office of Economic Development.

Regional Development Perspectives

Several states have designed programs to encourage communities to view their economies and their economic development resources from a broader regional perspective, allowing them to become competitive in ways that they cannot individually. For example, many small communities do not have the resources to afford professional economic development personnel exclusively for their area, but they may be able to get such services through a cooperative arrangement with other neighboring communities. Additional economies of scale are available for local government administration, thereby freeing resources for other priorities.

West Virginia's Partnerships for Progress is one of the newest efforts and is changing and adapting to the needs of West Virginia communities. The program established regional Partnership Councils in nine multicounty regions of the state, chosen to reflect economic similarities and common interests. Council members were appointed by the governor and represent business, labor, education, and government. Directors of regional development districts were also asked to participate on the councils. In conjunction with West Virginia University Extension, the Governor's Office of Community and Industrial Development provided a series of training sessions for the council members. The training provided the councils with basic economic information about their regions, and began a process of determining regional economic development priority projects. Several regions are currently implementing council recommendations and putting together region-oriented projects.

State development programs can make regional cooperation a priority and provide incentives to communities that work together. In reviewing applications, the Iowa Department of Economic Development scores those that include elements of multicommunity cooperation higher than those that do not. The state began to encourage multicommunity cooperation after development officials noticed a trend among small communities to form coalitions to meet specific needs, especially leadership and economic development. The Iowa Department of Economic Development has encouraged such cooperative arrangements through a conference that explains the issues that arise between communities trying to develop common objectives and cooperative strategies. The conference provided a forum for multicommunity organizations to present their experience and for local leaders to ask questions of state officials and local counterparts. The Department is also developing a multicommunity economic development inventory tool; a refinement of the more traditional community profile. The multicommunity inventory will provide communities with information from a regional perspective that includes neighboring communities. This should help to facilitate constructive cooperative partnerships.

One area in which economies of scale generally elude small communities is infrastructure finance. Illinois has created a Rural Bond Bank to buy and pool the bond issues of small towns and other units of local government in rural areas of the state. The Bond Bank will help communities get the financing they need, but may not be able to get on their own, because their individual bond issue is too small.

Access to State Government for Rural Citizens

Improving state government responsiveness to rural communities has been the goal of the Kansas Center for Rural Affairs. A 1988 Governor's Task Force on the Future of Rural Communities found that many citizens and community leaders were not aware of the resources available at the state level. The Center has undertaken an intensive promotion program to inform the public about the development services and programs that are available to rural communities. Located in the State Department of Commerce, the Center provides a one-stop information service for rural residents via a toll-free hotline. Rural development specialists are compiling a rural assistance database to improve referral service, creating outreach materials, and conducting followup activities with businesses and individuals who use the center in order to evaluate its services.

Innovative Business Financing Initiatives

Rural business assistance programs, especially in smaller states, have been limited to federally funded programs through the Community Development Block

Grant or the Farmers Home Administration (FmHA). Several interesting state-funded models are being tested. One is the Rural Economic Development and Initiative (REDI) Fund in South Dakota. The REDI revolving loan fund was capitalized in 1987 through the use of a 10-month 1 percent sales tax that yielded $40 million for low-interest loans to South Dakota businesses.

The revolving loan fund has also been used to match FmHA funds to create the Agricultural Processing and Export Program (APEX), which targets businesses adding value to raw agricultural products through processing. The APEX program gives priority consideration to businesses that are located or will locate in towns with under 2,000 population. The program also emphasizes employment of low-income persons, farm families, and displaced farm families. Operational in October 1990, the program has made three loans thus far for a total of $280,000, all for expansions of South Dakota firms.

State cooperation with private and foundation efforts is another innovative way to provide rural businesses with capital assistance. The Minneapolis-based McKnight Foundation's regional organizations are the result of a 2-year planning process that was based on the premise of local control and administration. The foundation began its Initiative Funds program in March 1986 with grants totaling $15 million. The six Initiative Funds make grants and loans for human services, economic development, education, leadership development, health, and community services. The foundation followed up on its original commitment with an additional grant of more than $41 million.

The Minnesota Rural Development Board's Challenge Grant, part of the state Department of Trade and Economic Development, also provides funding for locally operated revolving loan funds. The Initiative Funds programs were the only regional organizations that applied to administer the state's six $1 million Challenge Grants, which carry a one-to-one matching requirement. The Challenge Grant program covers all of greater Minnesota, approximately eighty counties excluding the Twin Cities metro area.

The program gives the local Initiative Funds board full discretion over the loans. It requires 50 percent participation by private sources; creation of job opportunities for low-income individuals, to be demonstrated by listing newly created jobs with the local Job Service and Job Training Partnership Act offices; and demonstration of an existing financing gap.

In conclusion, state rural development policy initiatives are emphasizing building local knowledge about economic development, identifying and supporting local leadership, encouraging regional cooperation, and improving access to state services. State governments are looking for ways to include other development partners, such as universities and extension services, in providing information and technical assistance to rural communities. The CGPA Rural Academy is assisting states in the development of comprehensive rural development policy; the experience and policy work of the ten academy states will be helpful to other state policy makers.

RECENT FEDERAL RURAL DEVELOPMENT POLICY

Federal funding for rural development activities has decreased steadily throughout the 1980s. Programs like the Community Development Block Grant, Farmers Home Administration grant and loan programs, and Environmental Protection Agency wastewater treatment funds have all been reduced, greatly limiting the options available to rural communities for financing new or improved infrastructure or for assisting new or expanding businesses.

In the current federal budget climate, the possibility of large amounts of new federal aid to rural areas appears remote at best. The president and Congress are opting for initiatives that emphasize the coordination and more effective use of existing resources, though even these modest attempts at change have been limited by their own complexity.

Presidential Initiative on Rural Development

The president announced his rural development initiative in January 1990. The goal of the initiative is to make better use of federal resources by coordinating across agencies within the federal government and with state and local governments, as well as with the private sector. The initiative has no new federal funds to invest in rural areas, but emphasizes achieving better use of existing programs. In the organizational efforts to date, federal officials have shown a recognition of the importance of local knowledge, control, and investment, which is manifesting itself in efforts to build partnerships with governors and state economic development officials.

Eight states have been chosen as pilot projects for initial implementation of the initiative: Kansas, Maine, Mississippi, Oregon, South Carolina, South Dakota, Texas, and Washington. A central feature of the president's initiative is the establishment, in each state, of councils of state- and/or regional-level directors of federal agencies that administer programs that impact upon rural areas. These councils will meet regularly, with a parallel panel of state government policy makers and administrators, to find ways to coordinate federal resources with state resources in order to implement development plans that are consistent at the federal, state, and local levels.

One example of the kind of coordination that is sought by federal rural councils is South Dakota's APEX fund described earlier. Creating the fund required negotiations between state officials from South Dakota's Governor's Office of Economic Development, the state FmHA director, and FmHA officials in Washington. The negotiations took nearly 2 years to complete, but the resulting program is tailored to meet the specific needs of South Dakota's small agricultural communities.

Rural Development Legislation

Over the past two years, Senate and House Agriculture Committee staff have been negotiating federal rural development legislation. Several radical and far-reaching ideas were under serious consideration by the House or the Senate committees, but the final compromise that became part of the Food, Agriculture, Conservation and Trade (FACT) Act of 1990, the Farm Bill, contains much more modest provisions for rural development.

The 1990 Farm Bill establishes the Rural Development Administration within the Department of Agriculture. This reorganization is intended to separate the rural development programs of the Farmers Home Administration (FmHA) from its farm operating and ownership programs.

Two new policies will be tested in pilot projects to be established in five states (Conference Committee Report on FACT, 1990, Chapter XXIII). The first pilot project will focus on the coordination of state, federal, and local rural development programming and financing. State rural economic development panels composed of state, federal, local, and private-sector representatives will establish priorities for the use of FmHA funding for projects within the state based on state and locally developed economic development plans created at the state or local level. A limited amount of funds will be allowed to be shifted from category to category. The second pilot project will test rural revolving loan funds as a means to increase rural capital availability. In five states, state, local, and private entities will be eligible to apply for federal seed money to establish revolving loan funds. Both pilot projects are authorized to begin October 1, 1991. It should be noted that an appropriation for the revolving loan fund was not made for fiscal year 1991.

These two pilot projects are interesting from a policy perspective, because they are, in principle, based on the idea that decision making about rural development priorities should take place at the state and local levels. In each instance, the legislation intends that project decisions be made by local organizations or panels of state, local, and private-sector representatives. Although many will find flaws in these models, they do represent a significant shift in thinking about the federal role in rural development.

FUTURE STATE AND FEDERAL ACTIVITIES

Debates over rural development policy will continue, as states and the federal government try to find effective and affordable ways to assist rural communities. These issues will be facing policy makers in the next few years, as a slowing national economy results in slow growth and possible declines in state revenues. Given all the competing priorities and interests vying for state and federal funds, how will rural areas fare?

There are several serious questions to be answered: Is the current emphasis on rural development a fair-weather phenomenon? Were state policy makers only willing to look beyond their urban constituencies because of the relative prosperity of the late 1980s? What will happen to rural areas in the period of slower growth and possible recession many are predicting for the early 1990s? How will the population shifts of the 1980s and the resulting shifts in congressional and statehouse representation affect the rural policy debate?

CONCLUSIONS

Rural development policy in America is changing to reflect the critical importance of local initiative and involvement in successful economic development. This recognition can be seen in a number of states involved in leadership programs, in the restructuring of community development programs to emphasize local capacity building, and in the inclusion of local government and private-sector participants in rural policy development activities at the state and federal levels. The increasing recognition of the important contribution of local businesses and local entrepreneurial activity and in many communities, a decreasing reliance on recruitment as the only development strategy are also indications that the real responsibility and capacity for community development must be based in the community.

At a time when federal resources for rural development have been declining and when many states are facing tight budgets, state and federal development officials are realizing that government cannot be the only player in the rural development game. Private-sector involvement is key to many of the efforts described before, from policy development to financing.

States are continuing to innovate to meet the varying needs of their diverse rural areas. New policy initiatives are being designed to be flexible, and states are working harder to make sure that rural citizens have access to rural development assistance.

The federal rural development initiatives have been described by some federal officials as "getting our act together" and "learning how to do business differently." It is certainly a difficult but essential challenge to face when resources are limited. The initiatives are focusing on building constructive, cooperative partnerships with states, local government, and the private sector to focus limited resources on rural problems in a coordinated fashion that takes into account local and state development plans. This certainly represents an ambitious and positive step for the federal government.

NOTES

1. For examples of new state spending or tax programs to aid general-purpose local government, see Marcia Howard, *Fiscal Survey of the States*, National Governors Association, National Association of State Budget Officers, September 1990, p. 7.

2. Survey released at a press conference January 2, 1991, National Governors Association of State Budget Officers.

3. The CGPA Rural Academy project was funded by the Ford Foundation, the Aspen Institute, and the W. K. Kellogg Foundation. Cooperators for the Academy included the Corporation for Enterprise Development, the National Governors Association, the Western Governors Association, and the Economic Research Service and the Extension Service of USDA.

4. At this writing, the new administration in Michigan had not taken a position on the Academy team's report.

5. Funders include the W. K. Kellogg Foundation, University of Illinois Cooperative Extension Service, Soyland Power Cooperative, GTE, Illinois Bell, the Illinois Rural Affairs Council, Illinois Institute for Rural Affairs, and the Illinois Department of Commerce and Community Affairs.

10. Local Economic Development Projects: Key Factors

Jan and Cornelia Flora

INTRODUCTION

The many factors that contribute to economic and community development can be divided into two major categories: economic infrastructure and social infrastructure. Economic infrastructure includes man-made structures, such as streets, buildings, and utilities; economic institutions, such as banks and service production firms; and economically significant locational characteristics, such as distance from and transportation links to a major city, and natural resource attributes. Social infrastructure includes intangible social factors, such as culture, entrepreneurship, the quality of social interaction, and social equality (Swanson, forthcoming).

The social infrastructure of communities can be conceptualized in three parts. The first is social institutions including local government, social service institutions, voluntary organizations (including civic groups, churches, political groups, recreational associations, and so on). The second is human resources, which include attributes of inhabitants, such as their technical expertise, organizational skills, educational levels, and even social structure (class, race, ethnicity, gender, and so on). The third is the characteristics of social networks including innovativeness, ability to mobilize resources within the community, and ability to link up with outside expertise and information.

Although all of the elements mentioned are important contributors to community development, this chapter will focus specifically on two factors: location characteristics and characteristics of social networks. To this end, this chapter begins with an examination of measures of economic development, looking in detail at the definition of economic development implied in each measure. Secondly, a series of social infrastructural characteristics are explored, with particular attention paid to those characteristics that are present in communities that have successfully generated economic development, in spite of locational limits.

A case study of a community-based attempt at economic development is used to illustrate how the networks function.

MEASURES OF ECONOMIC DEVELOPMENT

Since Effrat (1974), rural communities have been conventionally defined as ''the complete territorial community . . . (where) the residents comprise a community that is a relatively self-contained social environment supplying its members with a wide range of services.''[1] Midwestern communities are generally considered examples of the complete territorial community (Lynd, 1929; Lynd and Lynd, 1937; Moe and Taylor, 1942; West, 1945; Gallaher, 1961; Lyford, 1962). The idea of the ''complete territorial community'' has been criticized (Stein, 1960), but from a theoretical, not an applied, standpoint.

However, it can be argued that from the initial period of white settlement, midwestern territorial communities did not serve as the singular locus for residence, work, social, and consumption activities. In particular, residence and place of work often shifted depending on economic conditions. For example, place of work shifted suddenly in response to droughts or bumper crops, macroeconomic shifts, or the emergence or decline of particular modes of transportation. Consequently, household size expanded and contracted as members left or returned to their residences (Flora and Stitz, 1985). Likewise, places where people chose to shop shifted as the railroad came, and went, and as motor cars and improved roads reduced the limitations of space and time (Hudson, 1985).

In the post-World War II period, the combination of improvements in the personal automobile and the development of the interstate highway system, and technical changes in agriculture, particularly mechanization, leading to a replacement of capital for labor in farming, contributed to important shifts in location of employment. People were further freed from the need to live and work in the same place.

The retail merchandising revolution, based on name brand advertising, coupled with chain store and franchise development, loosened the linkage between residency and shopping location. School consolidation immediately after World War II and hospital consolidation in the 1980s are examples of the separation of residence and location of services. Beginning in the 1970s and accelerating in the 1980s, deregulation of transportation and banking, the weakening of the bargaining power of labor, and the development of a virtually worldwide labor market contributed to employment shifts. The relationship between where people worked and where they lived in the rural Midwest was further weakened.

Because of this weakening of the territorial community, the assumed interchangeability among indicators of community economic development no longer applies. By the late 1980s, research in one midwestern state, Kansas, found no correlation between any of the three different kinds of measures of economic development relating where one lived, worked, or shopped. Changes in popu-

Table 10.1
Comparison of Measures of Community/Economic Development

Development Strategy	Indicator	Function
Industrial attraction	Employment change	Where people work
Amenity/service enhancement	Population change	Where people live
Advertising/downtown improvement	Change in retail sales/ establishments	Where people shop

lation size, in retail trade, and in income were unrelated to one another using correlation analysis (Flora, Tan, and Flora, 1989). Further, even if those efforts to influence one variable, such as employment, are successful, the assumed concomitant improvement in the other variables, such as population and retail trade, may not follow and quality of life may not improve.

Economic/community development practitioners and many rural community theorists have assumed the existence of a single locus for residence, production, and consumption activities. As a result, they have rarely analyzed the implications of alternatively emphasizing different indicators for economic development efforts. For example, the thorough literature review of determinants of economic growth prepared for the National Governor's Association (John, Batie, and Norris, 1989) carefully classifies studies on economic growth in terms of the independent variables used: increasing resource availability, advancing technology, expanding markets, conquering geographic space, and building institutions, after Edwards (1981). This review, however, is not clear on what indicator of economic growth was used as a dependent variable.

The indicator of success chosen—population retention (residence), employment creation (work), or vitality of retail trade and service activities (consumption)—influences the strategy chosen for economic development. The literature on each indicator of economic development in the rural Midwest shows the significance of selecting each approach over the others (see Table 10.1).

Factors Influencing Employment Change

John, Batie, and Norris (1989) examined contributors to employment change in nonmetropolitan counties of seven farm belt states between 1979 and 1984. They found that location (presence of an interstate highway, adjacency to a metropolitan area, presence of a state university in the county) was not related to change in employment. Industrial mix, well-being of the population (measured by percent of adults with some postsecondary education and by per-capita income), and federal spending on development programs also had no significant impact on change in employment. The only significant location variable was percentage of commuters. This was attributed to commuters bringing money back to their county of residence, which then turns over several times in the community, thereby generating jobs. Other significant variables included employment change in the state (positive relationship) and dependency ratio (the higher the dependency ratio, the more likely employment was to grow). This finding suggests that transfer payments to retired people have generated jobs, much as occurs with commuters. Not unexpectedly, past employment growth during the 1970s fostered continued employment growth.

Many scholars examined only one aspect of employment growth. The factor most often used to indicate economic development is manufacturing growth. Eberts (1985) reported that a variety of public investments in roads, airports, water and sewage systems, and education were related to growth in manufacturing. Young (1986) found that industrial location was influenced by the presence of highways. McGranahan, in examining communities in Northwest Wisconsin, found that growth in manufacturing in the 1970s, the period of the migration turnaround, occurred in smaller communities and those with the least manufacturing employment at the beginning of the period. Receipt of state and federal economic development and infrastructure grants also contributed to manufacturing employment growth (McGrananan, 1984, p. 537). These results indirectly suggest that social networking with the outside was more important than central location in generating industrial employment growth.

More recent studies have found that industries other than manufacturing are related to employment growth in midwestern rural communities. Retired persons have had a positive impact on employment generation in rural communities through transfer payments that they receive—principally Social Security retirement benefits and Medicare payments (Flora et al., 1990, p. 98). The elderly are also more likely to shop and use services close to home than are younger members of the community. Thus, the retired population may be an important base for employment generation, particularly in service and retail sectors (Li and MacLean, 1989).

The employment generation approach has as an implicit assumption that one job is as good as another. Thus, the emphasis on increasing employment frequently results in efforts to attract low-wage industrial and service-sector jobs. In the current segmented employment system, these are generally ''female,'' or what are called euphemistically ''secondary'' jobs. Although they may increase family income, they are not effective in bringing in new families or in retaining those who are on the verge of leaving. Although some employment may be generated for people who are from outside the community, commitment to the new job often is insufficient to encourage the occupant to move to the community where the job is located. Thus, low-wage employment contributes to the separation of residence from employment.

A more sophisticated approach than indiscriminate industrial recruitment or a generalized retention and expansion program aimed at existing businesses and one that permits industrial targeting is shift/share analysis. The community or county is compared with the nation, the region, or (although this is rarely done) with other similar communities to determine which categories of firms (defined in at least two-digit SIC codes) in the community (county) are severely lacking (Hustedde, Shaffer, and Pulver, 1984, pp. 45–58). This analysis indicates the types of firms that could be recruited or established.

This mechanism is not based on theory and fails to answer the question, "Is the present distribution of income or output from the various sectors in the comparison group/unit desirable?" It does not define the comparative advantage of the community/county under consideration. Only by placing the sectoral comparisons into a dynamic historical context can prescriptive action follow. A smaller share for a specific sector in the community under study compared with the region may indicate that community "X" is in the advance guard or the rear guard. One cannot tell from the ratios alone, but must also have some knowledge of growth sectors. A related question involves selecting the comparison group/unit. What is an appropriate comparison group?

Finally, once a community/county identifies a "deficiency"—a potential growth area for a community—how then can that gap be filled? These questions all seem self-evident, but in reality, are often not asked, or certainly not answered satisfactorily. However, when these larger questions are answered, shift/share analysis is a useful tool in targeting industries or service firms that provide "primary" jobs and that the community has a chance of obtaining.

Population/Migration Change

Focusing on population change assumes that communities with population growth, or actual inmigration, are undergoing community or economic development. Communities with declining populations are viewed as experiencing a decline in viability as a community. Many studies by rural sociologists have examined population change as an important indicator of development (Beale, 1975; Beale and Fuguitt, 1985; Cook, 1987). However, development practitioners and community leaders who identify a declining or stagnant population as a problem often do not pursue development strategies appropriate to the perceived problem.

Practitioners and community leaders generally emphasize job creation as a means of population retention, but the growing separation of residence from work makes this an inefficient approach to population retention, for the geographic community. Thus, the peculiar phenomenon arises of places engaging in industrial recruitment and tax abatement generating as much employment for their neighbors as themselves. In a study of northwestern Wisconsin by Mc-

Granahan, when controlling for ecological and relevant social and political variables, manufacturing employment growth during the 1970s made no contribution to population growth; the standardized regression coefficient was zero (McGranahan, 1984, p. 537).

Johansen and Fuguitt (1990) report that because of commuting, population growth may not be a very useful indicator of economic growth. The use of Labor Market Areas (LMAs) as units of analysis is one method of dealing with this problem, but LMA research, although growing in importance, is rarely linked to the community research tradition.[2] Furthermore, there may be little social reality to a LMA. The *only* thing linking one to the larger area is a paycheck.

Often, communities facing a population loss seek to recruit, expand, or start firms that pay low wages, because those firms are the easiest to attract. Although this may improve family incomes, it is an inefficient way of attracting inmigrants. Krannich and Humphrey's 1983 study of Pennsylvania in the 1970s, confirms this.[3] They examined the relationship between mobilization for growth and population change. Mobilization was strongly associated with a critical mass of managers, proprietors, and officials. It was measured by a scale that included organizing a committee to seek new businesses, developing contacts with outside firms, applying for government funds to expand local business activities, and seeking private investors to expand local business activities. The results showed a slightly negative relationship between mobilization and subsequent population change, with controls for such factors as previous population change, population size, and centrality. The study does not determine whether mobilization led to job creation; we only know that it was not successful in generating population growth.

Often community leaders define the population problem as a lack of employment opportunities for young people; they would like to reduce the number of young people exiting the community. A study of inmigrants, outmigrants, and stayers in rural counties of Kansas in the late 1970s indicated that a strategy to retain youth is difficult, and probably not desirable. Inmigrants during this rural renaissance period were predominantly families with young children who had significantly higher educational levels than did either outmigrants or stayers (Flora et al., 1978). Thus, a better strategy than preventing youth outmigration is to attract families in the ''full-nest'' stage of the life cycle, thereby increasing the quality of human resources in the community. This requires a two-prong strategy: creation of quality jobs and amenity/service enhancement. In particular, the quality of schools is especially important to this age group.

Basing economic development on population retention or growth can relate, in specific ways, to employment generation. The employment generated should bring in new families. Thus, this approach should result in the generation of ''primary'' jobs, those that pay well enough to support the primary income earner in the family (who may be of either gender) rather than ''secondary'' (largely female or youth) jobs.

An alternative population-attraction approach is to recruit retirees, many of whom have adequate disposable incomes and skills useful to the community. According to Glasgow, "Older people who move from an urban to a rural area are more affluent than the nonmigrant, long-term elderly populations they join" (Glasgow and Beale, 1985, p. 23). Li and MacLean (1989) studied changes in the rural elderly population and effects on small town economies in Saskatchewan between 1971 and 1986. They report that an increase in elderly population was correlated with an increase in retail sales, over and above the expected influence of distance from a major city, change in total population, and local economic conditions. Furthermore, midwestern counties (located principally in scenic areas of the Lake States, including Michigan, Wisconsin, Minnesota, and the Missouri Ozarks) attracting elderly also attract younger persons.

There are two main disadvantages to recruiting the elderly. The first is that the employment generated as a result of an influx of elderly residents is often in low-paying service jobs. Secondly, older inmigrants are less likely than younger inmigrants to support tax increases for social services (Glasgow, 1985, pp. 8–9).

Retail Trade and Services

In considering the economic development of a community, it is also important to assess how effective the community is in capturing retail purchases by its residents and those in neighboring communities. Using a set of indicators to measure retail trade activity yields yet a third approach to community development. This approach is associated with the functionalist concept of social differentiation and with the human ecological concept of central place function. It places emphasis on retention of functions or on obtaining new ones. Performance can be measured by changes in numbers or types of functionally separate consumer activities or by changes in more readily available measures of retail sales or other types of service-sector income (Young and Young, 1973, pp. 24–26). The dominant development strategy developed to increase retail trade is downtown revitalization/historic preservation.

Several studies have reported that proximity to urban centers negatively influences retail sales growth in rural towns (Harden, 1960; Johansen and Fuguitt, 1973). They suggest that urban centers often compete with small towns for business within a dynamic central-place hierarchy. Stone's study of the impact of retail merchandising chains—in this case Wal-Mart—on the trading area is a case in point (Stone, 1988). Stone found that acquisition of a Wal-Mart store contributed to a net increase in retail sales in a community, although certain kinds of existing stores, in direct competition with Wal-Mart, suffered. However, smaller towns in the outskirts of communities with a newly acquired Wal-Mart compared with other communities of a similar size experienced substantially greater declines in total retail sales.

Straightforward indexes such as the pull factor (Darling and Tan, 1988) have tracked the retail trade performance of counties. However, such data are not collected uniformly—and certainly not on an annual basis for nonmetropolitan places. Central places, such as trade centers, by definition have higher pull factors than places or counties on the outskirts, because certain goods and services are purchased too infrequently to support a firm devoted to the sale of that item or service in a smaller community.

The importance of a comparison of pull factors is often not explored. Why does community "X" have a low pull factor compared with its neighbors? If its pull factor is declining, does that imply a decline in quality of life? What can be done to restore the community to its previous grandeur or to return it to the same level as neighbors with similar characteristics? What control do communities have over siting decisions made by large-chain general-merchandise stores such as Wal-Mart?

The applied retail trade approach to economic development involves communities (counties) calculating their pull factors and comparing themselves with other similar communities (or with themselves at earlier points in time). They then seek to redress the imbalance by encouraging people to shop locally (advertising), by investing in downtown improvement (including historic preservation), and by recruiting retail or service firms. In a nationwide study of rural self-development projects, the historic preservation and renovation projects were found to generate the least jobs per dollar invested. Further, those jobs created tended to be lower-paying (Green et al., 1991).

SOCIAL INFRASTRUCTURE AND COMMUNITY ECONOMIC DEVELOPMENT

In assessing keys to community/economic development, it is important to keep in mind both means and ends. Population retention, job creation, and retail trade all are means to an end. The ends include improved quality of life, as well as intangible elements, such as job satisfaction, a feeling of efficacy, and participation in decisions affecting one's life.

Scholars are coming to view social infrastructure as a major mechanism for overcoming the constraints of economic infrastructure (Swanson, forthcoming). As more and more responsibility is placed on local communities to generate needed resources, the human capital and social organizations and institutions present in a community become key elements in economic development (Blakely, 1989).

Several key factors of social infrastructure influence community economic development (Wall and Luther, 1987; Flora and Flora, 1990). By using a case study approach, social infrastructure has been identified. This, in conjunction with location in a central-place hierarchy and access to natural resources, can explain why certain communities are successful at community/economic development and others are not.

Crucial social infrastructure variables for community development revolve around several types of internal and external community linkages (networks). These linkages foster information flow and participation by a large proportion of the local citizens that, in turn, enhance the development process. The presence of the linkages discussed leads to numerous attempts at community economic development. Not all such efforts are successful. Yet the participatory nature of a high density of linkages within and among communities allows a fairly high proportion of activities attempted to take root in the community and to add to its social fiber.

Midwestern communities (Flora et al., forthcoming) have structural characteristics that contribute to strong internal linkages, although the level and kinds of linkages vary from community to community. Fallows' (1989) concept of "radius of trust" is helpful in understanding the propensity of midwestern communities to collaborate, for community economic development. Radius of trust defines boundaries between one's own kind and those who are outsiders. The radius of trust extends to the entire geographic community, and often beyond, in the rural Midwest.

By contrast, it is much more difficult to encompass the entire geographic community in rural communities in the South. There are several reasons for this including greater stratification in the rural South, economic inequality, the legacy of race, and, in particular, the cultural recognition of clearly distinct social groups based on race and class. In the Midwest, even though important class differences exist, because those differences are not socially recognized, the radius of trust extends to all groups in the community. These differences between the two sections of the country arise from the way in which they were settled. Settlement of the rural Midwest occurred during conditions of labor scarcity, whereas slavery in the South guaranteed abundant labor. Thus, a permanent subservient class did not develop in the Midwest, and although social mobility was limited, there was a dominant belief that people could ascend in the social order, and if they did not do so, the blame rested as much on them as on the social structure itself. Pfeffer (1983) provides a discussion of the historical differences between the two regions.

The term "just plain folks," used by Vidich and Bensman (1958) with regard to a northeastern village, also captures the essence of midwestern rural communities quite well. Settlement patterns in the Northeast were much like the Midwest. The survey of nonmetropolitan self-development projects showed that a disproportionate number of such projects were in the Midwest. Further, the type of projects that predominated in the Midwest were ones that "represented" the entire geographic community; self-development projects in the South were more likely to be projects of a particular social class grouping that did not reach the entire community (Green et al., 1991). This concept is similar to what is at least a rudimentary level of community solidarity (Young, 1970). Obviously, some midwestern communities manifest this characteristic to a greater degree than do others. Wall and Luther (1987, p. 26) suggest that this is an important clue to rural community survival and call it "evidence of community pride," seen in neatly trimmed yards, well-kept parks, community festivals, and events that emphasize history and heritage (John, Batie, Norris, 1989, p. 43).

The existence of social linkages is examined through a case study of Decatur County, Kansas, and its county seat, Oberlin. Decatur County, a farming community located in the northwest corner of Kansas, has fewer than 5,000 residents, and its population is declining. Decatur has developed social linkages over the past 25 years, qualifying it as an entrepreneurial community.

Decatur County has a history as an entrepreneurial community begun in the early 1960s. Economic development efforts originated with the formation of the Oberlin Industrial Development Company in 1962. In quick response to the establishment of regional planning commissions throughout the state, a Decatur County planning commission was formed in 1968. In 1969, the county planning commission became involved in regional hospital planning, which included a survey of hospital facilities for participation in Hill–Burton funding to improve the hospital and add a long-term nursing care unit. In 1970, the Decatur County Area Chamber of Commerce (DCCC) was formed, replacing the Chambers of the three towns in the county. The first projects of the newly formed DCCC were a countywide community-betterment committee, construction of aluminum canopies over the sidewalks on the principal block of the main street of Oberlin, commissioning and erecting a pioneer statue at the entrance of Oberlin, and organizing a feedlot and a dairy. Another project, which was not part of the original plan, was a home-grown carnival. These projects came to fruition in the early 1970s.

The fact that the radius of trust extended to the entire county contributed to Decatur County's ability to organize a home-grown carnival. In turn, the carnival has contributed to the expansion and deepening of that radius of trust over the years, as groups from all over the county cooperate in working at the carnival. Likewise, the economic benefits of the carnival are spread throughout the county. This has facilitated other economic development projects.

The county's most important festivals are the 4-H fair and the community-run carnival. In 1972, the contracted carnival notified the Decatur County 4-H Fair Board that it would not come that year. This notice precipitated a trip by two carloads of people from Decatur County to Hydro, Oklahoma, during their carnival to see how a locally owned carnival functioned.

The Decatur County Amusement Authority was formed as a nonprofit corporation within the DCCC. The carnival started in 1973 with a ferris wheel, locally constructed kiddy rides, a pony ride, and locally built game stands. A grandstand, a miniature train ride, and numerous other rides were added over the years, with local contributions of labor, supplies, and money. The carnival has operated every year for 5 days in August since 1973. Booths are staffed by local organizations and individuals in 2-hour shifts. All profits go to the Amusement Authority for community projects, including subsidizing maintenance costs of the community-owned movie theater.

Radius of trust is necessary for development-oriented linkages to occur. More specific characteristics of entrepreneurial communities are discussed in what follows with examples from Oberlin/Decatur County.

Flexible, Dispersed Community Leadership

Formal and informal leadership posts are rotated, with newcomers (those who have not lived in the community all their adult lives) accepted into leadership positions. The Heartland Center describes it as a participatory approach to community decision making—a situation in which power is deliberately shared. This approach includes such elements as a deliberate transition of power to a younger generation of leaders and an acceptance of women in both elected and appointed leadership roles.

This participatory approach contrasts with the findings of John et al., who report, "It was commonly found that one individual plays the role of 'sparkplug,' maintaining the partnership [of local leaders] through good times and bad" (John, Batie, Norris, 1989, p. 40). Although certainly towns have depended on one individual to keep things going, current research indicates that community leadership for successful economic development must depend on more than one person.

In the early 1970s, Decatur County citizens organized a feedlot and a dairy by selling shares to residents. In the mid–1980s, in response to the farm crisis, community investors provided seed money to establish a bus coach factory and a boat factory. In each case, local leaders organized the firms. More recently, a group of younger leaders has emerged to organize the boat-building company. The leadership in the bus coach firm included many who had been involved in the feed yard and dairy. The person who bridged the old and the new groups was a former county extension agent who took on the managership of the faltering dairy. When the dairy failed, he subsequently became the partner in a local elevator and feed, seed, and fertilizer store. As an outsider (although he had married into a local family), he had obtained positions of leadership in the community. His predecessor as county agent had also played an important role in community leadership and is still viewed with respect. In this midwestern farming-dependent community it is difficult—but certainly not impossible—for outsiders to assume positions of leadership.

However, persons living outside the community obtained positions of leadership only through technical expertise. Three of the five members of the board of directors of the bus coach firm are outsiders, and one is a woman. She also directs the Small Business Development Center in the area. Otherwise, the integration of women into the leadership structure is incomplete.

The flexibility in accepting new people in leadership positions was threatened by a controversy over the salary of the city administrator, who was recruited from outside of the community. The position was created in the mid–1980s and included economic development efforts on behalf of Oberlin. Many thought he was paid too much, although compared with other professionals in the state, the salary was quite modest. The salary controversy masked a deeper issue—resentment by voluntary community leaders that they had all worked for free. After more than 3 years on the job, the city administrator resigned. How the successor will fare is uncertain. Serious conflicts seem to emerge when a community attempts to make the transition from economic development volunteers to a paid staff. Strategies for sustaining a moderate to high level of volunteerism once a professional staff person is hired need to be investigated.

Private Investment and Local Infrastructure Improvements

John, Batie, and Norris (1989) describe several characteristics of a progrowth attitude. First, key people must be willing and able to commit the necessary time, effort, and resources to help firms solve problems. Second, they must be willing to take risks to create wealth. They also mention the contribution of local banks in nearly half of the communities where rapid job growth has taken place. The Heartland Center promotes a willingness to invest in the betterment of the community for future generations through sound and well-maintained infrastructure, and careful use of fiscal resources, implying frugality, but accompanied by a willingness to spend appropriately (Wall and Luther, 1987, pp. 27–9).

Decatur County, although its agriculture is based on family farms, has farms larger than average in that area of the state. In general, Decatur is a prosperous county. This ''surplus'' capital appears to have facilitated wealthier investment in community-based enterprises, several of which were rather risky ventures. The approximately $500,000 raised from among local citizens through contributions averaging approximately $1,000 each for the bus coach and for the boat companies was quite remarkable. Local bankers also supported economic development efforts, although they required a first mortgage when they invested bank funds.

Similar fund-raising efforts occurred for the feedlot and the dairy. In spite of having taken those earlier risks, ''investors'' were willing to take the plunge again during the crisis of the mid–1980s. The dairy had failed and investors received only part of their investment. Investors would have lost money in the feedlot venture had not a local man—also one of the initial investors—agreed to buy out his partners at 100 cents on the dollar. Considerable volunteer time was spent on these private for-profit community efforts, as well as on the carnival.

Acceptance of Controversy and the Depersonalization of Politics

In rural communities, members know one another in various roles. This role homogeneity often leads to a tendency to repress controversy, because of a fear that confronting people (or their relatives) in one of their roles may lead to problems in another setting. Hence, rather than issues being aired, they remain pent up. When they do emerge, an explosion is likely and possibly a community rift. Similarly, because everyone knows each other, discussion of politics in rural communities tends to emphasize personalities rather than issues.

Although several other institutions, such as churches, can ameliorate or exacerbate these tendencies, the local newspaper is particularly important in setting the tenor for handling controversy in the community. By regularly airing controversial issues, it can serve as a safety valve, allowing controversy to be a normal part of community life.

In Decatur County, the newspaper editor (there have been two in the period under consideration) has been active in economic development issues. He has also reported issues fully and has not let biases overwhelm the reporting. Thus, although considerable controversy arose among investors as to how the dairy should be managed, its failure did not prevent community leaders from trying new projects in the mid–1980s. Even after the loss of some $500,000 of citizens' money in the bus and boat schemes, participants voiced few recriminations. The weekly progress and setbacks of the bus and boat factories were reported in the newspaper with only modest boosterism, and no effort to cover up bad news.

Thus, politically oriented networks are likely to contribute to an antidevelopment orientation, through emphasis on personalities rather than policies, and through the suppression of the healthy controversy. However, the character of those networks can be mediated by institutions such as the newspaper.

Vertical and Horizontal Linkages

Entrepreneurial communities seek information and resources from similar communities and from state and federal sources. The Heartland Center lists several clues to survival that relate to information seeking and alliances. The first is knowledge of the physical environment and the competition. The second is an awareness of the importance of location. The third is sophisticated use of information resources to provide knowledge about one's own community, beyond the knowledge base within the community. Finally it is essential to be willing to seek help from the outside (Wall and Luther, 1987, pp. 27, 29).

John et al. (1989) also indicate that external support is important. They found 64 instances of federal or state assistance to the 102 growth firms in the 16 rapid-growth counties that they studied.

McGranahan related linkages with the larger system to population growth. He found that communities in which top politicoeconomic elites made regular (nonshopping) trips outside the community were more likely to increase both manufacturing employment and to experience population growth (McGranahan, 1984, p. 537). McGranahan concludes that extralocal participation is a more successful growth strategy than mobilization. In more precise terms, "a major part of growth promotion activity takes place outside of the public domain through the privately coordinated actions of developers, bankers, utility owners, and others with strong proprietary interests in growth" (McGranahan, 1984, p. 538).

This complex of interests is what Molotch (1976) has called the "growth machine." He suggests that linkages with the outside can be individual, rather than collective, and do not contribute to the strengthening of internal social networks. It may be that different kinds of external linkages predominate in different periods. The latter part of the 1970s—the period of McGranahan's study—was a rather quiescent time with respect to community/economic development efforts; thus, individual linkages with the outside would have predominated.

Oberlin/Decatur County has generated both vertical and horizontal linkages. Leaders in the county stay informed on state programs, and apply for them whenever appropriate. They are well-experienced in using horizontal linkages to gain project-specific know-how from neighboring communities. Individuals or groups of residents are often sent to similar communities to learn about projects, which are then adapted to the home community. These residents are carefully selected, with an eye to the type of support they may offer to the project. For example, when Decatur County decided to institute a "home-grown" carnival, among the residents sent to investigate the proceedings in another community were a banker and a newspaper publisher. Both of these members were then able to provide practical support for the Decatur carnival project.

It is important to note that while Oberlin/Decatur County seeks information and resources from the outside, they are willing to combine those resources with resources from their own community.

Importance of Social Infrastructure

The Heartland Center describes a surviving community as one with a strong belief in and support of education, coupled with a problem-solving approach to providing health care. They argue that in communities with effective survival strategies, good schools are a point of pride; the school is also a center of social activity. Sporting and other school events are well-attended.

An opposing point of view holds that in entrepreneurial communities there is an emphasis on academics not on sports. Strong boosterism in sports can divert attention and resources away from academic programs. John, Batie, and Norris (1989) emphasize that business leaders interviewed in their high-growth farm-belt communities were also committed to excellence in the school system, not only as a drawing card for recruiting efforts, but as a way of maintaining a well-educated work force and citizenry. Oberlin is a good example of a community that invests in social infrastructure: its concern with economic development does not distract it from recognizing the importance of schools, hospitals, and other infrastructure.

During the oil boom of the 1970s, Haliburton, one of the world's largest oil field service companies, located a regional office in Oberlin, partly because of its location near the center of several oil fields, but also because of Oberlin's good school system. Haliburton was not recruited (although it did locate in the industrial park), but Oberlin's preparedness paid off. For its size and location, Oberlin has quite extraordinary health care facilities. It has a county hospital, five medical doctors (including a surgeon), and two long-term care facilities, one skilled and one intermediate. In 1989, a bond issue to expand the hospital passed when other rural county hospitals were struggling merely to survive. It is interesting to note that the bond issue passed during the same period that the bus coach and the boat factories were in serious trouble, and investors were in danger of losing their money.

Ability to Expand the Geographic Boundaries of a Community

As population declines and/or services are shared or consolidated, there often is a need to collaborate beyond the geographic community and to recognize that the boundaries are flexible and variable.

In 1970, a dynamic and organizationally minded County Extension Agent organized a meeting of the Decatur County Planning Commission (established 2 years earlier), and the Chambers of Commerce of Oberlin, Norcatur, and Jennings (the two smaller communities in the county). The result was the abolition of the individual Chambers of Commerce and the creation of the Decatur County Area Chamber of Commerce (DCCC). The carnival, the dairy, the feedlot, and some smaller ventures were all projects of the DCCC. The Amusement Authority, which runs the carnival and manages funds generated from the carnival for social and economic development projects, is an arm of the DCCC and assists projects in all three communities. The conflicts often found among the towns in Midwestern counties have been significantly moderated because of the creation and activities of the DCCC.

Decatur County has done less well in extending its boundaries to include other nearby counties or communities. When its industrial park was full in the mid–1970s, the county dropped its membership in the North West Kansas Regional Planning Commission (NWKRPC), although the county still sought advice from the NWKRPC! Only recently has the county reactivated its membership.

CONCLUSIONS

Midwestern rural communities face enormous obstacles in a changing economic climate biased against the rural heartland. However, they have many advantages, based on a high level of social infrastructure that facilitates local community economic development efforts. Although location and economic infrastructure remain important, mobilization of the local population with an increased flow of information is important also. Increasing the density of local and extralocal networks can overcome functional limitations.

The results of these local community development efforts, however, are likely to be modest. One cannot expect dramatic increases in employment, population, or retail sales. Efforts often focus on improving one element, and are most successful when designed primarily to meet the local population needs, rather than to attract new residents. The modest population increase that may result is accomplished without the attraction of low-wage employment. Emphasis on information flow through networking often leads to a wider spread of development benefits, although the total growth in any individual indicator may not be as large as with externally generated change.

Attention to building human infrastructure means that communities systematically evaluate the impact of past actions, are aware of the larger social and economic context, and adjust strategies based on past experience. This not only ensures improvement in the general quality of life in the community, but also the process itself increases the quality of life of community residents.

NOTES

1. Effrat places the following approaches within that tradition: Human ecology [and the related central-place theory, we would argue], research based on the rural–urban continuum, community power-structure studies, and the functionalist ''community as social system'' approach (1974, p. 5).

2. The Economic Research Service of the U.S. Department of Agriculture has taken the lead in rural LMA research. Examples include Bloomquist and Killian (1988) and Killian and Hady (1988) .

3. Although they do not indicate whether the communities that they studied were actually seeking firms that paid low wages, it is probable that, because the communities were ones that were less central in the system and tended to be composed of persons of lower than average socioeconomic status, they were not in a position to be selective about the firms and activities that they recruited.

11. Rural America in the 1990s: A Tale of Two Cities

Mark Drabenstott

In his novel, *A Tale of Two Cities*, Charles Dickens began with these now famous words, "It was the best of times, it was the worst of times." These words described the dissimilar lives of two men who lived in different places but shared a common identity. So it is today in rural America. While the nation experienced eight years of economic expansion, the best period of peacetime economic growth in our nation's history, rural America did not participate fully in this economic journey. It has lagged far behind, with many farm and business victims.

The story, however, does not end with a simple contrast of the urban and rural situations. In rural America itself, we find a story within a story. Some rural places in the 1980s enjoyed the best of times. Retirement communities and some rural areas adjacent to our cities have enjoyed uninterrupted growth nearly matching, and in some cases exceeding, growth in the national economy. At the very same time, other rural places have suffered the worst of times. From closed farm-equipment dealers in Illinois to shut-down clothing factories in the small towns of Missouri to oil rigs stretched flat on the red earth of Oklahoma, traditional rural communities have keenly felt the downside of the 1980s.

The past decade shattered comfortable myths about rural America. Rural America is not a common farm economy; it is many economies, each with its separate strengths and weaknesses. In a world where complex global economic forces enter the deepest reaches of the heartland, the rural economy becomes a patchwork of strengths and weaknesses. Communities with leadership, skilled workers, and current technology will prosper as their products compete well on world markets. Communities with no leadership, unskilled workers, outdated technology, and inferior products will languish.

Confronted with a diverse rural economy that contains some pronounced pockets of weakness, policy makers at all levels are turning to rural development with renewed interest. Rural development is a topic with many lives—it last surfaced in the 1960s, only to be made seemingly redundant by the farm and energy booms of the 1970s.

What is it that spurs this new call for government intervention? Is it a desire to help the rural communities that have been left in the wake of economic expansion? Or is it a desire somehow to put rural America together again—into an economic whole that preserves all that we hold dear about these out-of-city places? It is in answering these questions that we begin to find the rudder that will guide policy measures for rural America.

To address this fundamental policy debate, three questions are relevant. First, how has the rural economy changed during the past decade? Second, given that change, what is the economic outlook for rural America in the decade ahead? And third, what, if anything, should policy makers be doing to change that outlook?

THE CHANGES IN THE RURAL ECONOMY IN THE 1980s

The disparate performance of the various parts of the rural economy is widely documented and broadly understood (Henry, Drabenstott, and Gibson, 1986; U.S. Department of Agriculture, 1987). A more useful starting point for this analysis may be a quick review of *why* rural economic growth has been uneven and generally weak. Three factors stand out in explaining the trend: international competition, the integration of rural places into national markets, and agriculture's drive toward concentration.

International Competition

Rural America was blindsided by world markets in the 1980s. In retrospect, it was the events of the 1970s that brought this about. In the 1970s, America's farmers came to believe that the world was running out of food, and that the 1980s would usher in a golden age when America's abundant farm resources would feed the world (at handsome rates of return). Similarly, in the 1970s, energy companies, whose development and production activities are concentrated in rural places, came to believe the world was running out of energy, and made enormous investments to expand production in the 1980s. Finally, America's rural factories grew complacent in the 1970s, as investment and productivity sagged.

In the 1980s, rural America learned that the products it makes not only are made elsewhere in the world, but they are also made more inexpensively and, in some cases, better. The world market in commodities became extraordinarily competitive, bringing hard times for rural businesses. U.S. farm exports fell more than a third from 1982 to 1986. The rural unemployment rate climbed above 10 percent in the early 1980s, as rural factories shut down. Since then, the rural jobless rate has remained above the urban rate, a turnaround from previous patterns.

The transition to a competitive international economy proved difficult in the 1980s because most rural places depend on just one industry. When the global market turns against that industry, the rural place has no safe harbor in other economic activity.

Thus, rural America enters the 1990s as part of an international market for food, energy, and other products. Competitiveness is the key word, causing new emphasis to be placed on technology, trained workers, and productivity.

Integrating Rural Places Into National Markets

Taken alone, the internationalization of rural America's major industries would have presented a stiff challenge in the 1980s. However, the challenge was compounded by other developments that removed some of the insulation in which rural America had historically wrapped itself. Simply put, a wave of deregulation in the 1980s brought rural America face to face with national market forces. In some cases, it was a rude introduction.

Financial market deregulation brought national money markets to rural savers and borrowers. Historically, country banks had paid little for their deposits and correspondingly charged low interest rates to farm and rural borrowers. Today, however, country banks must compete with Merrill Lynch, Sears, and Citibank for deposits. For most savers, the nearest bank can be reached by dialing a toll-free number. This has revolutionized rural financial markets and forced rural borrowers to compete for capital in national money markets. In short, rural businesses no longer have an indigenous interest-rate subsidy. Thus, the increased outflow of capital from rural places is not surprising.

Deregulation of the transportation industry has had a similar effect on rural places. Airfares to most rural places are higher than rates between major cities because there is less competition. It simply costs more to go to out-of-the-way places. And whether good or bad from an equity point of view, that is a market reality. In short, deregulation means rural America is no longer insulated from the rest of the economy. It has become part of the mainstream and, for better or for worse, rural America will feel the ebb and flow of the national economy much more than in the past.

Agriculture's Drive Toward Concentration

The third factor that is contributing to an uneven rural economy in the 1990s is agriculture's drive toward greater concentration. Spurred on by the farm financial crisis, agriculture underwent great structural change in the 1980s. Farm income and farm assets are now much more concentrated. The largest 300,000 farms control three-fourths of U.S. farm production. A marked decline in the number of farms and the corresponding concentration of farm production has profoundly affected rural America.

The decline in the numbers of farms means that farm production can be supported with less public and private infrastructure in rural places. Large farms tend to make business decisions based on a much larger market area. They may have direct marketing contracts, for example, with food processors some distance away, or they may arrange financing with major credit institutions in large cities. Thus, a concentration in farm production is being matched by a consolidation of agribusiness. Indeed, consolidation in the farm input and grain industries was a hallmark of the farm economy in the 1980s. With this consolidation has come a decrease in local agricultural businesses needed to sustain small farm communities. In short, the trend toward fewer farms is leading to fewer viable farm communities and to a general decline in public infrastructure in rural areas.

Put another way, farm prosperity will not bring prosperity to all farm communities. The weak businesses still found in many farm communities, after 4 years of record and near-record farm income, are evidence of that trend. Larger farms point toward fewer small rural communities in farm-dependent rural counties. Those communities large enough to serve as market centers for a large region will enjoy continued growth, as agribusiness services concentrate there.

Together, international competition, deregulation, and structural consolidation in agriculture go a long way toward explaining the unevenness of the rural economy in the 1980s. These factors describe a new rural reality: the rural economy is an integral part of national and international markets. No longer is the heartland insulated from the ups and downs of the macroeconomy.

THE RURAL ECONOMIC OUTLOOK FOR THE 1990s

After a decade of generally weak growth that was not shared equally, what is the outlook for the rural economy in the 1990s? The outlook suggests more unevenness, but given some painful adjustments in the 1980s, many segments of the rural economy appear well-positioned as the new decade unfolds.

Farm-Dependent Counties

Farm-dependent rural America enters the 1990s on comparatively solid footing. Farmers are in sound financial shape, after 4 years of robust recovery. Farm incomes are high, farmland values have recovered somewhat, and farm exports are rebounding. The recovery has been shared by farmers of nearly all commodities. Crop producers have generally done well, despite a severe drought in 1988. And livestock producers have put together the longest string of profitable years in memory.

Although this is a generally positive picture, two farm issues will have great impact on rural development: changes in farm and trade policy and the diminishing link between farm income and rural activity.

The agricultural outlook for the mid- and late–1990s will be heavily influenced by the outcome of the Uruguay Round of the General Agreement on Tariffs and Trade (GATT) negotiations, originally slated to conclude in December 1990.

No agreement could be reached on agriculture, however, so talks were suspended. Agriculture negotiations reached an impasse when the European Community resisted calls by the United States to end trade-distorting farm subsidies.

The round was recently revived by two actions. First, Congress gave the administration two more years to negotiate an agreement under favorable "fast-track" authority. Such authority requires Congress to vote up or down on an entire trade agreement without amending it. The original fast track authority granted when the Uruguay Round began was set to expire in June 1991. Second, the European Community has shown new willingness to table new proposals for reducing its internal farm subsidies. A new GATT accord to lower farm subidies is still not in focus, but there appear to be new forces moving the round toward an agreement.

The United States faces two possible outcomes. If the Uruguay Round succeeds, the United States will utilize its agricultural resources effectively and will stand to benefit from growth in world markets. Success in the GATT will mean fuller use of U.S. farm resources in total, a positive factor for many rural areas, but it will also mean shifting U.S. production to regions that are more competitive. This bodes well for central Illinois, but not for parts of Missouri, for example. If the Uruguay Round fails, the United States will face a world market crowded with supplies, and in all likelihood, U.S. producers will be called upon to take more acres out of production, causing serious damage to businesses in farm regions. Furthermore, if biotechnology unlocks new growth in the productivity of U.S. agriculture, the need to idle resources might be compounded still further.

The second farm-rural issue is the diminished link between farm income and rural economic activity. The record farm incomes of the past 4 years are testimony to a different economic multiplier in farm country. Farm income is now found in fewer pockets, and those individuals who have successful farms tend to spend their money further from home.

This trend probably will continue in the 1990s. Towns big enough to serve as trade centers for a sizeable farm region will prosper at the expense of the smaller towns nearby. Overall, population will decline in farm-dependent rural areas, a long-term trend that resumed in the 1980s after a brief hiatus in the 1970s.

Can farm-dependent communities reverse this economic decline? In general, the answer appears to be no. However, the one avenue that farming regions can consider is to add value to farm production before it leaves the region. Farm states are already singling out food processing as an economic development strategy (Barkema and Drabenstott, 1990). For many farming communities, the success of value-added efforts will determine their future. Producing bulk farm commodities will likely be a low-margin business in the 1990s; many other countries will be vying for world markets. Those farmers and rural businesses that are innovative in adding value to their farm output will benefit handsomely, relative to bulk commodities. States where the food industry is already well-established, such as Illinois and Wisconsin, have a sizeable lead in this race to process more food nearer to farms. Still, the number of food products for which this strategy will work is probably less than rural advocates would like to admit.

Manufacturing-Dependent Counties

Rural manufacturing counties will have a difficult decade again in the 1990s. Rural manufacturers will continue to face unrelenting competition from foreign producers. Simply stated, foreign labor is cheaper than rural U.S. labor. To compete more effectively, the labor-intensive factories now scattered across rural states must update their plants, relocate, or shut down. Investment in new plant and equipment may be impractical if long-term interest rates are held high by the ongoing credit demands of the federal government. At best, rural manufacturing may advance slightly in the 1990s. At worst, the number of rural factory jobs could erode substantially.

Retirement-Dependent Counties

Retirement communities should continue their robust growth in the 1990s. The aging U.S. population will result in an ever-growing number of consumers seeking retirement amenities. By the year 2000, the number of U.S. citizens over 65 will grow nearly 15 percent to about 35 million. Many of these retirees were born in rural America and they may remember its virtues when choosing a place to enjoy their golden years. However, this trend will not translate into a general boom for all rural communities. Rural communities with scenic amenities, adequate infrastructure, and first-rate health services will prosper and could be the real frontrunners of the rural economy.

In sum, the rural outlook will continue to have winners and losers. In the long run, traditional rural industries—farming and manufacturing—will benefit from some painful cost alignments experienced in the 1980s. Nevertheless, both will operate in a keenly competitive world market. What might be called the "new" rural economy, dependent on retirement, trade, and services, will find continued success in the 1990s. Demographic and economic trends will contribute to solid growth in this small but growing segment of rural America.

THE RURAL ECONOMIC POLICY DILEMMA

The new rural economic reality is a tale of two cities. Rural America has been slow to realize that in the 1980s, and economic trends suggest that diverse economic performance will continue in the 1990s. The question now is, what can and should policy makers do in response?

Rural development policy poses a dilemma to citizens and policy makers. The root of the dilemma is the mixing of new market realities with old social values. The new market reality suggests that not all rural communities will survive. The old social values say all things rural are worth preserving. Or, put another way, rural development policy tries to encourage economic activity in the very places where market forces are taking it away. This poses a fundamental paradox: Should it be a national public policy to lean against these rural winds?

The answer is both yes and no. There is a place for public policy to encourage economic growth in some rural places. Our nation has done this for more than 100 years—through a widesweeping network of land-grant universities, the extension service, rural electric power generation, subsidized mail delivery, and subsidized credit through the Farmers Home Administration and other federal agencies. All of these institutions will continue, but with what mission?

The issue becomes one of deciding what our goal for rural policy is and what the target for policy efforts then becomes. Is our goal to preserve all rural places? If so, the target for assistance is large and widespread and the corresponding effort must be enormous. Is our goal to encourage economic growth in those rural places that appear to have sufficient market attributes to survive? If so, our target is much smaller and requires fewer resources to reach.

The answer is clear. We do not have the luxury of preserving all rural places. The winds of change are too stiff. Many rural communities in the farm belt reached their peak population at the turn of the century, and even major efforts in the last decade of the twentieth century will not reverse this trend. Yet all too often,the discussion of rural development proceeds before this fundamental founding principle gets resolved.

It is curious that there appears to be greater concern about rural development today than in the 1950s and 1960s, when the rural economy actually underwent a bigger transition, as measured in population. The issue can be well illustrated in agriculture. In 1950, 23 million people lived on farms. By 1960, that number had fallen to 15.6 million, a farm exodus of 7.4 million people. In the 1960s, another 6 million people left the farm and another 3.7 million people left farming. In the 1950s, 1960s, and 1970s, the farm exodus occurred quite smoothly. This was because most farm families *profited* economically in the process. Most left small and medium farms for well-paying factory jobs. Most required little additional training to enter the industrial work force at a relatively high level.

Today, there is legitimate anxiety because the transition for farmers and other rural dwellers is much more difficult. The industrial jobs of the past are extremely hard to obtain. Today, jobs are created in the service industries and many people leaving rural America do not have the skills to fit quickly into high-wage service jobs. Thus, an opportunity gap has arisen for those being forced out of rural America.

What then can and should rural development policy do in the 1990s? Four principles may be helpful in formulating a policy response.

Target Policy Efforts

Targeting public effort will be one key to successful rural development. Funds will be scarce at the federal, state, and local levels. Decision makers must resist the temptation to spread these limited funds too widely. Diluting policy efforts will not achieve the desired result in communities lacking the economic assets to survive and it could jeopardize success in those communities that do.

The problem with targeting is that it forces policy makers to make hard choices. Often, information is insufficient to support a rigorous selection process. The answer, then, is to put the onus on rural communities themselves. Allocate state funds on the basis of competitive bidding, but help all communities in putting proposals together. The great advantage of this approach is that it implicitly recognizes those rural communities with vision and leadership, and these may be the most vital qualities for rural communities to prosper.

Prepare the Work Force

The rural work force was unprepared for the 1980s. Workers lacked the skills necessary to leave rural places and move quickly into attractive jobs elsewhere in the economy. The road to the industrial workplace was blocked.

What is needed is a redoubling of public efforts to outfit rural people with the additional skills to make them versatile and flexible in today's workplace. Rural residents have some superb job qualities: they work hard, they are resourceful, they have perseverance, and they are honest. However, to survive and prosper in today's job market, a worker or a manager must also have flexible analytical skills, computer skills, and communication skills.

This training effort should be comprehensive. Rural schools must outfit students with more flexible skills, and perhaps provide less vocational training. Adult education programs will occupy greater attention, paving the way to utilize the extension service and rural community colleges more fully. Finally, leadership development programs of various types will become even more important to rural businesses that hope to prosper in a more competitive rural economy.

Encourage Entrepreneurship

Many rural states are already well along in implementing strategies that foster entrepreneurship. Many states recognize that rural areas are more likely to grow through the success of home-grown companies than by attracting branch plants of large corporations. Small companies remain the principal source of new jobs in our economy, and that holds equally true for rural places as for urban places.

Rural America has a rich heritage of entrepreneurship and risk taking, and this provides a firm foundation for growth. To succeed in the 1990s, entrepreneurs will need assistance from government in two areas: technical assistance and startup capital. Because they are isolated from large markets, rural businesses often need help in one or more phases of their business plan. Public agencies, whether economic development agencies or universities, can be extremely helpful to young companies. This is a low-cost, high-benefit exercise for government.

The second area where government can help is startup capital. The word "startup" should be emphasized because a misperception persists about the availability of rural credit in general. In general, rural businesses do not lack credit (Morris and Drabenstott, 1989). To the contrary, most country banks are awash with funds. What is lacking is venture capital. Government can play a role here in supplying matching funds for new rural businesses. States, such as Kansas, already do this. However, the effort must be targeted at startup capital and not made generally available to businesses with good credit lines already.

New Directions for Research and Development

Finally, rural development policy should pay attention to new directions for researching and developing new rural products. As discussed earlier, many farm communities will need to add value to farm production in order to prosper. Universities can play an important role in identifying these products and developing the technologies necessary to support them. New processing and packaging technologies will be necessary to make food processing at the farm level more attractive. In addition to finding new market niches for farm-level food products, researchers may be able to unlock new industrial uses for farm products. This may be the greatest rural development opportunity on the horizon. In short, agriculture must be driven by marketplace opportunities, not by the goal of merely increasing the production of bulk commodities.

CONCLUSIONS

Rural America trailed urban America in the 1980s. Although the gap will not be as large in the 1990s, it will persist. However, the tale of two cities can be found even within rural America. Some rural places are prospering even as others die. This is not a new trend; it has continued since the turn of the century. However, the opportunity gap that rural workers now face when they leave rural America in search of a better living in the city is raising the stakes for rural policy makers.

Rural policy must be guided by the principle that not every rural place will survive the new rural economic reality. Rather, effort must be concentrated on those communities with the leadership and economic assets needed to prosper in an economy where international competition will be the byword. Farm communities will have to explore new ways of adding value to their farm production in order to arrest the decline in farm-related businesses.

Rural policy can benefit from the application of four guiding principles. First, efforts must be clearly targeted. Second, entrepreneurship must be encouraged and supported in rural America; technical assistance programs and venture capital will be useful public programs. Third, the rural work force must be better prepared for a dynamic job market that requires more flexible skills. Finally, universities should investigate and develop new ways to process and package farm and food products.

NOTE

The views expressed in this chapter are strictly those of the author and do not necessarily represent those of the Federal Reserve Bank of Kansas City or the Federal Reserve System.

Bibliography

Ahern, Mary C., and Michelle D. Fryar. 1985. *Physicians in Nonmetro Areas During the Seventies*, Rural Development Research Report 46. Washington, D.C.: USDA, Economic Research Service, Economic Development Division.

Almquist, Julie, Mary Foley, and Betty Wells. 1990. *Tomorrow's Leaders Today Resource Notebook.* Ames, IA: Iowa State University Extension.

"Americans on the Move." 1976. *Time*, March 15.

Barkema, Alan, and Mark Drabenstott. 1990. "Processing Food in Farm States: An Economic Development Strategy in the 1990s." *Economic Review* 75(4) (July/August): 1–23.

Barringer, Felicity. 1990. "Census Bureau Places Population at 249.6 Million." *The New York Times* (December 27): A1, A10.

Beale, Calvin L. 1975. *The Revival of Population Growth in Nonmetropolitan America,* ERS–605. Washington, D.C.: USDA, Economic Research Service, Economic Development Division.

———. 1985. "U.S. Population Trends Break with Past." *Rural Development Perspectives* 1 (April): 4–6.

———. 1988. "Americans Heading for the Cities, Once Again." *Rural Development Perspectives* 4 (June): 2–6.

Beale, Calvin L., and Glenn V. Fuguitt. 1985. *Metropolitan and Nonmetropolitan Growth Differentials in the United States Since 1980*, Working Paper 85–6. Madison, WI: University of Wisconsin Center for Demography and Ecology.

Bellah, R. N., R. Madsen, W. M. Sullivan, A. Swidler, and S. M. Tipton. 1985. *Habits of the Heart.* Berkeley: University of California Press.

Bender, L. D. 1987. "The Role of Services in Regional Development Policies." *Land Economics* 62(1): 62–72.

Birch, David L. 1987. *Job Creation in America.* New York: The Free Press.

Blakely, Edward J. 1989. *Planning Local Economic Development: Theory and Practice.* Newbury Park: Sage.

Bloomquist, Leonard E., and Molly S. Killian. 1988. "Specialization Is Tied to Natural Resources, People." *Rural Development Perspectives* 4(2) (February): 34–5.

Bluestone, Herman, and Stan G. Daberkow. 1985. "Employment Growth in Nonmetro

America: Past Trends and Prospects to 1990." *Rural Development Perspectives* 1 (June): 20, 34–7.

Booth, Douglas E. 1986. "Long Waves and Uneven Regional Growth." *Southern Economic Journal* 53(2): 448–60.

Bowker, J. M., and James W. Richardson. 1989. "Impacts of Alternative Farm Policies on Rural Communities." *Southern Journal of Agricultural Economics* 21 (December): 35–46.

Brown, David L., J. Norman Reid, Herman Bluestone, David A. McGranahan, and Sara M. Mazie, Eds. 1988. *Rural Economic Development in the 1980s: Prospects for the Future*, Rural Development Research Report No. 69. Washington, D.C.: USDA, Economic Research Service.

Burns, James MacGregor. 1978. *Leadership*. New York: Harper & Row.

Buttel, Frederick H., and Mark Lancelle. 1986. "Emerging Agricultural Technologies, Farm Structural Change, Public Policy, and Rural Communities in the Northeast." In *Technology, Public Policy, and the Changing Structure of American Agriculture, Volume II: Background Papers*. Washington, D.C.: U.S. Department of Commerce, National Technical Information Service, pp. 213–372.

Buttel, Frederick H., Steve H. Murdock, F. Larry Leistritz, and Rita R. Hamm. 1987. "Rural Environments." In *Advances in Environment, Behavior, and Design*, Ervin H. Zube and Gary T. Moore, Eds. New York: Plenum Press, pp. 107–28.

Campbell, Rex, and Lorraine Garkovich. 1984. "Turnaround Migration as an Episode of Collective Behavior." *Rural Sociology* 49 (Spring): 89–105.

Carlsson, B. 1989. "The Evolution of Manufacturing of Manufacturing Technology and Its Impact on Industrial Structure: An International Study." *Small Business Economics* 1(1): 21–37.

Chicoine, David L., and Norman Walzer. 1984. *Financing Rural Roads and Bridges in the Midwest*. Washington D.C.: USDA, Office of Transportation and Agricultural Marketing Services.

———. 1985a. "Governmental Structure, Service Quality, and Citizens' Perceptions." *Public Finance/Finances Publiques* 3: 363–80.

———. 1985b. *Governmental Structure and Local Public Finance*. Boston: Oelgeschlager, Gunn and Hain.

———. 1986. "Governmental Structure and Property Tax Reliance." *Public Choice* 49: 17–28.

Christenson, James A., and Carolyn E. Sachs. 1980. "The Impact of Government Size and Number of Administrative Units on the Quality of Public Services." *Administrative Science Quarterly* 25(1) (March): 89–101.

Coffey, W. J., and M. Polese. 1989. "Producer Services and Regional Development: A Policy-Oriented Perspective." *Papers of the Regional Science Association, 1989* 67: 13–27.

Colgan, Charles S. 1990. *Merging Planning and Politics in the Development of Policy: The Policy Academy*. Unpublished manuscript, The Edmund S. Muskie Institute of Public Affairs, University of Southern Maine.

Committee of 34. 1990. *Growing North Dakota*. Bismark, ND: State Legislature.

Cook, Annabel Krischner. 1987. "Nonmetropolitan Migration: The Influence of Neglected Variables." *Rural Sociology* 32 (Fall): 409–18.

Crihfield, John B. 1989. "A Structural Empirical Analysis of Metropolitan Labor Demand." *Journal of Regional Science* 29 (August): 347–71.

———. 1990. "Measuring Imbalances in a State's Local Labor Markets, and Implications for Rural Labor Market Policy." Working Paper, University of Illinois at Urbana-Champaign, November.

Darling, David L., and Jin-Song Tan. 1988. *Capturing Retail Sales Dollars in Rural Kansas Communities*, Community Development Study Report No. 36. Manhattan, KS: Kansas State University, Cooperative Extension Service.

Data Resources, Inc. 1990. *U.S. Markets Review: Midwestern Focus, Second Quarter, 1990*. Lexington, MA: Data Resources, Inc.

Deavers, Ken. 1990. "Why Care about Lagging Rural Development." *ARED Newsletter* (Winter): 4–5.

Deller, S. C., and C. H. Nelson. 1991. "Measuring the Economic Efficiency of Producing Rural Road Services." *American Journal of Agricultural Economics* 73(1) (February): 194–201.

Deseran, Forest A., William W. Falk, and Pamela Jenkins. 1984. "Determinants of Earnings of Farm Families in the U.S." *Rural Sociology* 49 (Summer): 210–29.

Dillman, Don A., and Kenneth R. Tremblay, Jr. 1977. "The Quality of Life in Rural America." *American Academy of Political and Social Science Annals* 429 (January): 115–29.

DiLorenzo, Thomas J. 1981. "The Expenditure Effects of Restructuring Competition in Local Public Service Industries: The Case of Special Districts." *Public Choice* 37(3): 569–78.

Doeksen, G. A., and C. W. Allen, Jr. 1990. "Infrastructure and Economic Development." Paper presented at Revitalizing the Rural South: Extension's Role in Enhancing Quality of Life, Birmingham, AL, January.

Drucker, Peter F. 1989. "The Futures That Have Already Happened." *The Economist* 313 (7625): 19–24.

Duncan, Marvin. 1990. "The Provision of Agricultural and Agribusiness Credit." Paper presented to the Third Annual Symposium on Agricultural and Agribusiness Credit, Farm Credit Administration, April.

Dunford, R. W., D. L. Chicoine, and D. E. Ervin. 1986. "Farmland Use-Value Assessment in the United States: A Summary and Critical Review." *Assessment Digest* 8(3) (May/June): 21–7.

Dynarski, Mark, Robert Schwab, and Ernest Zampelli. 1989. "Local Characteristics and Public Production: The Case of Education." *Journal of Urban Economics* 26: 250–63.

Eberts, Randall W. 1985. "The Role of Public Investment in Regional Economic Development." Paper presented at the Association for Public Policy Analysis and Management, Washington, D.C.

Edelman, Mark A., and James J. Knudsen. 1990. "A Classic Comparative Analysis of Average School Costs: Iowa Case Study." *North Central Journal of Agricultural Economics* 12 (January): 99–108.

Edwards, Clark. 1981. "The Bases for Regional Economic Growth: A Review." In *A Survey of Agricultural Economics Literature*, Vol. 3, Lee R. Martin, Ed. Minneapolis: University of Minnesota Press.

Effrat, Marcia Pelly. 1974. *The Community: Approaches and Applications*. New York: The Free Press.

Erickson, R. A. 1976. "Nonmetropolitan Industrial Expansion: Emerging Implications For Regional Development." *The Review of Regional Studies* 6(1): 35–48.

Fallows, James M. 1989. *More Like Us: Making America Great Again*. Boston: Houghton Mifflin.

Flora, Cornelia B., and Jan L. Flora. 1990. "Developing Entrepreneurial Rural Communities." *Sociological Practice* 8: 197–207.

Flora, Cornelia B., Jan L. Flora, Wayne White, Richard Leiker, Tommy Garnett, and Karen Albach. 1978. *Kansans On the Move*. Manhattan, KS: State of Kansas Department of Administration, Division of State Planning and Research.

Flora, Cornelia B., Jinsong J. Tan, and Jan L. Flora. 1989. "Highway Impacts on Local Economic Development." Mimeo. Blacksburg, VA: Virginia Polytechnic Institute and State University, Department of Sociology.

Flora, Jan L., and Cornelia Butler Flora. 1986. "Emerging Agricultural Technologies, Farm Size, Public Policy, and Rural Communities: The Great Plains and the West." In *Technology, Public Policy, and the Changing Structure of American Agriculture, Volume II: Background Papers*. Washington, D.C.: U.S. Department of Commerce, National Technical Information Service, pp. 168–212.

Flora, Jan L., Cornelia B. Flora, Yu-ching Cheng, Dwight Dickson, Muhammad Amin ul-Karim, and Yun-Ji Qian. 1990. "The Changing Structure of Farming-Dependent Communities in the 1980s: The Kansas Case." In *Sustainable Rural Communities in Canada*, Michael E. Gertler and Harold R. Baker, Eds. Saskatoon, Saskatchewan: The Canadian Agriculture and Rural Restructuring Group, pp. 89–99.

Flora, Jan L., Gary P. Green, Edward A. Gale, Cornelia B. Flora, and Frederick E. Schmidt. Forthcoming. "Self Development: A Viable Rural Development Option." *Policy Studies Journal*.

Flora, Jan L., and John M. Stitz. 1985. "Ethnicity, Persistence, and Capitalization of Agriculture in the Great Plains During the Settlement Period: Wheat Production and Risk Avoidance." *Rural Sociology* 50: 341–60.

Foster, William. 1989. "Toward a Critical Practice of Leadership." In *Critical Perspectives on Educational Leadership*, John Smyth, Ed. Philadelphia: The Falmer Press, Taylor & Francis, pp. 39–62.

Fox, W. F., and T. R. Smith. 1990. "Public Infrastructure Policy and Economic Development." *Economic Review* (March/April): 49–59.

Fuguitt, Glen V. 1985. "The Nonmetropolitan Population Turnaround." *Annual Review of Sociology* 11:259–80.

Gallaher, Art J. 1961. *Plainville Fifteen Years Later*. New York: Columbia University Press.

Gardner, John W. 1989. "The Tasks of Leadership." In *Contemporary Issues in Leadership*, William E. Rosenbach and Robert L. Taylor, Eds. Boulder, CO: Westview Press, pp. 24–33.

Garkovich, Lorraine E. 1989. "Local Organizations and Leadership in Community Development." In *Community Development in Perspective*, James A. Christenson and Jerry W. Robinson, Jr., Eds. Ames, IA: Iowa State University Press, pp. 196–218.

Gibb, C. A. 1954. "Leadership." In *Handbook of Social Psychology*, G. Lindzey, Ed. Cambridge, MA: Addison-Wesley, pp. 877–920.

Giertz, J. F., and D. L. Chicoine. 1984. "Tax Valuation of Farm Land: Non-Neutrality with Respect to Inflation." *National Tax Journal* 37(2) (June): 253–8.

Glasgow, Nina. 1985. "Newcomers From Cities Support Rural Growth and Development." *Rural Development Perspectives* 1(2) (February): 7–9.

———. 1990. "Attracting Retirees as a Community Development Option." *Journal of the Community Development Society* 21(1): 102–14.

Glasgow, Nina, and Calvin L. Beale. 1985. "Rural Elderly in Demographic Perspective." *Rural Development Perspectives* 2(1) (October): 22–6.

Glasmeier, Amy. 1988. "Bypassing America's Outlands: Rural America and High Technology." Paper prepared for the Rural Economic Policy Program of the Aspen Institute and the Ford Foundation, December.

Godwin, Deborah, and Julia Marlowe. 1990. "Farm Wives Labor Force Participation and Earnings." *Rural Sociology* 55: 25–43.

Goldschmidt, Walter, 1978. "Large-Scale Farming and the Rural Social Structure." *Rural Sociology* 43 (Fall): 362–6.

Gray, Thomas, A., and Bruce D. Phillips. 1983. "The Role of Small Firms in Understanding the Magnitude of Fluctuations in the Economy." Paper presented at the Atlantic Economic Society Meetings, October.

Green, Gary P., Jan L. Flora, Cornelia Flora, and Frederick E. Schmidt. 1991. "Local Self-Development Strategies: National Survey Results." *Journal of the Community Development Society* 21(2): 55–73.

Hackett, J. C., and T. Busson. 1986. *Managing Rural Infrastructure: State Assistance to Small and Rural Governments for Public Works*. Lexington, KY: Council of State Governments, State Research Institute, Center for Agriculture and Rural Development.

Hady, Thomas, and Peggy Ross. 1990. *An Update: The Diverse Social and Economic Structure of Nonmetropolitan America*. Washington, D.C.: USDA, Economic Research Service.

Hanushek, Eric A. 1981. "Throwing Money at Schools." *Journal of Policy Analysis and Management* 1: 19–41.

———. 1986. "The Economics of Schooling: Production and Efficiency in Public Schools." *Journal of Economic Literature* 24 (September): 1141–77.

Harden, Warren. 1960. "Social and Economic Effects of Community Size." *Rural Sociology* 25 (Summer): 204–11.

Harrington, Michael. 1962. *The Other America*. New York: Macmillan.

Hart, John F. 1988. "Small Towns and Manufacturing." *Geographical Review* 78(1): 272–87.

Harvesting Hometown Jobs. 1987. Washington, D.C.: National Association of Towns and Townships.

Heady, Earl O., and Steve Sonka. 1974. "Farm Size, Rural Community Income and Consumer Welfare." *American Journal of Agricultural Economics* 56: 534–42.

Henry, Mark S. 1988. "Southern Farms and Rural Communities: Developing Directions for Economic Development Research and Policy." *Southern Journal of Agricultural Economics* 20 (July): 13–28.

Henry, Mark, Mark Drabenstott, and Lynn Gibson. 1986. "A Changing Rural America." *Economic Review* 71(7): 23–41.

———. 1987. "Rural Growth Slows Down." *Rural Development Perspectives* 3 (June): 25–30.

Henry, Mark S., Agapi Somwaru, Gerald Schulper, and William Edmonson. 1987.

"Some Effects of Farm Size on the Nonfarm Economy." *North Central Journal of Agricultural Economics* 9: 1–12.

Hess, Beth B. 1983. "New Faces of Poverty." *American Demographics* 15 (May): 26–31.

Hudson, John C. 1985. *Plains Country Towns*. Minneapolis: University of Minnesota Press.

Hustedde, Ronald J., Ron Shaffer, and Glen Pulver. 1984. *Community Economic Analysis: A How To Manual*. Ames, IA: North Central Regional Center for Rural Development.

Illinois Department of Commerce and Community Affairs. 1989. *Rural Development Resource Guide*. Springfield, IL: Illinois Department of Commerce and Community Affairs.

Illinois Public Schools Financial Statistics: 1986–87 School Year. 1988. Springfield, IL: Illinois State Board of Education.

Iowa Academy Team. 1990. *Iowa Policy Academy on Rural Economic and Community Development, Project Overview*. Iowa City, IA: University of Iowa, Cooperative Extension Service.

Jacobs, Jane. 1984. "Why TVA Failed." *New York Review of Books* 31(8): 41–7.

Jenkins, W. O. 1947. "A Review of Leadership Studies with Particular Reference to Military Problems." *Psychological Bulletin* 44: 54–79.

Johansen, Harley E., and Glenn V. Fuguitt. 1973. "Changing Retail Activity in Wisconsin Villages: 1939–1954–1970." *Rural Sociology* 38 (Summer): 207–218.

———. 1990. "The Changing Rural Village." *Rural Development Perspectives* 6 (February): 2–6.

John, DeWitt, Sandra S. Batie, and Kim Norris. 1989. *A Brighter Future for Rural America?* Washington, D.C.: National Governors Association, Center for Policy Research.

Kelley, Robert E. 1989. "In Praise of Followers." In *Contemporary Issues in Leadership*, William E. Rosenbach and Robert L. Taylor, Eds. Boulder, CO: Westview Press, pp. 124–34.

Killian, Molly S., and Thomas F. Hady. 1988. "What Is the Payoff for Diversifying Rural Economies?" *Rural Development Perspectives* 4(2) (February): 2–7.

Klimasewski, T. 1978. "Corporate Dominance of Manufacturing in Appalachia." *Geographical Review* 68(1) 94–102.

Krannich, Richard S., and Craig R. Humphrey. 1983. "Local Mobilization and Community Growth: Toward an Assessment of the 'Growth Machine.' " *Rural Sociology* 48(1) (Spring): 60–81.

Lesser, B., and Peter Hall. 1987. *Telecommunications Services and Regional Development: The Case of Atlantic Canada*. Victoria, British Columbia: Institute for Research on Public Policy.

Li, Peter S., and Brian D. MacLean. 1989. "Changes in the Rural Elderly Population and Their Effects on the Small Town Economy: The Case of Saskatchewan, 1971–1986." *Rural Sociology* 54 (Summer): 213–26.

Lonsdale, Richard E. 1981. "Industry's Role in Nonmetropolitan Economic Development and Population Change." In *Population Redistribution in the Midwest*, Curtis E. Roseman, Andrew J. Sofranko, and James D. Williams, Eds. Ames, IA: North Central Regional Center for Rural Development, pp. 129–48.

Luther, Vicki, and Milan Wall. 1989. *Ten Ideas for Recruiting New Leaders*. Lincoln, NE: Heartland Center for Leadership Development.

Lyford, Joseph P. 1962. *The Talk in Vandalia: The Life of an American Town*. New York: Harper and Row.

Lynd, Robert S. 1929. *Middletown: A Study in Modern American Culture*. New York: Harcourt, Brace, and World.

Lynd, Robert S., and Helen Merrell Lynd. 1937. *Middletown in Transition: A Study in Cultural Conflicts*. New York: Harcourt Brace Jovanovich.

Lyons, W. E., and D. Lowery. 1989. "Governmental Fragmentation Versus Consolidation: Five Public-Choice Myths About How to Create Informed, Involved, and Happy Citizens." *Public Administration Review* (November/December): 533–43.

Majchrowicz, Alexander T. 1989. "Rural Areas Fall Further Behind in Jobs." *Rural Development Perspectives* 5 (June): 34.

Malecki, Edward J. 1990. "New Firm Formation in the USA: Corporate Structure, Venture Capital, and Local Government." *Entrepreneurship and Regional Development* 2(3) (July/September): 247–65.

Mann, R. D. 1959. "A Review of the Relationship Between Personality and Performance in Small Groups." *Psychological Bulletin* 56: 241–70.

Mazie, Sara Mills, Ed. 1990a. "Nonmetro Population Growth Improves" and "Nonmetro Areas with Urban Settings Remain Attractive in the 1980's." *Rural Conditions and Trends* (Spring): 18–21.

———. 1990b. "Poverty Severe in Nonmetro Areas." *Rural Conditions and Trends* (Spring): 16–17.

McGranahan, David A. 1984. "Local Growth and the Outside Contacts of Influentials: An Alternative Test of the 'Growth Machine' Hypothesis." *Rural Sociology* 49(4) (Winter): 530–40.

———. 1986. "Crime and the Countryside." *Rural Development Perspectives* 2 (February).

———. 1988a. "Rural Worker at a Disadvantage in Job Opportunities." *Rural Development Perspectives* 4(3) (June): 7–12.

———. 1988b. "Rural Workers in the National Economy." In *Rural Economic Development in the 1980's: Prospects for the Future*, David L. Brown, et al., Eds. Washington, D.C.: USDA, Economic Research Service, Rural Development Research Report No. 69, pp. 29–47.

McGranahan, David A., and Linda Ghelfi. Forthcoming. "The Education Crisis and Rural Stagnation in the 1980's." In *Strategies for Rural Development*, Richard Long, Ed. Washington, D.C.: USDA, Economic Research Service, Chapter Two.

McGranahan, David A., John C. Hession, Fred K. Hines, and Max F. Jordan. 1985. *Social and Economic Characteristics of the Population in Metro and Nonmetro Counties, 1970–80*, Rural Development Research Report No. 58. Washington, D.C.: USDA, Economic Research Service, Agriculture and Rural Economics Division.

Miller, James P. 1987. *Recent Contributions of Small Businesses and Corporations to Rural Job Creation*, Staff Report. Washington, D.C.: USDA, Economic Research Service.

Miller, James P., and Herman Bluestone. 1988. "Prospects for Service Sector Employment Growth in Nonmetro America." *The Review of Regional Studies* 18(1): 28–41.

Miller, Lorna Clancy, Boyd E. Rossing, and Sara M. Steele. 1990. *Partnerships: Shared Leadership Among Stakeholders.* Madison, WI: The University of Wisconsin–Madison.

Mills, David, and Allan E. Schuman. 1985. ''Industry Structure and Fluctuating Demand.'' *American Economic Review* 75(4) (September): 758–67.

Moe, Edward O., and Carol C. Taylor. 1942. *Culture of a Contemporary Rural Community: Irwin, Iowa*, Rural Life Studies 5. Washington, D.C.: USDA, Bureau of Agricultural Economics.

Molotch, Harvey. 1976. ''The City as a Growth Machine: Toward a Political Economy of Place.'' *American Journal of Sociology* 82 (September): 309–32.

Morris, Charles, and Mark Drabenstott. 1989. ''Financing Rural Business: What Role for Public Policy.'' *Economic Review* 74(8): 30–45.

National Council on Public Works Improvement, 1988. *Fragile Foundations: A Report on America's Public Works.* Washington, D.C.: U.S. Government Printing Office.

National Governors Association. 1987. *Making America Work: Productive People, Productive Policies*, Report of the Task Force on Jobs, Growth, and Competitiveness. Washington, D.C.: National Governors Association.

Nelson, Arthur C. 1990. ''Regional Patterns of Exurban Industrialization: Results of a Preliminary Investigation.'' *Economic Development Quarterly* 4(4): 320–32.

Osborne, David. 1988. *Laboratories of Democracy.* Boston: Harvard Business School Press.

Perspectives. 1989. *Farmline* 11(1): 2.

Pfeffer, Max J. 1983. ''Social Origins of Three Systems of Farm Production in the United States.'' *Rural Sociology* 47: 540–62.

Phillips, Bruce D., Bruce A. Kirchoff, and H. Shelton Brown. Forthcoming. ''Formation, Growth and Mobility of Technology Based Firms in the U.S. Economy.'' *Entrepreneurship and Regional Development.*

Porterfield, Shirley L. 1990. ''Producer Services: A Viable Option for Rural Economic Development?'' Paper presented at the annual meetings of the Southern Regional Science Association, Washington, D.C., March.

Pulver, Glen C. 1988. ''The Changing Economic Scene in Rural America.'' *Journal of State Government* 61(1): 3–8.

Rasmussen, Wayne D. 1985. ''90 Years of Rural Development Programs.'' *Rural Development Perspectives* 2 (October): 2–9.

Reed, B. J., and David F. Paulsen. 1990. ''Small Towns Lack the Capacity for Successful Development Efforts.'' *Rural Development Perspectives* 6 (June/September): 26–30.

Reid, J. Norman, Herman Bluestone, T. Alexander Majchrowicz, James P. Miller, and Celeste A. Long. 1988. *Economic Realities in Rural America: Recent Trends, Future Prospects.* Washington, D.C.: USDA, Economic Research Service and National Governors Association.

Rodefeld, Richard. 1974. ''The Changing Organization and Occupational Structure of Farming and the Implications for Farm Work Force Individuals, Families, and Communities.'' Ph.D. dissertation, University of Wisconsin.

Roseman, Curtis C. 1984. ''Illinois Migrants: Where They Go and Where They Come From.'' *Illinois Community and Resource Development Report* 8 (July): 6.

Ross, Doug, and Robert E. Friedman. 1990. ''The Emerging Third Wave: New Economic

Development Strategies in the '90s.'' *The Entrepreneurial Economy Review* 9(1) (Autumn): 3–10.

Schaeffer, Peter V., and William Sander. 1987. ''Schooling and Urban Employment Growth: 1980–1984.'' Working Paper No. 1, University of Illinois Institute of Government and Public Affairs.

Senf, David R. 1989. ''Measures of Shifts in Retail Trade.'' *The Review of Regional Studies* 19(3): 18–23.

Seroka, J. 1989. ''Public Administration and Planning in Rural Areas.'' *Journal of Planning Literature* 1(4) (Autumn): 430–44.

Smith, Eldon D. 1988. *Economic and Social Infrastructure in the Strategy of Regional Economic Development: An Alternative Theoretical Perspective Relevant to Open Economies*, Staff Paper No. 250. Lexington: University of Kentucky, Department of Agricultural Economics.

———. 1989. ''Reflections on Human Resources in the Strategy of Rural Economic Development.'' *The Review of Regional Studies* 19 (Winter): 13–22.

Sofranko, Andrew, J., Mark Flotow, and John C. van Es. 1985. ''Three Decades of Rural Community Growth and Decline.'' *Illinois CRD Report* 11 (August): 1–7.

Sofranko, Andrew J., James D. Williams, and Frederick C. Fliegel. 1981. ''Urban Migrants to the Rural Midwest: Some Understandings and Misunderstandings.'' In *Population Distribution in the Midwest*, Curtis C. Roseman, Ed. Ames, IA: Iowa State University, North Central Regional Center for Rural Development, pp. 97–127.

Stam, Jerome M., Steven R. Koenig, Susan E. Bentley, and H. Frederick Gale. Forthcoming. *Farm Financial Stress, Farm Exits, and Public Sector Assistance for the Farm Sectors in the 1980's*, Agricultural Economic Report. Washington D.C.: USDA, Economic Research Service.

Stein, Maurice R. 1960. *The Eclipse of Community: An Interpretation of American Studies*. New York: Harper and Row.

Stone, Kenneth E. 1988. ''The Effect of Wal-Mart Stores on Businesses in Host Towns and Surrounding Towns in Iowa.'' Unpublished paper, Iowa State University, Ames, Iowa.

Storper, M., and S. Christopherson. 1987. ''Flexible Specialization and Regional Industrial Agglomerations: The Case of the U.S. Motion Picture Industry.'' *Annals of the Association of American Geographers* 77(1): 104–17.

Survey of Municipal Officials. 1987. Macomb, IL: Illinois Institute for Rural Affairs.

Swanson, Lou. Forthcoming. ''Rural Social Infrastructure.'' In *Foundations of Rural Development Policy*, J. Norman Reid, David Sears, Glenn Nelson, Thomas J. Rowley, and Mervin Yetley, Eds. Boulder, CO: Westview Press.

The People Left Behind. 1967. President's National Advisory Commission on Rural Poverty. Washington, D.C.: U.S. Government Printing Office.

Thistlethwaite, Paul, Rob Wendland, and Craig Conrad. 1990. *Rural Life Panel: Summary Report* 1 (Spring). Macomb, IL: Illinois Institute for Rural Affairs.

Thomas, Margaret G. 1988. *Profiles in Rural Economic Development: A Guidebook of Selected Successful Rural Area Initiatives*. Kansas City, MO: Midwest Research Institute, p. 138.

U.S. Bureau of the Census. 1972. *Government Finances in 1970–71*, series GF–71–5. Washington, D.C.: U.S. Government Printing Office.

———. 1978. *Government Finances in 1976–77*, series GF–77–5. Washington, D.C.: U.S. Government Printing Office.

———. 1980. *County Business Patterns 1980: Illinois*. Washington, D.C.: U.S. Government Printing Office.

———. 1982. Census of Governments, Government Organization. Washington, D.C.: U.S. Government Printing Office.

———. 1983. *Governmental Finances in 1981–82*, series GF–82–5. Washington, D.C: U.S. Government Printing Office.

———. 1988a. *1987 Census of Governments, Government Organization*. Washington, D.C.: U.S. Government Printing Office.

———. 1988b. *County and City Data Book 1988*. Washington, D.C.: U.S. Government Printing Office.

———. 1988c. *Governmental Finances in 1986–87*, series GF–87–5. Washington, D.C.: U.S. Government Printing Office.

———. 1989a. *Current Population Survey*. Washington D.C.: U.S. Government Printing Office.

———. 1989b. *Governmental Finances in 1987–88*, series GF–88–5. Washington, D.C.: U.S. Government Printing Office.

———. 1989c. Jointly with the Department of Agriculture. *Rural and Rural Farm Population, 1988, Current Population Reports*, Series P–20, No. 439. Washington D.C.: U.S. Government Printing Office.

———. 1989d. *Population Profile of the United States: 1989, Current Population Reports,* Series P–23, No. 159. Washington, D.C.: U.S. Government Printing Office.

———. 1989e. *Poverty in the United States, 1987 Current Population Reports*, Series P–20, No. 163. Washington, D.C.: U.S. Government Printing Office.

———. 1990a. *Census of Population* (data tapes). Washington, D.C.

———. 1990b. *Residents of Farms and Rural Areas: 1989. Current Population Reports*, Series P–20, No. 446. Washington, D.C.: U.S. Government Printing Office.

———. 1990c. *Statistical Abstract of the United States: 1990*, 100th ed. Washington, D.C.: U.S. Government Printing Office.

U.S. Congress. 1989. Congressional Research Office. Joint Economic Committee. *Towards Rural Development Policy for the 1990s: Enhancing Income and Employment Opportunities*. Washington, D.C.: U.S. Government Printing Office.

U.S. Department of Agriculture, Economic Research Service. 1987. *Rural Economic Development in the 1980s; Preparing for the Future*. ERS Staff Report No. AGES–970724. Washington, D.C.: U.S. Government Printing Office.

———. 1988. *Economic Indicators of the Farm Sector, National Financial Summary*. Washington D.C.: U.S. Government Printing Office.

U.S. Department of Commerce. 1982. *Survey of Governments. Annual Finance Statistics* (computer tapes). Washington D.C.: U.S. Government Printing Office.

———. 1987. *Survey of Governments. Annual Finance Statistics* (computer tapes). Washington, D.C.

———. 1989. *Bureau of Economic Analysis* (data tapes). Washington, D.C.

U.S. Department of Labor, Bureau of Labor Statistics. 1980–1990. *Employment and Earnings Data* (data tapes). Washington D.C.

U.S. Small Business Administration, Office of Advocacy. 1988. *1976–1986 Linked USEEM User's Guide*. Washington, D.C.: U.S. Small Business Administration.

Vidich, Arthur J., and Joseph Bensman. 1958. *Small Town in Mass Society: Class, Power, and Religion in a Rural Community*. Princeton: Princeton University Press.

Vonder, Tim. 1989. *Three Leadership Models: Transactional, Transformational and Community-Based.* Paper presented at World Future Society Sixth General Assembly, Washington, D.C., July.

Waldrop, Judith, and Thomas Exter. 1990. "What the 1990 Census Will Show." *American Demographics* 12 (January): 20–30.

Wall, Milan, and Vicki Luther. 1987. *Clues to Rural Community Survival.* Lincoln, NE: Heartland Center for Leadership Development.

Waller, Maxine, Helen M. Lewis, Clare McBrien, and Carroll L. Wessinger. 1990. " 'It Has to Come from the People': Responding to Plant Closings in Ivanhoe, Virginia." In *Communities in Economic Crisis: Appalachia and the South,* John Gaventa, Barbara Ellen Smith, and Alex Willingham, Eds. Philadelphia: Temple University Press, pp. 19–28.

Walzer, Norman. Ed. 1990. *Economic Development in Small Illinois Communities.* Macomb, IL: Illinois Institute for Rural Affairs.

Walzer, Norman, and Nancy Baird. 1989. *Administration and Finance of Illinois Townships.* Macomb, IL: Illinois Institute for Rural Affairs.

Walzer, Norman, and David L. Chicoine. 1989. *Rural Roads and Bridges: A Dilemma for Local Officials.* Washington, D.C.: USDA, Office of Transportation.

Walzer, Norman, and Shawnelle Kapper. 1989. *Issues and Concerns of Small Community Officials.* Macomb, IL: Illinois Institute for Rural Affairs.

Walzer, Norman, and Ralph Stablein. 1981. "Small Town and Regional Centers: Implications for Growth." *Growth and Change* 12 (July): 1–8.

Weber, Bruce A., Emery N. Castle, and Ann L. Shriver. 1988. "Performance of Natural Resource Industries." In *Rural Economic Development in the 1980's: Prospects for the Future,* David L. Brown et al., Eds. Washington, D.C.: USDA, Economic Research Service, Rural Development Research Report No. 69, pp. 103–33.

Weber, Max. 1947. *The Theory of Economic and Social Organization.* New York: The Free Press.

Weinstein, G. L., H. T. Gross, and J. Rees. 1985. *Regional Growth and Decline in the United States.* New York: Praeger.

Wells, Betty. 1990. "Social Identity as a Tool to Build Multi-Community Clusters." *Sociological Practice* 8: 157–66.

West, James. 1945. *Plainville, U.S.A.* New York: Columbia University Press.

Wheelock, Gerald, 1979. *Farm Size, Community Structure and Growth: Specification of a Structural Equation Model.* Paper presented to the Annual Meetings of the Rural Sociology Society, Burlington, VT.

Wolman, Harold, and Kenneth Voytek. 1990. "The State Government as a Consultant for Local Economic Development." *Economic Development* 3(4) (August): 211–20.

Young, Frank W. 1970. "Reactive Subsystems." *American Sociological Review* 35 (April): 297–307.

Young, Frank W., and Ruth C. Young. 1973. *Comparative Studies of Community Growth,* Rural Sociological Society Monograph No. 3. Morgantown: West Virginia University.

Young, Ruth C. 1986. "Industrial Location and Regional Change: The United States and New York State." *Regional Studies* 20: 341–69.

Zaleznik, Abraham. 1977. "Managers and Leaders: Are They Different?" *Harvard Business Review* (May/June): 67–8.

Index

I

J

K

L

M

About the Contributors

John B. Crihfield is assistant professor in the Department of Agricultural Economics and the Institute of Government and Public Affairs at the University of Illinois at Urbana–Champaign. His current research focuses on problems in community and regional economic development and public finance.

Steve Deller is assistant professor of community development at the University of Maine. His work focuses on community and regional economic development and local public finance issues with attention to the efficient allocation of public resources. Deller's work has appeared in *The Review of Economics and Statistics, Regional Science and Urban Economics*, and *American Journal of Agricultural Economics*.

Mark Drabenstott is an assistant vice president and economist with the Federal Reserve Bank of Kansas City, where he heads the Regional Economics Group in the Economic Research Department. In that role, he is responsible for directing and monitoring the Bank's research on the seven-state Tenth Federal Reserve District and its principal industries—agriculture and energy. He is an author of numerous articles on such subjects as farm policy, rural development, farm exports, and agricultural finance. Dr. Drabenstott currently serves as chairman of the Federal Reserve System Committee on Agriculture and Rural Development.

Cornelia Flora is professor and head of the Department of Sociology at Virginia Polytechnic Institute and State University. She was previously University Distinguished Professor at Kansas State University. She is a past president of the Rural Sociological Society and current Editor of the *Newsletter* of the Association of Women in Development. Her recent books include *Sustainable Agriculture in the Temperate Zones* and *Rural Policy for the 1990s*.

Jan Flora is professor of agricultural economics at Virginia Polytechnic Institute and State University. He previously was Professor of Sociology and Acting Director of the Kansas Center for Rural Initiatives at Kansas State University. He has done extensive research on community development in both the United States and Latin America. He has recently completed a nationwide study of self-development rural communities in the United States. His most recent book is *Sociology of Developing Societies: Central America*.

John Gruidl is research associate with the Illinois Institute for Rural Affairs at Western Illinois University. His research focuses on regional economic development with an emphasis on the role of small business.

Ronald J. Hustedde is an assistant extension professor in the Department of Sociology and a public policy specialist at the Appalachian Center at the University of Kentucky in Lexington. He is directing a public policy program about Appalachian issues. He has 10 years experience working with rural communities in domestic and international settings.

Molly Sizer Killian has been a sociologist with USDA's Economic Research Service since 1985. She is a coauthor (with Charles Tolbert at Florida State University) of *Labor Market Areas for the United States*. She is currently investigating the importance of local educational characteristics for employment and earnings growth in metro and nonmetro commuting zones.

David A. Lins is a professor of financial management at the University of Illinois. Prior to joining the University in 1982, he was an agricultural economist with the Economic Research Service, U.S. Department of Agriculture.

Sara Mills Mazie is assistant director of the Agriculture and Rural Economy Division in the Economic Research Service of USDA and editor of *Rural Development Perspective*, a journal that reports on recent rural research, and *Rural Conditions and Trends*, a new quarterly that presents the most current information available on economic, demographic, and socioeconomic conditions in rural America. Previously, she served as a policy analyst of the Office of Rural Development Policy at USDA and as a research associate at the Urban Institute.

James P. Miller is an economist with the Economic Research Service, U.S. Department of Agriculture. He is currently employed by the Agricultural and Rural Economic Development Division of the Economic Research Service.

Bruce D. Phillips has been director of database development for the Office of Advocacy of the U.S. Small Business Administration where he supervises a staff and budget that creates, maintains, and disseminates economic data on trends in small and large firms from the Small Business Data Base. In this position, and his prior position as Senior Economist at SBA from 1979–85, he conducts research on a variety of employment and small business development issues; these include preparation of an annual chapter in *The State of Small Business*, an annual report from the President to the Congress on economic conditions in the small business sector. He is also the coauthor of *The Supply of Labor in Lower Level Occupations* with Harold Wool.

Andrew J. Sofranko is professor of rural sociology and agricultural economics, University of Illinois, Urbana–Champaign. For the last 15 years, he has been teaching and conducting research in Illinois on rural communities and on rural demographic trends. For 4 years he edited and contributed to the Illinois CRD Report.

Tom Unruh is a policy analyst for economic development at the National Governors' Association Center for Policy Research. His recent work has included research, analysis, and technical assistance on state rural development policies through NGA's Rural and Agricultural Policy Program, state use of the Community Development Block Grant for economic development, and state international trade initiatives. Before joining the NGA staff in 1988, Mr. Unruh was a special projects manager for the Kansas Department of Commerce.

Norman Walzer is professor of economics at Western Illinois University and director of the Illinois Institute for Rural Affairs. He has coauthored or coedited six books, including *Financing Economic Development in the 1980s* (with David Chicoine) and *Financing Rural Health Care* (with Lavonne Straub), both published by Praeger.